CARLISLE'S

CULT HEROES

PAUL HARRISON

Know The Score Books Limited

www.knowthescorebooks.com

KNOW THE SCORE BOOKS PUBLICATIONS

CULT HEROES	Author	ISBN
CARLISLE UNITED	Paul Harrison	978-1-905449-09-7
CHELSEA	Leo Moynihan	1-905449-00-3
MANCHESTER CITY	David Clayton	978-1-905449-05-7
NEWCASTLE	Dylan Younger	1-905449-03-8
NOTTINGHAM FOREST	David McVay	978-1-905449-06-4
RANGERS	Paul Smith	978-1-905449-07-1
SOUTHAMPTON	Jeremy Wilson	1-905449-01-1
WEST BROM	Simon Wright	1-905449-02-X

MATCH OF MY LIFE	Editor	ISBN
ENGLAND WORLD CUP	Massarella & Moynihan	1-905449-52-6
EUROPEAN CUP FINALS	Ben Lyttleton	1-905449-57-7
FA CUP FINALS (1953-1969)	David Saffer	978-1-905449-53-4
FULHAM	Michael Heatley	1-905449-51-8
LEEDS	David Saffer	1-905449-54-2
LIVERPOOL	Leo Moynihan	1-905449-50-X
MANCHESTER UNITED	Ivan Ponting	978-1-905449-59
SHEFFIELD UNITED	Nick Johnson	1-905449-62-3
STOKE CITY	Simon Lowe	978-1-905449-55-2
SUNDERLAND	Rob Mason	1-905449-60-7
SPURS	Allen & Massarella	978-1-905449-58-3
WOLVES	Simon Lowe	1-905449-56-9

GENERAL FOOTBALL	Author	ISBN
2007/08 CHAMPIONS LEAGUE YEARBOOK		
	Harry Harris	978-1-905449-93-4
BURKSEY	Peter Morfoot	1-905449-49-6
The Autobiography of a Football God		
HOLD THE BACK PAGE	Harry Harris	1-905449-91-7
OUTCASTS	Steve Menary	978-1-905449-31-6
The Lands FIFA Forgot		
PARISH TO PLANET	Dr Eric Midwinter	978-1-905449-30-9
A History of Football		
MY PREMIERSHIP DIARY	Marcus Hahnemann	978-1-905449-33-0
Reading's Season in the Premiership		
TACKLES LIKE A FERRET	Paul Parker	1-905449-47-X
(England Cover)		
TACKLES LIKE A FERRET	Paul Parker	1-905449-46-1
(Manchester United Cover)		
2006 WORLD CUP DIARY	Harry Harris	1-905449-90-9

CRICKET	Author	ISBN
GROVEL! The 1976 West IndiesTour of England	David Tossell	978-1-905449-43-9
MOML: THE ASHES	Sam Pilger & Rob Wightman	1-905449-63-1
MY AUTOBIOGRAPHY	Shaun Udal	978-1-905449-42-2
WASTED?	Paul Smith	978-1-905449-45-3
LEAGUE CRICKET YEARBOOK North West edition	Andy Searle	978-1-905449-70-5
LEAGUE CRICKET YEARBOOK Midlands edition	Andy Searle	978-1-905449-72-9

RUGBY LEAGUE	Editor	ISBN
WIGAN WARRIORS	David Kuzio	978-1-905449-66-8

FORTHCOMING PUBLICATIONS

CULT HEROES	Author	ISBN
CELTIC	David Potter	978-1-905449-08-8

MATCH OF MY LIFE	Editor	ISBN
ASTON VILLA	Neil Moxley	978-1-905449-65-1
BOLTON WANDERERS	David Saffer	978-1-905449-64-4
DERBY COUNTY	Johnson & Matthews	978-1-905449-68-2

GENERAL FOOTBALL	Author	ISBN
ANFIELD OF DREAMS	Neil Dunkin	978-1-905449-80-4
THE BOOK OF FOOTBALL OBITUARIES	Ivan Ponting	978-1-905449-1
MANCHESTER UNITED RUINED MY WIFE	David Blatt	978-1-905449-81-1
MARTIN JOL: THE INSIDE STORY	Harry Harris	978-1-905449-77-4
RIVALS: INSIDE THE BRITISH DERBY	Douglas Beattie	978-1-905449-79-8
UNITED THROUGH TRIUMPH AND TRAGEDY	Bill Foulkes	978-1-905449-78-1

RUGBY LEAGUE	Editor	ISBN
MOML LEEDS RHINOS	Phil Caplan & David Saffer	978-1-905449-69-9

To Mandy,
'you are everything to me
(except where Carlisle United
are concerned)'

CARLISLE'S

CULT HEROES

PAUL HARRISON

Series Editor: Simon Lowe

www.knowthescorebooks.com

First published in the United Kingdom
by Know The Score Books Limited, 2007
Copyright Paul Harrison, 2007

First published in the United Kingdom by Know The Score Books Limited, 2007

Know The Score Books Limited
118 Alcester Road
Studley
Warwickshire
B80 7NT
Tel: 01527 454482   Fax: 01527 452183

www.knowthescorebooks.com

A CIP catalogue record is available for this book from the British Library
ISBN-13: 978-1-905449-09-7

Jacket and book design by Lisa David

Printed and bound in Great Britain
By William Clowes Ltd

Jacket Photographs
Front centre: Jimmy Glass – his entire career will be remembered for just one thing, scoring the club's most important goal ever.
Left: Peter Beardsley – the formative days of his career were spent at Brunton Park, United's favourite adopted son.
Right: Bob Stokoe – Loyal and innovative aren't sufficient words to describe him, possibly United's best ever manager.
Inset: Malcolm Poskett – Eagles, Rams and Saints couldn't stop him, Mally plundered goals at will and cared little for reputations.

Rear
Left: Jimmy McConnell – United's most lethal striker ever, scored two goals in the club's first ever league game.
Right: Chris Balderstone – possibly the most complete footballer to grace a United shirt, Bill Shankly certainly thought so.

Author's Acknowledgements

I make no bones about the fact that this book is all about my gods. Anyone who pulls on the shirt of Carlisle United is special, very special, but this is a book about twenty superhumans. They may not be the greatest footballers ever to play for Carlisle United, but in one way or another they are extremely special. Without them, this book could never have been written. My first and initial thank you goes to each and every footballer to have played football for Carlisle United FC (except Jim Tolmie, of course). I also want to give special praise and thanks to both Stan Bowles and Kevin Gray, absolute quality the pair of you.

Appreciation goes to Mandy Harrison for suffering months and years of reading draft chapters, transcribing written interviews and other important information on ex-players and for being the ideal travelling companion on my crusades the length and breadth of the British Isles to research this book. Next in line has to be the late Bob Stokoe. I got to know Bob extremely well in his latter years and his personal insights into football and Carlisle United in particular were a real motivator to the completion of this book. Bob, I assure you, you will never be forgotten.

My thanks go to Fred Story and Andrew Jenkins, not forgetting John (Doc) Haworth, John Nixon, Steve Pattison and Dick Young, all of whom were influential and real inspirations to me with their kindness, openness and real passion and desire to see the club move forward. There is no finer board of directors in the professional game of football. Also thanks go to David Mitchell for making Brunton Park so special, he is a man of pure class and distinction. I shouldn't forget Andy Hall and Barbara Abbott for being great colleagues and associates, a great media team.

It goes without saying that it would be extremely rude of me not to mention the thousands of supporters of Carlisle United that are spread across the globe in this age of the internet and instant messaging, you are simply the best. My special thanks also go to the Carlisle United Online message board members, many of whom are knowledgeable about all things United and who provoke many a lively discussion.

Unlike many other authors who have penned works on the club, and who, for some personal reason choose to ignore the often valid input of the works of their peers, I independently want to mention the rest of the writing best. High in that league comes author and friend Neil Nixon, a true blue and a great writer. All his works are a pleasure to read and a welcome addition to my library. I also want to mention an old friend from many years ago, Keith Wild, who above all others (myself included) added so much to the United literary canon. Further, I want to mention 'The Doc', whose companionship (in my occasional visit to the United Directors box) I truly enjoy. He is a fine ambassador for the club and someone who lives and breathes Carlisle United.

The illustrations contained within this work are mainly from my own personal collection, which I confess is vast. However, of those provided from other sources, primarily of note are those supplied by Mike Capps from Kappa Sport pictures in Kettering – as always fantastic, thanks to the *Evening News and Star* and the *CumberlandNews* for further provision of illustrations and to Cumbrian Newspapers also. Appreciation goes to Jonathan Becker and Loftus Brown who remain in my honest opinion, truly the elite of Carlisle United photography. Last but not least to my publisher Simon Lowe at Know The Score Books, for believing in this project and seeing it through. He is a hard task master but a genuine lover of the game.

If I have omitted anyone from these notes then I can only apologise, my thanks anyway.

Paul Harrison
September 2007

Contents

Introduction

> 'We are all capable of infinitely more than we believe.'
>
> David Blaine

HOW MANY TIMES AS a supporter of Carlisle United do you see a football book on the shelves of your local bookstore that looks like it could be a really good read? You pick it up and go straight to the index and eagerly scan the pages looking for the two words which may well mean you will buy the book, Carlisle United. Then it dawns on you, they aren't there! Cardiff City always get a mention, as do Charlton Athletic, but the alphabetical listing where the name Carlisle United should appear does not possess those two very important words. It has always amazed me why we are so often ignored and don't make the pages of published football books and other football-related memorabilia. Take for example back in the late 1960s and early 1970s when a national petrol chain gave away team badges of 91 league clubs, the one missing? You guessed it, Carlisle United.

Well there are no worries about absentees in this volume, it's all about Carlisle United, the players and individuals who have made their mark at Brunton Park and will forever be regarded as Cult Heroes. Here at least, the rest of football plays a bit part role. Welcome to my football dream land, a place where I can delve back through the passage of time and bring together for the first time, all the Cult Heroes and legends that have graced the blue (and occasionally red, yellow and deck chair striped) shirt of who, in my opinion are the world's greatest football team, Carlisle United.

In the introduction to my previous book based upon the history of Carlisle United, *The Lads in Blue*, which was published in 1995, I told how my first ever live professional football experience had, essentially, charted the rest of my life. Since then many important circumstances in my life have changed. As surreal as it may sound, back in 1968 to a mere nine year old, my personal perceptions of life with Carlisle United seemed so beautifully clear, it was comfortable, an awe-inspiring experience that I fully embraced. It instilled within me a real feeling of togetherness with my Brunton Park peers, there was a real sense of complete unity between players and supporters, I became as one with Carlisle United.

One of my first memories of a match day in the late sixties at Carlisle United was that of our then mascot, an eccentric character known as 'Twinkletoes', who, dressed in a blue and white silk top hat and long tailed blue suit complete with matching waistcoat and white trousers and huge Carlisle United rosette pinned to his lapel, would scamper onto the pitch just as the team was about to come out for kick off. Firmly gripped beneath his arm was OLGA (anagram of the word GOAL) the stuffed fox. Olga would be then ceremoniously placed on the centre spot, only to be removed by him seconds before the referee started the game. Twinks would wander round the cinder track which surrounded the playing area, pre-match and at half-time, chatting to supporters, getting them motivated and generally instilling a carnival atmosphere throughout the ground. From time to time he would often be wearing his slippers! I'm not sure; perhaps he suffered from painful feet? Perhaps he had forgotten he still had his slippers on? More likely that Twinks simply didn't care what people thought, he just wanted to be there with his football heroes.

As I grew older I got to know that 'Twinkletoes' wasn't his real name, he was actually George Baxter, a corporation road sweeper. Whatever, everyone knew him as being Carlisle United through and through. I once saw him in the Denton Holme area of the city, close to where he lived; he recognised me, and shouted "C'mon Ye Blues". As daft as it sounds, I was thrilled that someone, who was literally an institution at Carlisle United, should recognise me as one of their own. George has passed away, but his memory will live forever in the legends of United supporters. Ultimately, Twinks has become a symbolic figure who supporters associate with the 1960s at Brunton Park. In his own way a Cult Hero, certainly one of mine.

Carlisle United is not just about footballers, it's about memories. It's about how it makes us, as supporters, feel. It's about how those we hero worship inspire us, how they impact(ed) upon our lives, either as leaders or team players or as people. We can scream our lungs out desperately pleading with the team to do well, it doesn't make that much difference on the pitch if the players won't, don't, or simply can't perform to our expectation levels, which, I hasten to add are always extremely high. It's about commitment to the cause, the kind of player or club and officials who want us to succeed in all we do, who don't understand the meaning of the word defeat, those who give everything they can and a bit more thereafter.

This book then is about twenty such individuals. Twenty men who believed they were capable of genius, and, thankfully, produced enough of it to delight United fans to elevate themselves from mere good players into truly heroic status. It will, I hope, take on a real life adventure, often sublime, often ridiculous, often humorous, always emotive. Each of the Cult Heroes selected is there on their own merit. Don't skip any or you may just miss out on some of the incredible action recollected on virtually every page. Here you will find twenty of the most intriguing characters ever to have plied their trade on the Brunton Park pitch or in the dug out. They may not be everyone's choice, they may not be the greatest players or managers or club officials we have ever had. However, the one thing they do have is charisma and more importantly Brunton Park cult status. For most of us, that counts for just about everything.

Paul Harrison
September 2007

Foreword

Carlisle United is a football club that will always remain very close to my heart. I really enjoyed my time at Brunton Park and I would like to think that I had a special relationship with the club's supporters throughout that period – we achieved a great amount in a short space of time.

When Paul Harrison first approached me about including a chapter on me and my time at the club in this book, I was ecstatic. Then to be asked to write the foreword was really quite unbelievable. I liked nothing better than reading Paul's programme notes each week as did most of the other players at the club. The thing I enjoy about Paul's writing is that it is honest and he always says it as it is. He's well respected too and that matters a lot in football. As a result of his writing, I know many football people who want him to write their autobiographies. So for me personally I can think of no one better placed to have researched and written this wonderful volume. I am truly honoured to be covered in this book and seeing my name featured alongside such cult heroes as Ivor Broadis, Peter Beardsley, Stan Bowles, Alan Ross and Kenny Wilson is fantastic.

Carlisle United has had some wonderful and not so wonderful times in the past. For me personally, getting relegated into non-league football was a low point, but we all pulled in the right direction and soon we were back in the swing of winning trophies.

The one thing that inspired us as a team and a club was the tenacious backing of our devoted support. Wherever we travelled, we seemed to take thousands with us, more often than not the blue army would out sing the home support on our travels. That was great for us as a team and as players, it made us more determined to do well. I think when you go through some of the chapters in this book, you will read of some of the passion, grit and determination that has run through the club for as long as history records it.

Paul has been in the fortunate position to have interviewed or spoken with many of the heroes no longer with us and others like myself too. He owns countless hand-written records of conversations with some of football's greatest and finest people, Bill Shankly, Stan Bowles, Alan Ross and Chris Balderstone to name but some contained in this book. Records which, for the first time in book form, will allow readers to get beneath the skin of many of the people who have made Carlisle United such a fantastic club.

For me, this is the book that needed to be published on the football club. This is the book that I would want to buy and read. Paul Harrison is a passionate supporter of Carlisle United and it's this passion that seeps through in just about every word. I hope you enjoy the book and find it as thoroughly enjoyable a read as I did.

Kev Gray
August 2007

JIMMY McCONNELL

'THE HAMMER'

1928-1932

UNITED CAREER

Games	150
Goals	126

MAGIC MOMENT

Carlisle scored eight, Jimmy three, but he could have had many more – all this within a week of joining the Football League.

THEY say that great players come and go, but legends live on. This then is our first particular Cult Hero, whose goalscoring exploits can stand up to any scrutiny and match just about anyone in the history of football worldwide. Today, his value on the transfer market would be counted in tens of millions, sad then that this phenomenal centre-forward and supremely confident footballer commanded fees of no more than a few hundred pounds, although it was, of course, an entirely different era.

There can be no doubting that Jimmy McConnell was the most dynamic and sensational striker in the history of Carlisle United football club. Despite this, he remains something of a football enigma. Whilst there can be no doubting that United had the very best out of him, at other clubs such as Kilmarnock, Crewe Alexandra and Rotherham United he struggled to settle. Added to that is the fact that the story of Carlisle United's greatest striker is clouded with curious inconsistency, mainly through misrepresentation and poor research which has been passed off for decades as official records. This, for the first time in print, is the true story of Jimmy's football career. I make no apology for eulogising about how good a footballer he actually was, as will be seen, and I am not alone in heaping such praise upon this fantastic footballer who simply fell in love with Carlisle United.

Born in Ayr on 23 February 1896, James McConnell grew up in a working class community where the major employment for the region was coal mining. As is well documented, this was a dangerous and physically and mentally testing occupation that made great demands upon those who worked down cramped and oppressive mines. Harrowing tragedy stalked the mining community, where the daily risks were high. Witnessing the harsh reality of losing life and limb in order to simply earn a living, young Jimmy quickly became street-wise, with a toughness about him which would stand him in good stead during his footballing years. As he grew up, the situation which faced many able bodied young men soon confronted him. There was a war going on – one of the bloodiest and most shocking conflicts of all time – but Jimmy had no hesitation in answering his country's call to arms in 1914, when he signed up for service with the Royal Horse Artillery aged 18. During the Great War, he served much of this time in Egypt, avoiding, more by luck than any kind of judgement, the carnage of Flanders.

On his return to Scotland McConnell trained hard and kept himself fit by running and playing in local football games between mining communities or simply running through the streets. The football he took part in was literally a kick-about, yet despite this practice mentality, Jimmy's ability soon attracted attention. Word spread of the skills of the 5' 9" centre-forward, who weighed in at around 12 stone 7 pounds. In 1920, one of Scotland's biggest junior local sides, Auchinleck Talbot, were informed of the goalscoring prowess of young McConnell and sent along a representative to informally look at him. Within a few minutes a decision was made and Jimmy was invited for trials at their Beechwood Park home. Auchinleck was then a small hamlet with less than 2,000 population. As a football club they had been formed in 1909, being named after Lord Talbot de Maldahide, who generously gave the club Beechwood Park as their football home. After folding in 1916 (mainly through the problems associated with the Great War) the club reformed in 1920.

In these humble surroundings the football career of Jimmy McConnell began. Jimmy was actually one of the first signings the reborn club made. Auchinleck, who have the curious nickname 'The Bot', completed their football comeback by winning the Ayrshire Cup for the first time in their history, beating Irvine Meadow 3-0 at Rugby Park in 1920 with McConnell on the score sheet. That same year the team set a club goalscoring record during a Scottish Cup tie when Jimmy played a major part in the humiliation of Craigbank. The game, which took place at Beechwood Park, ended 11-0. Before long, McConnell's cavalier and strong bustling style, which was neatly interwoven with some often arrogant ball trickery, saw him become of one of the most talked about players in the Scottish junior game. His goalscoring exploits added to the interest professional clubs began to show in him. He bagged five, scoring with both his feet and a couple of headers in one practice (friendly) game for Talbot, not forgetting the five minute hat-trick he once scored.

It wasn't too long before some of Scotland's more senior and established clubs were knocking on the Kyle-based club's door. Kilmarnock were by far and away the strongest suitors and wouldn't take no for an answer. Led by the then club secretary Hugh Spence, who later went onto manage the team, the Ayrshire club's committee showed the commitment to stick with it, persevering with their pursuit of McConnell. Eventually, after a few days of negotiations, an agreement to release the player was reached. The transfer cost Kilmarnock three pounds plus some old football kit. So it was that Jimmy McConnell took his first step up the football career ladder.

Unfortunately (or fortunately for Carlisle) Jimmy never fulfilled his ambition with the Rugby Park side. It was, in all reality, a huge step up in the standard of play. Kilmarnock played in the Scottish First Division and were established at that level. But there appears to be a reason for McConnell's failure to deliver which goes beyond that gap in class. Jimmy was seen by the committee which ran the club and picked the team as being a player with real potential. However, his reputation preceded him and when he was introduced to his new team-mates it became clear that tensions existed. Some players refused to shake Jimmy's hand, others welcomed him. The main body of dissent against him appeared to come from players who were, to be honest, distinctly average and were settled at the club and were clearly jealous and saw him as a threat to their own position. The rumblings of disharmony were not solely directed towards Jimmy, some players were of the opinion that the committee were not sufficiently qualified to select the first team week-in week-out. They probably weren't the first and they certainly weren't the last to hold that opinion of the managerial set up of many a club. On this occasion the situation seemed to have some impact as Hugh Spence was moved from secretary to team manager a short time later.

It also has to be said that Jimmy himself did not go out of his way to ingratiate himself with his new playing colleagues. In one of his trial games he is said to have made his team-mates playing against him (the Kilmarnock team were split into two teams and included any would be trialist) in the match, look utterly foolish, as first he turned them this way, then that way before leaving them in his wake. Others were shoulder charged out of the way, as Jimmy simply imposed himself on the game in the way he liked to.

After one practice/trial game, a delegation of a few of the players went to the club committee and expressed their concerns about the new man, saying that he was too rugged and not refined enough to play at a decent standard. The committee had few options open to them. An extraordinary meeting was called as they availed themselves of the harsh reality that faced them if they progressed their interest in McConnell. The last thing they needed was a player revolt or disharmony amongst the playing ranks. The outcome was perhaps inevitable, quantity outshone quality and the complaining players received the support of the committee, Jimmy McConnell was told that after deep consideration they arrived at the conclusion that he played no part in the future of the club and could leave. He had not played a single competitive game for Killie. One can only surmise what that experience did to McConnell, who must have been angry and disheartened. Thankfully, he had a strong character. The principles he'd learned during his upbringing in a strong and resilient community provided him with the strength to keep going. The tunnel vision of the Kilmarnock officials and, in particular, those of some of their average and ordinary players was not about to break his spirit. Jimmy still held serious aspirations to succeed in the game.

HE DIDN'T HAVE TO wait long to get out of Rugby Park. News of McConnell's release alerted a number of clubs, but Jimmy wasn't about to move too far afield. He chose to remain in Ayrshire, signing for Stevenston United, a decent side who played in the Western Football League. It was with this move that Jimmy realised that his confidence on the ball had taken a real hammering. He initially found it hard to get into any consistent form. He couldn't lose or drop his marker as easily as he had been used to. To further exasperate matters, rumour and gossip abounded that it was he who had caused trouble among the players at Kilmarnock and that this was the real reason he was released. Mentally tough, he ignored all such suggestions and set about the personal task of getting himself focused and fit enough to perform at his peak. Within weeks, he was again scoring goals for fun. Soon the talk of him being a disruptive character on the pitch was forgotten, as Stevenston supporters were thrilled by his swash-buckling style. Strong in the tackle and difficult to knock off the ball, he took no prisoners. Yet for Jimmy, it was all very simple; his mantra was to win fairly, but to win at all costs.

If his earlier move to Kilmarnock could be classed as courageous and a little too ambitious too quickly, then, on paper, the move to Stevenston United was without doubt a step backwards. However, it provided him with a platform from which he could re-establish his fine reputation as a goalscoring centre-forward. He was again high on confidence, dancing and weaving round opposition defenders on the pitch, scoring goals, and ultimately, once again, being monitored by more senior clubs.

Nithsdale Wanderers were a club side making real progress on and off the field around that time. An ambitious club, they had hopes of acquiring membership of Scottish League Division Three and thereby moving forward through the leagues. In 1923 when the Scottish Third Division was formed, Nithsdale received approval to join the newly-formed league. McConnell was one of the signings brought in to make them competitive at this new level, and what an impact he made. His personal tally of 45 goals from a total of 81 scored by the club that first league season was outstanding. During the 1924/25 season more McConnell goals steered them to the Scottish Third Division Championship and with it, promotion to the Second Division. The success was clinched in the most dramatic style. On the final day of the season Wanderers needed the two points a win would bring to secure promotion, but they faced a strong and extremely confident Montrose side. Cue Jimmy McConnell, as Wanderers were simply irresistible that day and romped to a very comfortable 8-0 victory. Jimmy was again amongst the goals and also acted as provider. Promotion meant that little Nithsdale were challenging amongst clubs with greater fan bases and support, such as Dunfermline, Clyde and Alloa Athletic and incredibly, they were very much holding their own, finally settling into a mid-table position, with Jimmy continuing his net-busting antics, weighing in with a further 37 goals from a total of 78 club goals scored in 1925/26.

It must have been something of a rollercoaster ride for the man and the player. Hero worshipped locally, he was now a man with a big reputation. He yearned for the big time. Yet when the opportunity to prove himself at the top level of the Scottish game had been provided to him, insecure jealousy of more average players had caused him to become alienated by his so called team-mates. This fact alone had forced him to return to lower league football. Many players would have been destroyed by such trauma, but Jimmy wasn't just any player; the ambition within him was burning. He aspired to success and knew he had to move on if he was to sample honours within the game. Football has often been referred to as an International language. This is clear as the basic methodology of getting the ball into the back of the opposition's net as many times as you can without retaliation exists globally. The passions worldwide are identical, with most players wanting to play for the top clubs. Clubs themselves want to be classed as top clubs, and everyone, supporters included, want their team to win every game they contest. All very simple, but the sad reality is that not every player can be successful, not every club can be a big club, and not every game can be won.

No-one could ever blame Jimmy for looking for the opportunity to progress his career and to potentially move to bigger and better things. As it was, this came sooner than he expected. After a training session one afternoon, two men approached the striker. They were scouts, sent on a mission by the man who wore a permanent grimace on his face, Glasgow Celtic supremo Willie Maley. The scouts invited Jimmy to Celtic Park for a spell as a trialist. Celtic were then, as they are now, a massive club, full of ambition and crammed with vastly experienced and quality players. For Jimmy McConnell it was the opportunity of a lifetime. Naturally he accepted and was soon on his way to Glasgow for what, one must assume, he thought would be his last crack at the big time, McConnell now being aged 30. Jimmy must have also hoped that this time he would be able to develop a harmonious football relationship.

Sadly, at the time of the Celtic trial, Jimmy was carrying an injury to his back. It may not have been too much of a problem had he told the doctor. However, desperate to prove himself at Celtic, he elected not to mention it to anyone in fear of it jeopardising his trial spell. He played three practice games fighting through the pain barrier. From all the Celtic people saw, the centre-forward wasn't of the standard they had anticipated. Jimmy, complete with back injury was anything but nimble or skilful on the ball. In fact he seemed unable to drop his shoulder and get past his man, while his heading lacked power and direction. So at the end of his trial games, the Celtic boss himself broke the news to him that he felt Jimmy wasn't up to Celtic's standard. It was only then that Jimmy elected to tell Celtic officials of his injury. It mattered little to them as they wished him every success in his future career.

AS IT WAS, ONE of the associates of Celtic had contacts in the United States where football (soccer) was in its infancy, but was steadily building a reputation as an enjoyable sport. As he made his way out of Celtic Park, Jimmy was approached again and asked if he would like the opportunity to play overseas. There was no transfer, and consequently no signing on fee, but the clubs there would be happy to give him a house, a decent footballer salary and potentially, an external job.

Within a few weeks he was on the move to the States. It was now the summer of 1926. It was culturally a massive move for him to make. However, he wasn't alone as a British-born player playing in America in the 1920s. Others like Archie Stark, Jock Marshall, Dave Edwards had all made the move and succeeded in making a good name for themselves and enhancing their own reputations. Initially signing for Springfield Babes, McConnell was an instant success, scoring an average of a goal every game. It wasn't too long before he was signed by the curiously named Providence Clamdiggers, who were managed by ex-Bethlehem Steel soccer star Sam Fletcher. At Providence he further developed his scoring reputation, making 21 appearances and scoring 17 goals. With such succcess behind him, Jimmy was again in demand and his football exploits were regularly commented upon in the pages of the local press. It came as no surprise that some of the top American Soccer League clubs were keen to sign him. So it was that in May 1927, Jimmy moved to Bethlehem Steel, historically one of the most successful US soccer teams to exist. The *Bethlehem Globe Times* of 17 May 1927 reported:

BETHLEHEM STEEL SIGNS NEW PLAYER
James McConnell, former Scottish soccer star, to be on forward line.

'A step in revamping the forward line of Bethlehem Steel soccer team to increase the goal scoring possibilities is forecast in the recent action of the management in signing James McConnell, last season with the Providence club, and regarded as one of the most dangerous goalscoring forwards in the American League. McConnell is a product of Scotland, and experienced by quite a few years of active participation in the sport. He is about 28 years of age and is the bustling type of forward. Negotiations for his acquisition were pending for several weeks for Fall River as well as other clubs were bartering with the management for his services. However, senti-ment probably prevailed in spite of keen rivalry developed in recent years and when disposition was made Fletcher [Providence coach and former Steel player] could not turn down his former team-mates.'

Two days later it was revealed that Jimmy was amongst the top twenty goalscorers in the entire American Soccer League for that season, with 14 league goals and further strikes added during exhibition games.

Under a broiling sun on Saturday 10 September 1927, 31 year-old McConnell made his home debut at Lehigh Field sports facility, the newly named home ground of Bethlehem, before a crowd of 10,000 against New Bedford. It was a typically exhilarating performance by the tough centre-forward as the *Bethlehem Globe Times* reported:

'With the opening whistle Bethlehem did the pressing and continued to attack for all of 15 minutes before their efforts were productive. Movement after movement was initiated before McConnell crashed through the goal. Cleverly trapping the ball in midfield, Stark advanced toward the visitors' net and in doing so drew the defence close to meet him. In a flash he slipped the ball up centre to McConnell, who was in position to meet it and then with a rifle shot drive a skimming shot over the ground, landing the sphere in the far corner, well out of reach of Geudert.'

The goal was apparently greeted with great enthusiasm both on and off the field. The bustling striker then went close with two further efforts. It appeared that all Jimmy's efforts had gone to waste when the visitors equalised, but little Johnny Jaap saved the day when he glanced a header home to ensure that Bethlehem won the game 2-1. The following day, Bethlehem faced Brooklyn. Unfortunately for Jimmy, he and his team mates were on the receiving end of a serious football lesson as they suffered a severe 5-0 thrashing.

Next up on the fixture list were J & P Coats, a game which as can be seen, well and truly allowed McConnell to make his mark and prove his worth to his new side. The newspaper headlines and coverage of the encounter said it all;

MCCONNELL STANDS OUT IN AGGRESSIVE GAME, NOTCHING A TRIO OF COUNTERS.

Johnny Jaap and James McConnell, sturdy and aggressive centre-forward, were material factors in notching goals to give Bethlehem Steel soccer team its second victory in its third American League start on the home slot on Saturday afternoon. McConnell accounted for three of the goals.

On 40 minutes McConnell notched the first goal, firing home a loose ball from a Jaap cross. In the second half, McConnell headed home a second, before scoring a third 20 minutes later when he burst through the Coats defence and had little trouble in beating Kerr in the visitors goal, with his speedy drive.

A game at Hartford a couple of weeks later saw Jimmy suffer a nasty muscle injury to his back, therefore putting the club's leading goal scorer out of action for a month or so. During this time, Tom Gillespie, a firm favourite at Bethlehem, returned, reclaiming the centre-forward position. On his own return, McConnell was moved from his customary centre-forward role to inside-forward and played in what was basically a reserve team for an exhibition match at New Bedford. The game ended in a 4-4 draw, with McConnell grabbing himself a brace and the headlines. Such exhilarating performances ensured an instant recall to the first team where he struggled to find form in a 3-2 defeat against Newark. He was substituted during this game and replaced by Archie Stark who went on to score one of Bethlehem's two goals.

The injury several weeks earlier seemed to have taken something from him. Certainly he must have felt a sense of uneasiness at the club, as his playing position altered so frequently and he found himself in and out of the team like the proverbial yoyo. Unsettled by his irregular appearances, he was released on loan by Bethlehem shortly after Christmas, in December 1927. The loan was to J & P Coats (the Threadmakers) of Pawpucket, and was subject to any recall Bethlehem felt necessary. One of Jimmy's great successes at the Threadmakers came on 26 February 1928 when he scored in the 2-1 Eastern Section semi-final victory over United States Soccer League Champions, Fall River. His goal proved to be the decisive one in the encounter and came from a free-kick from which 'McConnell headed the ball into the cage.'

During that 1927/28 season Jimmy played some 32 games for J & P Coats, and to his utmost credit had an incredible scoring return, with 19 goals. So it was that in March 1928, word got to him that George Bristowe, manager of Carlisle United was interested in bringing him back to Britain and to Brunton Park. McConnell returned home to speak with Bristowe and was quickly impressed by the astute awareness of the Carlisle boss. Bristowe gave him an in-house trial in which he scored three goals, and told him that if he signed for Carlisle he could make a real impact on the English game. A centre-forward such as him could not only enhance his reputation, but also find security (financial) at the right club. Jimmy needed no further per-suasion, the United States had been an adventure, but he missed his Scottish home, and the city of Carlisle was ideally located for him to soothe that particular want whenever he desired. The player himself was to later say of this decision: "It was the best football move I could make, Mr Bristowe was a real gentleman. He told me he wanted me at Carlisle and made me feel very welcome. I knew of Carlisle and some of my old team-mates in Scotland told me they had been inquiring after my contact details. I made sure Mr Bristowe knew how to get hold of me, so it wasn't a case of them hunting me down. I wanted to play for Carlisle. From that day on, Carlisle was the only place for me. I do love the place."

IT IS AT CARLISLE UNITED that football records are turned on their heads, as a real anomaly is encountered. According to FA Cup records on 27 November 1927, Jimmy McConnell was one of Carlisle's scorers in an FA Cup tie against Doncaster Rovers. Yet records I have searched through clearly have him playing in America during the same period. In fact he scored a couple of goals in America a few days earlier! Hence the overall totals for games played and goals scored in Jimmy's Carlisle career should be reduced by one in each column. Sorry Jimmy.

I have been really fortunate enough during my life to speak with people who could recol-lect this era. One player who featured around this time, regaled me with countless tales, anecdotes and memories which have until now remained securely locked in the family vault. Against much of what pundits and journalists delight in telling us about Brunton Park being an outpost, back in the 1920s Carlisle United wasn't a bad option. They were a club with a good reputation in the Northern game. With Football League status achieved in 1928 they really announced their arrival among the upper echelons of the game. George (Ginger) Harrison, who joined the club from West Stanley after a brief spell at Darlington in August that year, was hardly what could be described as a high profile signing, yet on arriving at the ground to sign his contract, he was literally mobbed by Blues fans desperate to see one of the stars who would be leading them into the Football League. Harrison told his family that there was a team spirit at the club which he found extraordinary and that he personally had never before encoun-tered during his time in the game.

Discussing personalities, there can be no doubt that one player stood out amongst his contemporaries: Jimmy McConnell was the man who George believed was indicative of every-thing good about Carlisle United at that time. He told me: "Jimmy was a true gentleman who would give everyone he passed in the street a nod and a wink, yet on the pitch he possessed a merciless side. His physical strength and quick feet would often leave defenders trailing in his wake. The goals he scored illuminated his life and that of thousands of others who cheered him on from the terraces. Jimmy would often enjoy a drink, but only if we had won. If we lost he took it personally and bemoaned his own performance in front of goal. He so desperately wanted Carlisle to win everything. He was a great example to us all."

So it was that Carlisle United played their first ever game in the Football League away at Accrington Stanley. It is said that close to a thousand Carlisle fans made the relatively short journey to Peel Park, Lancashire, special trains being provided to transport players and supporters. As befits a man who was to become the club's first true Cult Hero, it took Jimmy all of five minutes to introduce himself to the English Football League with an absolute screamer of a shot that left the Stanley keeper with no chance and sent United on their way to a 3-2 victory. For the historians, that goal was Carlisle United's first ever Football League goal. It wasn't the only record Jimmy McConnell was to have to his name at Carlisle United.

The press of the day were gushing with compliments about not only United's display, but that of the Carlisle centre-forward: "McConnell received a forward pass and immediately launched another run towards the Stanley goal. Suddenly, without warning, he unleashed a terrific shot which flew into the top corner of the goal causing those gathered behind the Stanley keeper to stoop down in fear of the ball bursting through the nets and taking off their heads... The centre forward is filled with confidence and determination, make no mistake. There is a good deal of skill to his game too, Jimmy McConnell was really too hot for Stanley to handle."

The compliments didn't end there as McConnell grew in stature and his performances became more and more phenomenal. A few months after an FA Cup third round game against Everton at Brunton Park in 1930, which sadly United ended up losing 4-2, the most prolific goalscorer in British football history, Dixie Dean, who continued his scoring ways by grabbing a brace against United that day, said of the Carlisle striker: "They [United] were tougher opponents than we expected. One player stands clear in my mind as being an exceptional talent. Jimmy McConnell was his name, a fantastic footballer. He had the same goalscoring ability that I possessed, but he had more pace and ability than I ever did. It still strikes me that he should have been one of football's better known centre-forwards."

The following season, 1930/31, Jimmy, who turned 35 that winter, scored 37 League goals plus a further four in the FA Cup and it was on 28 March 1931 that he entered the Carlisle United records books for quite a different reason – as he was presented with a Chesterfield three piece suite; a first and last for the club, no other player has ever received such recognition.

The reason behind this unusual gesture was the fact that he had become the first ever Carlisle player to score 100 goals. That same season the team scored an incredible 98 goals, again a club record, which now after all this time would seem unlikely to be beaten.

But it wasn't only the quantity of goals McConnell scored that made him such a Brunton Park hero, it was the style and gusto with which he defeated defender after defender with barnstorming runs and then despatched the ball – and remember this was the heavy old leather ball which weighed double what a modern ball comes in at – into the back of the net with incredible velocity. After his retirement McConnell said: "I was proud to represent Carlisle. It will always be my club. I really found it easy to play there. So many of our team had skill and determination to achieve. My confidence blossomed. During games I would tease opposition defenders about how I was going to leave them standing as soon as I got the ball. I would keep at them, reminding them I was there all the time. They got nervous when I got the ball and would try to snatch it away from me, I would drop my shoulder, duck this way then the other and move forward with haste. Other players backed off in fear of me conning them. As soon as I caught sight of goal I would smash the ball as best as I could. Sometimes it went in, sometimes it kept flying upwards! I think most people remember the powerful goals I scored for Carlisle, I remember them all."

Memorably, McConnell also scored in the club's first ever home league game at Brunton Park against Bradford City in what was described as a thrilling 2-2 draw. "Bradford were a decent side as I remember," he said. "I didn't expect to lose and knew I would score. Can't say why, just always knew when I was going to score. I had been kicked in the air by their centre-half and we were having a right old tussle. I told him if he didn't stop kicking me, I was going to make a chump of him and land him on his backside – and I did a few times in that game."

It was a truly memorable season for the centre-forward, who went on to score 42 league goals, including four hat-tricks, against Hartlepools, Southport and home and away and against Ashington. Add to this eight double strikes and a penalty and you can see why the club finished the season in a healthy eighth position in Division Three (North), not bad in their first ever league campaign. The amazing feat of scoring 42 league goals in one season is a record that has rarely been troubled since (only Hugh McIlmoyle coming close in the 1963/64 season with 39 league goals).

Jimmy's ability to score goals caused players to recognise him as a threat. He was as deadly with his left foot as he was with his right, he could head the ball too. Fast and strong, he was extremely difficult to get near once he had the ball under his control. Preferring the no.9 shirt, he always took the job seriously – goals were his sole objective and mission. "I can't really remember how many times I scored three or more goals in a game, a few I should think," he said. "I saw it as part of my job, to put the ball in the net. Fairly, of course. A couple of times I would clatter the keeper, trying to get him to drop the ball. Sometimes he would end up tangled in the back of the net. But a goal was a goal and I always enjoyed celebrating scoring a goal."

THE FOLLOWING SEASON, 1929/30, McConnell's exploits continued as he bagged three hat-tricks, scoring four goals on two occasions as United crushed Wrexham 5-1 (four for Jimmy), Chesterfield 6-0 (three) and Barrow 7-1 (four) all at Brunton Park. The destroyer, as he was called by opposition players, was ruthless and seldom wasteful. And yet there were those who proclaimed that his two seasons of goalscoring heroics would not and could not be repeated a third time. McConnell was after all now approaching his 35th birthday.

How wrong they were. The 1930/31 season saw him net an incredible six hat-tricks, scoring four goals in two of those games. In the last of a particularly good run of form he virtually single-handedly destroyed Rochdale at Brunton Park in January 1932, 4-0 the final score, including a McConnell hat-trick. However, many supporters of the time recalled not only the goals which defeated Rochdale, but how often the centre-forward went close or hit the woodwork with other efforts; it could easily have been six or seven McConnell scored that day.

The late Bill Shankly, who joined United in the same season as McConnell left, told the author in 1977: "Jimmy McConnell was the greatest centre-forward never to receive proper recognition. I saw him play many times, each time he left me awe-struck. If there was one player I could pick to have signed at any club I have managed, Jimmy McConnell would be very high on that list. He was a good man off the field too, sociable and mild mannered. On the field he was devastating, a real destroyer of defences. As a young player I once asked him for some advice. He told me: 'Keep out of my way if you ever face me as an opponent or I will knock you over the roof of the grandstand.' I think he meant it too. I couldn't understand at the time why he was never half the player at Crewe or later Rotherham. Now with my experience I know why, he just loved everything about playing for Carlisle. Some say Dixie Dean was a great goalscorer, I say Jimmy McConnell of Carlisle United could quite match him – on his day of course!"

MCCONNELL'S LAST GAME for the club came at Brunton Park on 23 April 1932, before a crowd of 3,412 in a rather limp 0-3 defeat by Lincoln City as the 1931/32 season drew to a close. Just a few weeks later, in May 1932, with finances not good at the club, the news no Carlisle United supporter wanted to hear was announced: Jimmy McConnell had been sold off to Crewe Alexandra for a sum in the region of £200. His goalscoring record for United bears some repeating:

1928/29 – 42 goals
1929/30 – 27 goals
1930/31 – 37 goals
1931/32 – 20 goals

A grand total of 126 goals in just four seasons.

The passion McConnell displayed when wearing the blue and white of Carlisle seemed strangely absent at Crewe. He found the going tough at Gresty Road and despite the perfectly adequate return of 22 league goals from 36 appearances, he never really settled in the railway town. The goals he scored attracted Rotherham and a little prying soon provided the information that the player was unhappy and unsettled. Rotherham was not a club with a great footballing record to their name. In fact they were a team who had failed to win a single away game the previous season. Manager Billy Heald saw McConnell as an option to fire them to victory. He described the reason he signed the centre-forward: "He (McConnell) is a player who can score goals from anywhere. Strong and with powerful shooting ability, goals come easily to him. If we can capture the play he managed at Carlisle we will be moving up the table."

Injury didn't help McConnell's career in South Yorkshire. He did still manage to make his mark despite making just 21 league appearance for the Millers, scoring four times, and a further three appearances in the FA Cup during which he found the net in a 2-1 second round win against Coventry City. But Rotherham wasn't Carlisle. Jimmy missed Brunton Park and was always keen to learn how they fared, even when playing elsewhere.

"A couple of my fellow team comrades at Rotherham had a bit of a go at me after I once got into conversation on a station platform with a Carlisle man. I asked how United were faring. He recognised me as McConnell and shook my hand. My fellows were incensed and told me that I needed to follow the rules, other teams don't matter. I told them I would always look out for how Carlisle fared. I think it sealed my fate at Rotherham, you know."

Despite Jimmy's assertion that wasn't the only factor contributing to his departure from Millmoor. Northern football was not in a healthy state, with many clubs struggling to make ends meet financially. Rotherham were one such club in serious financial difficulties. Within a season McConnell found himself released by the new Rotherham manager, Reg Freeman, who had been brought in to replace the failing Heald. With club debts now reaching the £15,000 mark, assets had to go. Jimmy was one disposed of and he eventually moved back to his native Scotland, where he re-signed for one of his earlier clubs, Nithsdale Wanderers and, now aged 37, continued to score goals for fun.

FOOTBALL STATISTICS HAVE BEEN used by the likes of Opta to form the basis of many a spurious argument in the modern era. Now you can learn the number of passes completed by any player in any particular game, number of tackles made, number of shots on and off target or number of minutes played. But goals win games. That is the most important statistic of all. And it is one that will never change. Jimmy McConnell is still king of stats and records thanks to his Carlisle goal hauls. But there's more. Incredibly, upon his retirement from the game in 1936, Jimmy had become the first footballer ever to score over 100 goals in both the English and Scottish leagues; a feat since only surpassed by Kenny Dalglish. He had bagged 107 in Scotland, 130 south of the border and, amazingly, had found the time to be able to also boast over a hundred in the American game (119).

After retiring from football, this legendary footballer and prolific goalscorer chose to settle in Carlisle, where he lived and later worked as a crane driver for Carlisle Electricity Undertaking until his sad death at the age of 53 on Sunday 15 May 1949. Jimmy died at about 1.15pm whilst talking about (of all things) Carlisle United, to staff in the Crescent Inn on Warwick Road, Carlisle. His wife, a childhood sweetheart Isabella Gallocher survived him until September 1963. She was buried in the same plot as Jimmy in Carlisle's Upperby cemetery – gone, but never forgotten.

BILL SHANKLY

1935 & 1949-1951

UNITED CAREER

as player

Games	16
Goals	0

as manager

Games	99
Wins	46

MAGIC MOMENT

'This is your manager speaking,' was how Shanks began his pre-match utterances

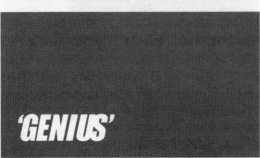

'GENIUS'

'I always knew that Carlisle was right for me, from the day I signed. I always looked out for their results.'

Bill Shankly

BILL Shankly OBE is still described by the vast majority of football commentators and journalists as one of the greatest football managers ever. If ever a man looked every bit of a leader and could be regarded as being the 'Special One' then it is he, not some jumped up overpaid prima donna who has had a transfer kitty twice the size of the new Wembley stadium and who knows little or nothing about all levels of the British game. Shankly meanwhile epitomised what being a footballer and a manager was all about, working his way through the lower leagues before proving himself in the big time, picking up and improving lower league players having personally monitored their progress and getting to know their personality traits. Shankly was a tough but resilient man-manager, with a smattering of all the skills necessary to make him a great leader.

On a visit to Scotland I elected to make a trip to Glenbuck in Ayrshire.This was the birth-place of Shankly and home to the legendary Glenbuck Cherrypickers, a side which had once been home to five of the Shankly brothers and incredibly had produced no less than 49 profes-sionals from their ranks. Glenbuck, from all I had read, was a small mining village about 30 miles east of Ayr, situated just off the A70. As I drove beyond Carlisle and onto the A74 trunk road on into Scotland, I felt the strange twinge of nervousness in my stomach. It was anticipa-tion of what Glenbuck would be like, would it have changed since a young Bill Shankly had first started kicking a football? What stories would the local folk tell me about football's greatest leader? I mulled over this and much more, my mind working overtime in anticipation of what Glenbuck held in store for me.

Soon I turned off the A74 at junction 12 and began to make my way along the winding and largely deserted A70. It wasn't too long before I hit the town of Muirkirk, which, according to my map lay to the east of Glenbuck. I must have missed a turning, I thought, so turning round I re-traversed the route and again I found no sign of the village of Glenbuck. Glenbuck, birthplace to Bill Shankly, had simply disappeared from the map. I continued my search, this time on foot. Looking round, I desperately scanned the area looking for any kind of sign of human habitation. This was a barren place with a cold, biting wind, the undulating landscape broken up by the odd clump of trees and single bushes. Nearby, a small loch, Douglas Water, looked cold and decidedly uninviting, rippling as the wind stroked its surface. The whole environment seemed grey and quite miserable, something like a Lancashire mill town of the 1960s, dreary and devoid of anything. Strangers on foot in these parts are not a familiar sight, and I was soon approached by a digger driver who was part of a local quarry workforce. Without hesitation he asked: "Fan of Bill Shankly are you?"

I nodded my head disappointedly and explained the reason for my journey: "Oh it's gone. All razed to the ground a few years back. There's nothing to see now." He pointed out a small flat area of grass and explained that it was once the home of Glenbuck Cherrypickers. I was shocked, was there really nothing to depict that this was once a small close knit community where countless footballers learned their trade? "Yes, there is," I was told, "a plaque on the side of the road over there," he said, again pointing to an indeterminable piece of the landscape. I thanked my guide and began the downhill journey to where I had left my car. I was demoralised and perhaps shocked that something like this could happen in my own lifetime. It's something you read about, but few ever experience first hand for themselves. How could an entire community simply be allowed to disappear? They call this progress! Like the great man himself, Glenbuck has gone, but one thing is for certain, in both cases, neither will ever be forgotten.

THE LEGEND STARTED MANY years ago when tailor John Shankly moved to Glenbuck from the nearby village of Douglas. Once settled in the small community he found himself attracted to local girl, Barbara Blyth, whom he married. She came from a family of undoubted sporting pedigree. Barbara's brother Bob was a top class sprinter who also had a football career with Glasgow Rangers, Middlesborough, Preston North End and Dundee before becoming player-manager and finally chairman at Portsmouth. A further brother, William, played football for Portsmouth, Preston, and then with Carlisle United, before moving into football administration as a director, and then chairman at Brunton Park.

Born on 2 September 1913, Bill Shankly was one of ten children raised by Barbara and John within the mining community of Glenbuck. He was also the youngest of five Shankly brothers who forged a career from professional football. The boys all did well for themselves. Alec, or Sandy as the family referred to him, was the oldest. He played inside-forward for Ayr United, this prior to World War I. Following the end of the war and with a continuing football career now beyond him, he was forced into a working life down the pit. Jimmy was a centre-half who became a centre-forward, playing for Portsmouth, Halifax Town, Sheffield United, Southend United and, finally, Barrow. John proved to be a useful outside-right, again playing for Portsmouth before moves to Luton Town, Alloa, Blackpool and Greenock Morton. Unfortunately ill health forced him to prematurely retire from the game, whereupon he returned to Glenbuck and the pit. In 1960, whilst watching the Real Madrid versus Eintracht Frankfurt European Cup Final inside Hampden Park, John suffered a massive heart attack and later died in hospital. Meanwhile, Bob Shankly, played for Falkirk, and went on to have a successful managerial career, initially with Dundee, whom he led to the latter stages of the European Cup and later with Falkirk and Alloa.

Unlike his elder brothers, Bill never got to play for his local team, Glenbuck Cherrypickers. After a trial when he was 17 he was told he needed more experience before he would be invited back. His early football development had been down to another local side Cronberry Eglinton, where he played as right-half in the Cumnock and District League. Carlisle United had then an excellent scouting network reaching out into the Scottish leagues. It was one such scout, Peter Carruthers, who spotted the raw yet majestic talent of Bill Shankly and got in touch with the then newly appointed manager of Carlisle United, Bill Clarke, advising him to take a look at the player himself. Clarke, who had previously been company secretary, did not have a playing career to speak of and relied heavily on the experience of others and his committee/board of directors for guidance. One of the directors at this time was a man called

Billy Blyth, who just happened to be Bill Shankly's uncle! Not that nepotism had anything to do with this transfer. Shankly had been putting in some outstanding displays in the local district league. Indeed, Carlisle were not alone in courting Shankly. Bobby Crawford, scout for Preston North End had tried to hijack the Carlisle bid, coming in with a late offer to Shankly to move to Deepdale. However, Carlisle was closer to home for the young player, who had not, up until that time, left Scotland before.

So it was that Shankly arrived at Carlisle and took part in a second class fixture against Middlesbrough reserves, which United lost 6-0. Whatever the result that day, Shankly did sufficiently well to impress and, in July 1932, was offered a one-year contract at Brunton Park worth a very reasonable £4 2s (£4.10p) a week.

Recalling that time, Shankly later said: "When I first got to Carlisle, they had a trainer there by the name of Tom Curry; he was everything I needed and more. Tom was as good as they came, a tough taskmaster who never let me get away with a thing. My first task at Brunton Park was to sweep up the litter around the ground and on the terracing; no easy task because there was a lot of cinder and debris around. Tom showed me how to do it, something I learned from him, never ask anyone else to do something you yourself would not be prepared to do. So he cleared up the lot, the entire ground in about half an hour. He bet me that I could never beat that time. No matter how hard I tried I never did beat it. Tom was an extremely proud man, he was proud of Carlisle United and spent time with every player, coaching and talking to them.

I spent a few months in the reserves learning the trade, I suppose, until Tom called me into his office to tell me I was in the first eleven for the next home game, against Rochdale. It was New Year's Eve 1932, cold and wet. We had a centre-forward called Bill Slinger. He was as good as anything I had seen anywhere, strong and fiercely competitive. He could really bang the goals in. It wasn't the greatest of debut games the fans will have seen. I was aware that I needed to play it safe, but get my tackling right. I always felt that timing and contact with the ball were an absolute skill. I made a few really good tackles and saw Tom Curry clapping me and cheering me on. That's when I knew I was doing okay. We drew the game 2-2 and Bill (Slinger) got both our goals.

I got a little run in the first team, five games I think, but we won just one of them, against Mansfield Town. Oddly enough it was a game when Bill Slinger was absent, injured I think. Bill was a tough man, who would chat to me about his role being difficult. He thought he had an impossible task in trying to fill the boots of the team's previous centre-forward, Jimmy McConnell. I think he did pretty well really, considering how phenomenal McConnell actually was…I was always a bit disappointed that I never got to play alongside Jimmy McConnell, he was devastatingly lethal, and people constantly talked of him and his goals. I told Bill to stick to his own game, that way he kept his confidence. My run in the team came to an end after I picked up a bit of a knock in a game against Rotherham at Millmoor."

For a young boy Shankly spoke some very mature words, not worried at all about giving advice to his peers and motivating the team even then.

"The Carlisle crowd were always a raucous lot, even then they made a lot of noise. The ground wasn't very good to be honest. It sufficed, but it needed knocking down and building again. The changing rooms could be freezing cold and hot water must have been scarce in Carlisle, as we hardly ever had any after a game. I think Tom (Curry) liked us to bath in luke warm water, he felt it was better for us. I remember after one game coming out of the changing rooms, the mud caked thick to my elbows and knees. The water was too cold to wash in, so I was just about to leave when I heard this voice bellow out, it was Tom Curry. 'Shankly, where do you think you are going? Don't you dare leave this ground without washing, clear that shit off your arms and legs now, then come to me afterwards for inspection.' I did too, Tom was a good man and I respected him and his word. I really enjoyed my time at Carlisle, it made me grow up and become the person I am."

At the end of that 1932/33 season, Shankly made his way back to Glenbuck, deeply satisfied with his performances in the 16 games he'd played for Carlisle. "I always knew that Carlisle was right for me, from the day I signed, I always looked out for their results."

Within hours, a telegram was received at the Shankly family home. It requested that the player return to Carlisle at once. Shankly did as was asked of him and upon arrival learned that Preston North End had come in with a bid of £500 for his services. The directors had accepted the bid and so Shankly was to speak with Preston urgently. He did and so ended his time as a player at Brunton Park. "I was highly ambitious. Carlisle was a good enough side. I loved the place, but Preston just seemed a better option. Sure, the money was more too, but it wasn't about that, I wanted the chance to win things. At Preston that chance was always there. That said, Carlisle needed the £500, so there wasn't really much of an option open to me."

Whilst it does not sit well with supporters of Carlisle United, it was the right career move for Shankly, who became a key member of the Preston side that won promotion to the First Division in 1934 and went on to appear in two FA Cup finals, losing one to Sunderland in 1937, but winning the trophy the following season in 1938. Further to these successes, he made his Scotland international debut in a 1-0 win against England in April 1938. As a player it was his most successful period, as four further international appearances were to follow, seven wartime internationals also featured Shankly. But the breakout of war in 1939 effectively ended his playing career. Like many professionals, he guested for a number of teams during the war, including Northampton, Liverpool, Arsenal, Cardiff City, Bolton Wanderers, Luton Town and finally Partick Thistle. He still found time to have a hand in Preston's victory in the 1941 Wartime Cup Final at Wembley. After the war, Shankly returned to Deepdale. He was now aged 33 and many at Preston believed he was coming to the end of his playing days. He gradually dropped out of the first team picture and found himself playing more reserve team football, which infuriated him.

It was February 1949 when Carlisle United made a formal approach to the Preston player, offering him the position of manager. It wasn't a straightforward decision for the 35 year-old and the player was uncertain that it was the right thing to do. Preston did not help matters and threatened to withhold his benefit (of about £750) if he left for Carlisle. Further to this he was offered a benefit game, but only if he agreed to stay with Preston. All in all a sizeable sum of money was on offer, money which would help provide financial security after his playing days were over. Eventually, Preston agreed to release the player if an assurance was given that he would never play competitive football for Carlisle. This was agreed and the deal closed without further complication. All that remained was the player to agree to move and financial terms. Money didn't enter into it, Shankly was grossly disappointed with the attitude of the Preston board and despite a last ditch effort by Tom Finney, pleading with him not to leave, Shankly walked out of Preston and returned to Brunton Park on 19 March 1949.

The salary he accepted to become manager of Carlisle United was the princely sum of £14 per week.

Shankly's first game in charge at Carlisle United took place on 4 April 1949. It was the Cumberland Cup final against local rivals, Workington Reds. United won the match 2-1, Shankly had won a trophy in his first ever game in charge as manager! That season was more or less over when the new boss arrived; safe from relegation with only seven matches to play, it was very much a matter of seeing the season out. The results weren't brilliant, four draws, two defeats, one victory. But the new boss was not about to allow his side time to settle. He breezed through Brunton Park like a maelstrom, getting rid of 'deadwood players' as he would call them and bringing his own staff in; players like Billy Hogan from Manchester City, John Billingham from Burnley, and Alex McIntosh from Barrow. Reg Simpson became Shankly's first signing as a football manager when he followed his new boss from Preston to Carlisle within days of Shankly pitching up at Brunton Park.

If anything, Shankly was ahead of his time as he set about re-branding United and changing their image into a smart and more disciplined body. He later mused: "If you treated your players as if they were the cream they might start to believe it and play like it. We were on our way back home from a game when I saw a new playing kit for sale in a shop window. I told the driver to wait and jumped off the team bus and bought a whole new playing kit. It was needed."

Shankly ensured that the club was doing all it could to attract better players and keep good ones. One scheme was for the club to buy a house and convert it into flats to help with the players' accommodation. His desire to keep the fans happy was well founded. He once said: "Keeping the fans happy is one of my priorities, these people keep me and my players in a job. It is for them we play, and no footballer should ever forget this point." To this end, he could be seen on Sunday mornings, clearing the terracing of weeds and other detritus, painting stands and generally smartening up the appearance of the whole ground

Perhaps though, Shankly will be immortalised at Carlisle because of his pre-match broadcasts to the crowd, informing them over the club Tannoy system of team changes and imploring them to give their support to the players. His discourses became an integral part of attending a match and he was not afraid to speak his mind. On one rumour linking an unnamed striker with the club, he said to thousands of people over the Tannoy: "There is no way Bill Shankly or Carlisle United are interested in signing this player. He is not fit to play in our colours. The man plays as though his feet are tied together, so you can forget all talk of him coming here." It is difficult to imagine that kind of thing happening in the modern age.

The end result was not wholly visible in the league as, after his first full season in charge Carlisle finished ninth in Division Three (North). In the FA Cup, January 1950 saw Leeds United visit Brunton Park in the third round of the competition. Goals from Dick and Lindsay were not enough to prevent the Yorkshire visitors from running out 5-2 winners. Shankly had originally been offered a bonus by Carlisle if he managed to get them into the top three of the league, but as the season progressed it was clear that the directors would not keep their part of the bargain. Despite this, Shankly the motivator was in full flow, as fans and players alike believed that under his guidance anything could be achieved. Geoff Twentyman, a player who was for many years to play under the man he referred to as 'the boss', once unwittingly suffered his manager's wrath. The Carlisle players trudged off the pitch at half-time in one game, that United were losing 2-0, during which Shankly had been screaming his head off on the touchline demanding more and more out of his team. As the players sat in the dressing room, in walked Shankly, who at once yelled at club captain Twentyman: "What did you call at the pre-match toss-up?"

"I called heads, boss," replied the startled Twentyman.

"Jesus Christ!" said Shankly. "NEVER call heads!"

But perhaps Bill Shankly's greatest gift to the public of Carlisle was hope. Season ticket sales for the 1950/51 season reached an all time record high as fans began to anticipate that the team was on the verge of something good. Shankly was a man of the people, he could easily stand on the terracing as one of them, as well as being a manager. They felt he understood them, and that he understood what it was about Carlisle United that made the club so special, so different from every other football club. The supporters were devoutly loyal to him. The league season began well, with Carlisle flying high, gaining five wins from the opening seven games in the league and progressing to the third round of the Cup after victories over Barrow and Southport. In the third round they drew the Arsenal at Highbury. Cup fever again gripped the city. It is said that over 5,000 United fans made the journey. No Carlisle side had ever before played in front of 57,932 spectators, but that day they did just that. Pre-match Shankly walked his players around the Highbury pitch, winding them up and continually telling them they were the best. As the crowd roared and Highbury rocked, the kick-off time soon came around. It was Carlisle who rose to the occasion. Billy Hogan was truly outstanding and continually waltzed past England left-back, Lionel Smith, as time and again he turned the defender this way then that. Phil Turner almost opened the scoring for the visitors, but somehow the Arsenal keeper twisted in mid-air and managed to push his ferocious effort over the crossbar. United never looked under pressure and coped well with any Arsenal threat. At full-time it was 0-0, a remarkable result by anyone's standards.

Arsenal's half-back, the late Joe Mercer, once said of that game: "Carlisle United are not one of my favoured clubs. They always appear to put me and my players in their place. This game was no different. It was always going to be a tricky tie. As I remember, Billy Hogan was the star of the game, he gave poor Lionel Smith a real roasting. It was as though he was floating on air at times and the ball seemed so comfortably attached to him! I cannot recall any other player ever doing that to Lionel. Carlisle were as unfortunate as we were ill prepared for their actual football style, which was way above what we expected. They could have caught us out had we not had element of luck and our keeper had not been right on top of his game."

The replay at Brunton Park before 20,900 screaming Blues fans was a different matter entirely. Arsenal were aware of the threat Hogan posed. Shankly always believed that Arsenal deliberately took him out of the game with some heavy-footed tackling. So, with the Hogan threat nullified, Arsenal went on to win the game 4-1. Shankly was angered by the Arsenal tactics, and vented his feelings afterwards. "We are playing our football in the Third Division (North); did they really have to kick my players off the park? It was a great shame they felt the need to kick Billy Hogan into the terracing, I felt we could have given them a good game up here. It's done now, we have all shook hands. Billy is naturally disappointed as he knows he had the beating of their England full-back. It's a tough lesson, but we have all learned from it. No team will physically outfight any team of mine again."

THERE CAN BE NO doubting that these two performances raised the profile of the Carlisle boss and, at the end of that season, Shankly would leave Brunton Park for good. "The problem I had at Carlisle was that the board of directors, all of whom were devoutly loyal to the club, could stand no more financial pressures. The buying of more experienced and better players never came into the equation. If I had wanted someone, somebody better than I had, then I would have to sell three, maybe four players to subsidise this. It was a never ending circle. All kinds of things had been promised to me, yet the reality was that they would never be delivered. We got some great fish suppers from Johnny Corrieri, but he didn't have the money to influence or bankroll the club, he was simply a businessman, a man who owned a fish and chip shop. Johnny was really disappointed when I left for Grimsby. I applied for the job at Liverpool around the same time as Grimsby. I got an interview, but didn't quite make the standard. I told Johnny then that I was looking to develop myself in management.

He agreed that whilst we were good friends neither he nor the board of directors would stand in my way if I wanted to leave. The entire Carlisle experience was excellent, no club will ever mean as much to me as they do. I was really made to work hard for everything there, character building at its extreme, but worth every moment."

At Grimsby Town Shankly still never fulfilled many, if any, of his ambitions. Within two years he was back in Cumbria, this time at Workington Reds. Two years later, in November 1956, he moved on again, this time to Second Division Huddersfield Town. In a twist of fate after Shankly had been rejected, Huddersfield hammered Liverpool 5-0 at Leeds Road in October 1958. Shankly watched as the directors and officials of the fallen giant trooped out of the ground, thoroughly dejected. A few weeks later, those same directors returned, this time with an offer of employment, which Shankly could not reject. He was now on his final football managerial journey, to Liverpool. The rest, as they say, is history. Though, in this case, not quite.

Carlisle United and Liverpool were to meet several times during Bill Shankly's tenure as manager of the Anfield club. The first of these came about in 1972/73 season, the Football League Cup competition had paired them in the first leg at Brunton Park. Carlisle fought valiantly to earn a 1-1 draw, Les O'Neill scoring Blues' all-important equalising goal.

"My team certainly knew they had a fight on their hands tonight." said Shankly after the encounter. "I think Carlisle showed why they are regarded as one of the better teams at this level. We did enough to hold them off. It may be different at Anfield, though." He was right too. Despite Alan Ross saving a penalty from Tommy Smith, United were heavily beaten. "I thought Alan Ross was fantastic for Carlisle this evening," said Shankly after the game. "I know he has let in five goals, but he saved another ten certainties. I think they [Carlisle] may have been a little overawed by it all."

The following season, it was the FA Cup competition that paired them, this time at Liverpool, in the fourth round proper. Liverpool had been in fine form that season, destroying all who faced them, so when Carlisle held them to a goalless draw it was a real surprise to football in general, let alone the ex-Carlisle boss. "What can you say, they thoroughly deserved it today, I thought we were going to lose," Shankly admitted. "Chris Balderstone was magnificent, but so was the rest of the team. Defensively they coped with us easily. It's going to be difficult up there next week in the replay. I have told my players they must be at the top of their game if they are to stay in the competition. Carlisle at Brunton Park is not a good tie for us, particularly after this." Typical Shankly psychology, lulling the opposition into a false sense of security.

Liverpool, of course, came to Carlisle steamingly motivated and won the tie comfortably by two goals to nil.

BEFORE HIS RETIREMENT from the game in the summer of 1974, after his side recovered from that 0-0 draw at Anfield against the minnows of Carlisle to lift the trophy for only the second time in its history, Shankly was asked about his former club, a team who had just won promotion to the highest echelon of the English game, the old First Division. He said of the achievement: "I would say it's the greatest feat in the history of the game, Carlisle United getting into the First Division of the English League." It was a comment he often repeated. The boy who had once arrived at Carlisle and called the dilapidated stadium 'a glorified hencoop' had witnessed a club he was extremely fond of achieve the impossible, all during his lifetime in the game. God bless you Bill Shankly.

BILLY HOGAN

1949-1956

UNITED CAREER

Games	191
Goals	27

MAGIC MOMENT

The mighty Arsenal were not prepared for the silky skills of Billy Hogan during the epic FA Cup battle of 1951. He ripped holes in the Gunners' defence each time he got the ball

'SIMPLY THE BEST'

AS a schoolboy at Kingmoor primary school in Kingstown, Carlisle, I was fortunate enough to have a teacher who loved football. I was probably no older than nine years of age, but even then, Carlisle United were extremely important to me. My school reports even contained a reference to Carlisle United within them. My teacher stating: 'Paul is a clever lad. If he took as much interest in his academic studies as he does in Carlisle United then he would be a genius. Sadly he doesn't, so he isn't.' I took it as a compliment. Unfortunately my parents didn't and all talk of Carlisle United and football was banned from my home for many weeks.

The teacher who wrote this report has, in my opinion, a lot to answer for. His name was William Graham. He was undoubtedly the best teacher I ever had during my school years. However, the catch is that he was also an ex-professional footballer with Carlisle United and a man who went to every game he could and would discuss them with me whenever the opportunity arose during school playtime breaks. I remember asking Mr Graham, as I then referred to him, who, in his opinion, was the greatest Carlisle United footballer? This was when I first heard the name Billy Hogan. "Billy Hogan was Carlisle United's Stanley Matthews," Mr Graham replied. "Although I think Billy was maybe a bit better than Matthews. What he couldn't do with a football wasn't worth knowing. He had swinging hips, all the skill you could imagine in fact, and he played for Carlisle United."

So it was with some intrigue that many years ago I commenced research into a footballer who has been voted as United's best player of all time and who an older generation of Carlisle supporters still speak of in awe.

WILLIAM HOGAN WAS BORN in Salford on 9 January 1924. He played his early football in the Lancashire leagues until the outbreak of war, which curtailed his playing career. He took up arms and served his country as an infantryman in Italy until war ended and he returned to his Manchester roots. First to notice his soccer skills were Manchester City. Their manager, John Ross (Jock) Thomson, an ex-Scottish International and Everton wing half, had heard of the young Hogan playing locally and went to watch him. After one viewing, Thomson made his move, signing Hogan on amateur terms. It wasn't the greatest of relationships. "Manchester City were going through a time of change," remembered Billy later. "I thought I was in with a shout of doing alright there, but for some reason, Jock never saw me as a long term option. They were a big club, but at the time didn't seem to have a great deal of direction under Jock's management." Putting it bluntly, Jock Thomson wasn't the man to take either Manchester City or Billy Hogan forward. He departed in January 1950 after the club was relegated.

With City now in Division Two and with no real chance to progress in the team, even under new manager Leslie McDowall, Hogan decided that to develop his playing career it was best that he move to another club; even though he didn't really want to leave his home area in Salford. So it was that Carlisle boss Bill Shankly broke the bank and the club record transfer fee by paying City £4,000 for the inside-forward. As part of the deal Hogan was allowed to continue to train with the Maine Road outfit thus enabling him to remain at home and travel to Carlisle for matches. Further, such was Shanks' desire to bring the player to the club, that he agreed to pay all Hogan's associated travel costs to Carlisle on match days.

Keen to do well, and made to feel extremely comfortable in his new surroundings, Hogan made his Carlisle debut in a 1-0 home win over Wrexham on 1 September 1949. Two days later he fired home his first goal for the Blues. He himself declared it was a: "simple tap in at the back post, but they all count don't they?" Hogan went on to make 39 appearances that season scoring six goals. More importantly he was the perfect provider for United strikers George Dick and Jacky Lindsay, both of whom benefited greatly from his wonderful delivery of a ball from wide positions.

Hogan had an aversion to heading the ball. Indeed he rarely did so, claiming it gave him awful headaches. It mattered little, for this was a footballer who enjoyed nothing more than getting the ball down, drifting first inside, then outside to the wing before being so devastatingly accurate with his crosses or shooting. By the December of the forward's first season at Carlisle he had already provided sufficient evidence to indicate that he was going to be the stuff legends are made of. United had been drawn at home to Third Division (South) Swindon Town in the second round of the FA Cup. The game had been in doubt due to heavy snow falling over the city, leaving Brunton Park under several inches of the stuff. Desperately keen for it to go ahead, staff and an army of keen volunteers cleared the terraces and the playing area of all residual snow, using shovels, brushes and hands right up to several minutes before the Saturday afternoon kick-off, a Herculean feat which allowed the fixture to go ahead. An attendance of 18,604 were not feeling the cold for too long. It was Carlisle who kicked off, with the ball almost immediately being played outside to Billy Hogan. Attacking the Warwick Road End of the ground he turned defenders the wrong way and left them despairing as he got to the touchline. Looking up, he crossed the a perfect ball into the penalty area where Jacky Lindsay ran in to meet the ball and thump it home with his head. It is claimed that just 24 seconds had elapsed from kick-off in the centre circle to the ball bulging the back of the Swindon net. Whatever the veracity of that, and of course it is uncheckable, this being 1950, it became the stuff that legends grow out of – and Billy was at the root of it.

Hogan, despite the treacherous conditions underfoot, was fleet of foot and had such perfect balance and poise when on the ball that Swindon just couldn't contain him. United fan Jimmy Baty recalls of that fixture: "I think the Swindon cup-tie was one to be remembered because of Billy Hogan. There was no stopping him that day. It was cold and the Swindon team had hardly got a chance to warm up before Billy had put them on their backsides, dancing round them and dropping crosses into their penalty area time and again. The only mystery is how we didn't score more than two goals. I spoke to Billy Hogan after the game and he said he had enjoyed it and never felt the cold one bit. I think that day every Carlisle supporter went home realising that Billy Hogan was not your average Third Division (North) player; he was absolutely magnificent."

And that tale explains another aspect to the Hogan legend. There was nothing that Billy enjoyed more than discussing the game with fans afterwards. Time and again they (the fans) would line up behind the grandstand waiting for their favourite player to emerge after a game. Billy would find himself surrounded by those eager to get his autograph or just to speak with him. The fans were extremely important to him and after away games he would return with other players to Brunton Park and hand out (free of charge) the programme from the game and ground of the team they had visited. He once said that he and a couple of other players were always tasked by Shanks at away games to go in search of as many programmes as they could find to hand out to United supporters back home.

"The fans are everything, without them there wouldn't be football," Hogan later said. "Bill Shankly always said that we should, as far as possible, be open and honest with fans. He was right too. I remember more than once how the fans lifted me and the team with their singing and chanting from the terraces. There was one bloke I remember who used to be below the main grandstand at Brunton Park week-in, week-out. I would hear him shouting for me to: 'get past him, get past the defender'. Every time I got the ball he shouted the same thing. I never knew who he was, but I always wondered what he looked like. One day I was in Scotch Street in Carlisle city centre when I hears this shout: 'get past him, get past the defender'. I stopped and looked around, but couldn't see anyone looking at me or anyone who might have said it. To this day it remains a mystery, but whoever that person was, he inspired me to do just what he said. I hope I sent him home happy."

THE FOLLOWING SEASON, 1950/51 was for Hogan, sensational. He had already become a terrace hero not only through his fantastic skills and ball control, but also through his outstanding relationship with the club's support. It goes without saying that the side he featured in was then regarded as one of the best in either section of the Third Division. McLaren, Twentyman, McIntosh, Lindsay, Turner; all were footballers of outstanding quality, assembled by a young manager going places. Billy played 45 games that second season, scoring 12 goals which included four goals in the first five games of the season. That form elevated Blues into the promotion pack. Shankly revelled in the limelight the signing of Hogan had provided him and later said of the player: "Billy Hogan was a sensational footballer, one of the best I ever signed or managed and that includes many of these I manage at Liverpool. I would have taken him with me wherever I could, but sadly he enjoyed life at Carlisle too much and didn't really relish the thought of moving further away from his Salford home The fans worshipped him, a few times I had to go out to drag him into the ground to get changed, because he was too busy chatting to supporters outside."

By the end of the 1950/51 season, all the hard work towards a push for promotion was lost when the team lost its penultimate league game at Halifax, dropping them down to third in the final table and missing out on the club's first ever promotion by just two points. Hogan had missed the crucial fixture through injury. "Halifax Town was a name we never uttered at Carlisle for a long time after that result," he said. "They were a struggling side near the foot of the table. We had beaten them at Brunton Park a couple of days earlier, 1-0 and should have had no problems with the return fixture at The Shay. But we did and lost it 1-0. Mansfield, our nearest rivals for promotion, won their game and moved up into second place. It was a very disappointing time. I know some supporters say that we lost out because I was out of the team, but that isn't true. After the Arsenal Cup result everyone in our league wanted to beat us. We were exhausted as a set of players and Halifax were obviously desperate not to finish bottom of the league. It was one of those things. It just wasn't meant to be."

The following season Hogan was an ever present, though his role changed dramatically. The arrival of a new manager, Fred Emery, to replace the departed Shankly meant an influx of fresh talent in the form of strikers Allan Ashman and Jimmy 'Wham' Whitehouse to add firepower to the United attack. Hogan was key to these signings. Both Ashman and Whitehouse were clinical goal scorers, but Hogan was the provider extraordinaire. Ashman, in particular, raved about the player. "Bill Hogan was the best footballer I played with during my time at Carlisle United. In fact I can't think of anyone at any club I have played for or managed who was more exciting, creative and loyal. Bill had everything and he was a real character too. Before one game I said I wanted the ball on my head at every opportunity and he delivered it every time to my head. Sometimes, even when there was a shooting opportunity, he would lay on a better chance for me with a header.

Afterwards when I moaned about him crossing to me all the time instead of passing, he would laugh and say: "But Allan, you said that you wanted crossed balls to head all the time, so that's what you got." Bill was lethal in his partnership with Jimmy Whitehouse, it was frightening really what the two of them could do. One game against Crewe Alexandria was a riot, he was as complete a footballer that day as I ever saw anywhere. The pair of them just read each other so well. I was really fortunate to be playing alongside them both. I learnt a lot from Bill. He was one of those people who just command respect. Players would listen when he spoke. I tell you, if I'd had a Billy Hogan in my First Division team then we wouldn't have been relegated, far from it. He was technically the most gifted player I knew."

Hogan recalls of the team Fred Emery built: "I was devastated when Billy Shankly left the club. He had taught me so much about self confidence and attitude. I know other players were disappointed too, but one thing that Shanks always told us was to get on with it, one man doesn't make a team or a club. I think where he was concerned we know a little different now. He was the ultimate where football management was concerned, the best, and always will be. Then Fred Emery came into the club as someone we never really knew a lot about. He was decent enough and had us all in as individuals. He told me that he was looking to bring in a couple of forwards to support me and that I was key to his thinking and plans for the future. It was a real nice thing to say and I appreciated his support. Team talks weren't quite the same after Shanks left us, and while Fred did all he could to keep us content, there was definitely a void he couldn't quite fill.

As for new players coming in, Allan Ashman was lethal. His first game with us was at Rochdale. I had one of them games where I just seemed to get space and room to do what I wanted. We won 4-0 and Allan grabbed a hat trick. I got a goal myself. We worked well together, but his goals weren't all down to me, no. Allan was more than capable of making and creating goals himself."

IN SEPTEMBER 1952 Crewe visited Brunton Park. It was an awful game, spoiled by the visitors, who kicked lumps out of the United forwards at every chance. Midway through the second half Billy Hogan hit the ground clutching his knee. A blistering tackle had literally bent the knee joint the wrong way, tearing the ligaments on impact. The tackle went unpunished and Hogan himself would explain it as: "Just one of those things that happen in football. Crewe were a tough side and had rattled us from the start. I think I took about seven or eight nasty, and I mean crudely nasty, kicks from their defenders during the game. Then, in the second half, I skipped past a couple of challenges and was about to pass the ball wide when I see this fellow coming in from my right. His foot was knee-high and I thought to myself: 'this is a leg breaker'. I tried to side-step, but he caught me full on. The pain I felt was worse than I had ever had in the game. But that's football I suppose."

Over the following three seasons Billy managed just 37 more appearances for United, the frantic pace which he enjoyed and the ability to turn, spin off defenders and run had clearly deserted him as the knee continued to cause problems. Despite this he never gave up and managed in his last season at the club to muster enough strength to play 34 games and score one final goal in a 4-1 drubbing of Stockport County. "The Stockport game in 1956 was a memorable one for me as I felt I was able to produce some of the skill I used to possess. My knee still hurt, but when you have a good sized crowd inside Brunton Park singing your name and applauding you as you leave the field you feel no pain, just total satisfaction."

His final game for the club came on 28 April 1956 away at Bradford. "It was really painful. I was pushing myself too hard," Billy recalled. "I just wanted to do well for the club and not let anyone down. But after the Bradford game my knee swelled to size of a balloon. All we had was a cold compress in them days, not the treatment facilities they have now. I had to get dressed and make my home with the other players. I think everyone realised it was all over for me. Later that week the boss said to me that he didn't think I was fit enough to play in the final game, I was relieved actually. The club was great to me, they talked through options, but generally speaking we all felt my playing career was over."

Retiring back to Salford, Hogan played local league football to the sprightly age of 62, still refusing to head the ball!

IN 1982, AFTER A survey in the local media, Billy Hogan was voted as the greatest footballer to play for Carlisle United. Forget Peter Beardsley, Jimmy McConnell or Chris Balderstone, Billy Hogan was the player most fans claimed to be the best ever. Sadly in June 2007, whilst this book was being compiled, news broke that Carlisle United's greatest ever player had passed away. It is more than apt then that he has a rightful place in this volume.

I was fortunate enough to meet and interview him in 1988 during one of his visits to Brunton Park and found him charming and somewhat reluctant to believe the adulation he was held in at the club. Despite this, when we sat and discussed his time with Carlisle there was a glint of passion in his eyes as he recalled the days when he was simply the best. "Allan Ashman and 'Wham' Whitehouse were a dream to play with," he recalled. "We had a cracking side then; full of power and skill throughout. As players it really felt as though we were one big family, watching out for each other and knowing what the others were going to do or where they would be on the pitch at any one time. I think the best manager I played for was that chap Bill Shankly. He was a real menace. He was tough and always wore his heart on his sleeve where Carlisle was concerned, but he knew his football. Shanks would say to me just as we were leaving the dressing room to go out onto the pitch: "Bill, you are the best player out there again, let them know it, show them how to play football." Comments like that really make you feel good about yourself as a player. Mind you, if I didn't perform he would give me what for afterwards. You wouldn't be able to print half of what he said, the swear words! Thankfully you couldn't understand the other half of what he said anyway with his accent, especially when he was upset and verbally laying into you, so, as such, it never really hurt too any great extent!

I think every player who ever played for Bill Shankly the manager can have nothing but respect for him. There was something special in the way he spoke to players and motivated them. When we played the mighty Arsenal, as they were then referred to, in the FA Cup in 1951, we had no right to go to Highbury and get anything, let alone a replay. But the boss got us all wound up before the game, walking us round the pitch in a then empty stadium, reminding us of some of the great players who played there. He would say: "That English defender Smith and Mercer, both lucky men to be playing football. I would never sign them, they aren't good enough for Carlisle United. You boys are here because I want you here. Let's get rid of this lot and get into the next round with no fuss."

It didn't end there. He kept at it right until kick-off. We were all a bit in awe by then as you could now hear the crowd inside the stadium. I was amazed to hear shouts for Carlisle every-where, it was wonderful stuff. As we got up to walk out of the dressing room, Shanks grabbed hold of me and said: "Billy, that Lionel Smith is nothing, understand, nothing. Get at him and get round him every time, you will terrify them with your skill, show him up for what he is, okay?"

That was enough for me, I did just as I was asked and felt I did alright. Afterwards, both Lionel and Joe Mercer came up to me and said I was the best forward they had come across that season, but nobody would get two chances to make fools of them. I didn't really under-stand what they meant by it then and I laughed it off."

Carlisle did in fact hold Arsenal to a 0-0 draw that day, but almost won it when Hogan slid through a pass to Phil Turner who hammered a goal-bound shot, which forced a wonder save out of Gunners keeper George Swindin. In the Brunton Park replay it was to be a totally different story.

"The Arsenal team that came to us in the replay had a separate mentality to the one we faced in London five days earlier, this time they meant business," Hogan continued. "I was a marked man. Each time I got the ball one and sometimes two Arsenal players clattered into me. It wasn't fun at all. I asked the referee for a bit of support, but he would just tell me to shut up and get on with the game. It wasn't as if I was deliberately throwing myself to the ground on each challenge. I was getting kicked up in the air.

All I remember is taking on the left back and seeing three players haring at me, not the ball, me! It bloody hurt I tell you. I thought I had broken something, I don't think Muhammad Ali could have hurt me more than them Arsenal players did. I knew I wasn't going to be able to continue; my right leg was painful and both pins were covered in bruises. Mighty Arsenal? More like mighty cheats that day. They really worked us over. They didn't win because of football skill, they won because they were tougher and harder. After the game, their manager came up to me and apologised for the treatment I suffered. He told me that sometimes football skills cannot be matched, so you must do what you feel right to contain a threat. In my case it was kicking me, nothing like sporting behaviour!"

MY LASTING THOUGHT OF a footballer who was clearly one of United's greatest players of all time will be when he let me into a personal secret he had held for countless years. "Some managers liked you to line up for team photographs as though you were in starting formation for a game. The goalkeeper would be central on the back row then his defenders and so on in each position thereafter; the forwards would all sit in the front row. If you want to know something unique about me, I was always a bit funny about team photographs. Obviously I wasn't the tallest of players and so would avoid standing next to someone like Geoff Twentyman or Jim McLaren. Instead, I would like to take my seat in all team photographs on the far right front row. I don't think you will find any pre-posed team photographs without me sitting there. It used to irritate some players that I always sat there, so I just did it for the amusement of it all."

Naturally I've checked and, sure enough, Billy Hogan can be seen in the same front row seat in all team photographs. One other curious point of note is that the player in later years referred to himself as an inside-forward, whereas supporters and other players relate to him as an orthodox winger. It matters little, Billy Hogan possessed sublime skill and, like his one time manager and mentor, Bill Shankly, where Carlisle United was concerned, he always wore his heart on his sleeve. In his own words: "The supporters are everything. Carlisle United's are among the best I played in front of. They deserve player loyalty, they deserve good players, they deserve to be winners."

One thing is for certain. In Billy Hogan, Cult Hero, terrace legend and potentiallythe greatest player ever to don the club shirt, we had a real winner.

IVOR BROADIS

'THE MASTER'

1946-1949 & 1955-59

UNITED CAREER

as player-manager

Games	111
Goals	52
Wins	41

as player

Games	250
Goals	84

MAGIC MOMENT

A brilliant creative display and two goals against York in 1957

> 'Ivor was fantastic. His goals were classy. The Mansfield players didn't know what to do when he got the ball. They tried to kick him but couldn't catch him. I will always remember that as Ivor's match.'
>
> Ted Holmes, United fan

AS a young boy I recall being in primary school at St Peters in Kingstown. These were the days when there was a maximum of about 30 pupils in the entire school and everyone knew everyone else. Playing football in the tight playground is best described as difficult, but somehow we managed it and often the teachers joined in. I cannot remember the occasion, but one day it was announced that ex-England international footballer Ivor Broadis would be visiting the school to talk to us. To be honest, I was only about eight years old and I had never heard of him. However, the male teachers were clearly very excited by it all. When the day came, I was surprised to learn that the visitor had also played for my team, Carlisle United. It proved indeed a spectacle. Ivor came along, and talked not only of football, but of discipline and good conduct which is (or was) an expected part of your behaviour if you were to succeed at a career in the game. He spoke of players who were clearly his friends, players I had only read of and seen pictures of in my *Football Monthly* magazines. More importantly to me, he discussed the appeal of Carlisle United. Even at my tender age I could see that it was clearly a club which was very close to his heart.

After his talk, Ivor gladly signed autographs and took time out to answer all our questions. As inane as they probably were, he gave them all a great deal of thought and replied honestly and openly. I remember him speaking to me, asking which team I supported. I gave him the only reply I knew: "Carlisle United". He seemed pleased to find someone who didn't follow the usual suspect, popular sides like Manchester United or Tottenham Hotspur. One thing above all stuck in my mind about that day; I felt that Ivor was what Carlisle was all about. He was a friendly man, who clearly had good links with schools and the local people. More importantly, he was one of us.

A few years later, well a couple of decades really, I was fortunate enough to meet Ivor again. This time it was outside St James' Park, Newcastle, another of his former clubs. By this time Ivor was a very skilful and revered journalist covering football in the north of England, writing for the *Journal* newspaper and a host of other top papers and magazines. I managed to get some time and the opportunity to speak with him, and, as is usual with me, discussed Carlisle United. Ivor was honest, despite the fact that we were surrounded by mad passionate Geordies, many wearing black and white striped shirts, all keen to touch him or pat him on the back. He was passionate about the Blues and openly said so. Ivor is that sort of person; he says it as it is, honest, frank and open. From that day forth, Ivor Broadis has held my ultimate respect. He is the consummate professional in all that he does. I wasn't alone that day in wanting to seek the knowledge of his invaluable experience. Despite the amount of people wanting to speak with him, he was still able to take time to talk to everyone. He was professionally courteous, despite the extreme pressure he must have felt placed upon him by the eager and enthusiastic screaming hordes.

I wondered that day how he maintained an ice cool composure. It also caused me to ponder if that was the way he played his football, with absolute control. As a supporter and keen historian of Carlisle United I have over the years thoroughly enjoyed researching many facts about the club, meeting and speaking with countless players and ex-players and managers, young and old. All know the name Ivor Broadis. All hold him in the highest esteem. Even when you move away from Carlisle United, his successful football career is acknowledged by countless writers and historians of the game.

I have been fortunate to speak to many football people who knew him as player and a manager. Not one has anything but the best compliments to say for everything Ivor achieved in the game. Some, including the late Bill Shankly, referred to him as 'The Master'; an accreditation of his absolute knowledge of the game and to the way he conducted his business. Disciplined and at times ruthless in his decision-making as a manager, Ivor Broadis was, and remains, a man of the people, respected and adored by the supporters of every club he played for. Spurs, Manchester United, Sunderland, Manchester City and Newcastle United are just a few who he can claim to have represented. Also, let's not forget England. He played and scored in a World Cup finals after all. Today, there are few people in football who can stake such a claim to national respect. Ivor is one such person who can. It makes me extremely proud to say that he is very much part of Carlisle United's history and undoubtedly, one of the greatest Cult Heroes we have ever had at the club.

IVAN ARTHUR BROADIS WAS born in Poplar, East London in 1922. His early football career started at Glengall Road School on the Isle of Dogs, before he moved to Cooper's Company School in Bow. As a young player he stood out amongst many of his peers, consistently scoring goals and with a turn of pace which would leave even the fittest schoolboy defender looking like he was wearing lead boots. Football in the London suburbs was popular. Competition to get into some of the better amateur teams was fierce. Young Broadis very quickly rose above much of the mediocrity that surrounded him and had a host of scouts watching him. It was notable amateur club Finchley who were first attracted to his potential, and signed him. It wasn't very long before he was scoring goals on the Glebelands sports field, where Finchley played their home games. Other, more high-profile clubs were soon alerted. Northfleet United, otherwise known as the Shrimpers, played their football in the Kent League alongside clubs like Gillingham and Dartford. North Kent was (and still is) a working class area and always has been somewhat neglected and apparently ignored by many of the upper classes living elsewhere in the county. These are people who still refer to Kent as the Garden of England. Working class or not, Central Avenue in Gravesend, which is where Northfleet United played their home games, would often enjoy attendances of a couple of thousand, who would turn out to watch their favourites.

There is something incestuous about the uninspiring region of Gravesend. Northfleet for example, claims to be a separate town. To the casual eye there is no clear division, it appears to be just another ward of the same conurbation. There was also a football club

simply called Gravesend. However, at the time, it was Northfleet who were the more promi-
nent of the two and who attracted some of the better players from the London area. For a
while after the war, the clubs amalgamated. Yet even today that peculiarity of the area continues. Blue Square Conference Premier league club Gravesend and Northfleet renamed itself
Ebbsfleet United in the summer of 2007, a move undoubtedly inspired by the nearby Ebbsfleet
cross channel railway link. The hope being, no doubt, to deflect some of the money being
poured into regenerating the area the way of the football club.

Back in the 1930s football in the Kent league wasn't as high profile as it was within the
capital boundaries. Travelling to and from north Kent wasn't the easiest of passages either, so
it is unsurprising to note that Ivor returned to play for Finchley FC within a short space of time.
But the experience had served him well and he was by now earning a decent reputation as an
inside-forward across the entire south east region. With the outbreak of World War II competitive football was temporarily forgotten. However, such was the desire of many to continue to
play the game and the welcome distraction it allowed from the hostilities that were taking
place around Europe, football was soon reinstated as regional wartime leagues were created.
This worked well for the football-supporting public as service personnel (some of whom were
professional footballers) would often find themselves posted to other parts of the United
Kingdom. It therefore provided an opportunity for players to sample football representing
other, often smaller clubs. Aldershot, for example, being based near the British Army's training
camp, boasted a team full of internationals for the only time in their history. For young Ivor, it
provided him with the opportunity to forge a name for himself in the game he excelled at and
so enjoyed playing. He was serving in the 1383 Transport Command of the Royal Air Force
and, as it so happened, he was to be moved around the country quite a lot, allowing him to
experience a wide range of clubs.

As he hailed from the Isle of Dogs it was only natural that his local club side Millwall,
would give him the opportunity to represent them. This was during the 1940/41 season and
Ivor made a total of 14 appearances for the Lions, scoring six goals. That same season he
also turned out for Tottenham Hotspur. His appearance/goal ratio was even better for the
north London club, where he notched ten goals in 12 appearances. The following season
saw a further 35 appearances and 12 goals in the white of Spurs. His reputation as a player
of outstanding ability was vastly enhanced during his spell at White Hart Lane. Over the
following three seasons he was to make a further 29 appearances, scoring 11 goals in the
process. It was while at Spurs that Walter Winterbottom first noted his talent. Unknown to
anyone at the time, Winterbottom would go on to manage the England national football team
from 1946 to 1962.

Manchester United were Ivor's next great admirers and between 1942 and 1944 he
turned out four times for the Old Trafford club, scoring three goals into the bargain. Clubs in
the north of England began to hear of the powerful inside-forward with a loaded shot and after
a brief stint (one game, one goal) at Bradford Park Avenue, he eventually arrived at Carlisle
United after being stationed at Crosby-on-Eden. During the 1945/46 season he made 20
appearances and scored 11 goals playing alongside players like Billy Adams, Jackie Cape and
the then-prolific, Dalston-born, Jack Connor.

Everyone at Carlisle United was impressed by the mild mannered Southerner, who had
made such an impact in the period of wartime football. Carlisle were effectively managerless

after Hugh Harkness, who it should be said had done a sterling job of work holding the club together as manager during the wartime era, had voluntarily stood down from the position. To be fair to Harkness, he didn't possess the experience or the knowledge to manage in league football and he was advised that this was the reason why he couldn't continue in the role as the club wanted someone with Football League experience. Company Secretary Bill Clarke temporarily stood in until the board found their man and struck a sensational deal with the 23 year-old Broadis to join the club as player/manager. Hugh Harkness could perhaps feel a little bitter about his replacement, as Broadis too was without a single Football League appearance! Ivor did, though, possess far greater experience of the game. Whatever the politics behind the recruitment, it was without doubt one of the best appointments and the right thing for the club to do in its history. Despite his tender age, Broadis had played with some of the country's leading players. He was tactically astute and had made many contacts within the game. For the record, he was and officially remains the youngest Football League manager. Sadly, given his excellence and ability, this, and his remarkable departure from the club, are what he is most remembered for during his tenure at Carlisle United.

THE YOUTHFUL BROADIS must have found life at Brunton Park extremely tough in those early days. For a start, the ground wasn't in the greatest of order. There was the playing surface itself, not well looked after, but still one of the best outside the top clubs. The problem was the unevenly-laid cinder track which surrounded the playing area. This harsh looking and spiteful stuff could and did cause injury to players. The club itself hadn't been in the best of shapes when Broadis arrived. It was financially strapped with no budget for transfers and had a chairman, Mr Reed, who, whilst being an ardent fan, wasn't the simplest person to negotiate anything with. A few years ago Broadis said: "It was doomed. Imagine a 23 year-old trying to work with a board of directors where the average age was about 70! Trying to get anything out of the board was like facing an inquisition. I had to justify everything three times over. I once asked for improved lighting for when the players trained in the evening and it was dark. Two 100 watt light bulbs were the solution the board arrived at. Two bulbs dangling from the old grandstand. Hardly floodlights!

What I will say though, is that they did back me with the signing of some players. They had to agree and want the players themselves, mind, but overall it was a baptism of fire. It certainly stood me in good stead for my future career in the game."

Despite all this, Ivor persuaded many players to come to the club, selling it to his targets through his own vision and ambitions of where he wanted to take it. However, his time as manager can only be regarded as average. His first season in charge, for example, was abysmal. United scored a total of 70 goals, Broadis himself scoring 19 of them, but, on the opposite side of the coin, they conceded 93 goals, the worst in the league. There were some remarkably inconsistent results. High-scoring victories such as the 5-1 thrashing of Hartlepools were countered by some horrible hammerings, such as the 9-2 defeat at Doncaster Rovers, a 5-1 reversal at home to Darlington, and a 6-0 defeat at Rochdale.

Whilst life at Brunton Park may not have been a bed of roses, Broadis the player was simply sensational with a ball at his feet. In the 1947/48 season he found the back of the net 20 times, including a hat-trick against Mansfield Town on the first day of the New Year. His performance during this fixture left supporters speechless. United supporter Ted Holmes recalled: "It was freezing cold and Mansfield were known as a bit of a tough team to break down; a side similar to ourselves. They had some sharp players, who could punish you if you let them get at you. They came to Carlisle and were all over us. For the first 45 minutes, we couldn't get a look in. Broadis had gone close about three times with shots, but it never looked like we were going to score.

Then, in the second half, he [Ivor] was absolutely fantastic. It was the first time I had seen a player totally dominate and dictate a game. He must have covered every blade of grass on the pitch. His goals were classy too. The Mansfield players didn't know what to do when he got the ball. They tried to kick him, but couldn't catch him. We won 3-1 in the end, but I will always remember it as being Ivor's game."

The team's performances on the field were vastly improved from when he first arrived at the club and off it things had really started to change. Proper training procedures had been adopted and a much-admired scouting system implemented, meaning that Broadis was alerted to all the best up-and-coming local talent, reaching into Scotland and the football factory that was the north east. The following 1948/49 season turned out to be a more than memorable one for both Broadis and Carlisle, as both hit the headlines. Sadly, for the club it was for all the wrong reasons. Results were again inconsistent. A heavy and traumatic 6-0 defeat at York City was not to be the worst suffered that season. In early December, high-flying Rotherham United smashed eight goals past United keeper Bill Sweeney at Brunton Park, in what is, thankfully, still the club's record home defeat (1-8). The flourish of the previous season when the team finished in ninth place in the league, now seemed a million miles away.

With the club financially struggling to make ends meet, there didn't appear to be any light at the end of the tunnel for Broadis, who was working night and day to try to sustain an effective team whose primary objective was to stay in the league. How frustrating it must have been to the young ambitious player/manager, still in his early twenties, to have to labour so hard under the restricted conditions he endured at Brunton Park. The board of directors themselves did all they could to subsidise the manager, however, there was a need for long term objectivity and a certain amount of pragmatism. Broadis wanted the opportunity to succeed. In truth he was too young to commit to the long haul of building Carlisle United.

For a number of weeks there had been mounting speculation that Broadis was being eyed up by other clubs. Preston North End, Manchester City and Blackburn Rovers were, it was claimed, all closely monitoring his situation. Then on 31 January 1949 news first broke in the north east of England, in Sunderland to be precise, that the local club had made a new signing. Ivan Arthur Broadis would be wearing the red and white stripes of Sunderland at Roker Park for the immediate future!

To say that there was absolute uproar in Carlisle and in football would be an absolute understatement. Questions of legality were asked as Broadis became the first ever Football League manager to transfer himself as a player to another club. He had negotiated and agreed his own transfer fee; the princely sum of £18,000 was deposited in the United coffers, meaning the club was left in its healthiest state ever. Despite the cash injection, however, Carlisle was in turmoil as their manager and also best player were gone in one fell swoop.

Emotions were mixed among the club's supporters. Some felt he had betrayed the club, while others felt he had done everyone, including himself, a huge favour, securing the stability of Carlisle in the process. Whatever the situation, Broadis' reign as player/manager at Brunton Park will not be remembered for affectionate football reasons, certainly not for success on the pitch. In fact he should be remembered by all United supporters as the man who saved Carlisle, pulling them from the precipice of financial meltdown.

No supporter who saw the raw talent of Ivor Broadis during his first spell at the club will ever forget the rough diamond, who led from the front and scored some great goals too. He will be widely regarded as the manager who laid the foundations for the club's future, as first Bill Shankly and then Allan Ashman picked up the baton and ran with it towards the heyday of the First Division.

LESS THAN TWO YEARS LATER, in October 1951, Broadis was on the move again; this time to Manchester City for a record-breaking fee of £25,000. City boss Les McDowall had been tracking the form of the inside-forward with the fierce shot for some time and was desperate to get his man. Within the space of two months Broadis was making his first full England appearance, the first of 14. During his time at Maine Road he played 79 games and scored just 12 goals, a lesser return in comparison to his other clubs.

The lack of goals did not deter Newcastle United, who signed him two years later for a fee of £20,000. The move back to the north east proved more positive than his first stint there, at Newcastle's neighbours, Sunderland. Most football writers when discussing Broadis' fine career rightly claim that he probably played his best football for Newcastle. There can be no doubting that he matured in his game whilst at St James' Park. The passionate Newcastle fans took to him and quickly accepted him as one of their own and to this day he is welcomed with open arms by the club's fanatical support. At Newcastle Broadis played in the same side as another Blues Cult Hero, the late Bob Stokoe, then a centre-half, who told me of his recollections of the confident inside-forward. Stokoe said: "There was a footballer who at times could dazzle and make you wonder: 'how the hell did he do that?' That player was Ivor Broadis. A right bugger of a footballer, he could out-run, out-jump and out-fox most players I knew. Give him half a glimpse of the goal with a ball at his feet and he would shoot too. Ivor is not only one of the best footballers I saw and knew, he was also a decent man and the most articulate and accurate football correspondent of his time. I would often read his columns and, when I could, listen to him talking about the game. He did well at Newcastle. The supporters really took to him and I know manager Joe Harvey had a lot of time for him as both a footballer and a man. Ivor is one of the game's great ambassadors even today."

Being the perfect gentleman and an ambassador is a recurrent theme throughout any conversation one has with anyone privy to Broadis' career. However, he did have his moments. At Newcastle he didn't get on too well with another player called Jimmy Scoular; indeed, few people got on with this gruff, tough Scotsman. The pair had many confrontations. On one particular occasion Scoular and another player were walking to the training ground as it was pouring down with torrential rain. Suddenly Broadis came hurtling around a corner, driving a brand-new car. Seeing the men, he blasted his horn, apparently to thoroughly hack Scoular off and to get them to move out of his way. Scoular let loose and shouted some profanities towards Broadis and continued the abuse when they both arrived in the dressing room, to which Broadis retorted: "Sorry James, but if you would like to relieve your feelings, feel free to urinate on my car bonnet."

The Newcastle dressing room apparently burst into hysterical laughter as once again Broadis had taken control of a volatile situation and put a humorous spin on it. Other players who played alongside the England International recall how he always maintained his calm and displayed a collected attitude in times of stress or confrontation. It was one of his real skills, keeping the dressing room calm when the pressure was on, and a technique no doubt learnt at the hard edge of management as a callow 23 year-old boss at Carlisle.

Perhaps, however, Broadis's greatest personal achievements in the game came during his appearances for England in the 1954 World Cup finals in Switzerland. On 17 June 1954 he scored two of England's goals in a 4-4 draw with Belgium in the first group game. Playing alongside the legendary Stanley Matthews, the wonderful Nat Lofthouse and the awesome Tom Finney, Broadis was outstanding. His control and power were perfectly integrated into a good side, led by that man Winterbottom. England progressed through the group stages to the quarter-finals of the competition where they met Uruguay. Sadly, albeit in typical fashion as we now know in major tournaments, England struggled, while the South American team hit their best form for the game and triumphed 4-2.

JUST OVER TWELVE MONTHS LATER, Ivor returned to his spiritual home as in July 1955 he came back to where his league career had started, Brunton Park, Carlisle. It was Fred Emery who had heard that the player might be available as he didn't fit into Newcastle manager Duggie Livingstone's long-term plans. Emery struck the deal which brought him back to Carlisle, signing him as player/coach for a fee of £3,500. His first season back proved to be very much a replay of when he had previously been at the club. Goals were being scored in abundance, but also being leaked like a sieve. Broadis was at his brilliant best when playing with the likes of Allan Ashman, Jimmy 'Wham' Whitehouse, Ian Atkinson and Billy Hogan. Despite such quality on the pitch, United boss Emery couldn't find a way to plug a defence which simply leaked goals. Over the next few seasons, Broadis looked every bit the player who had graced the international stage of the World Cup finals. Cultured on the ball, he was still deceptively effective without having the scintillating pace he had possessed in his younger days. The goals continued to flow, this time in conjunction with another devastatingly lethal strike partner in the form of Alf Ackerman. However, in his last season in the English game (1958/59) there were fewer appearances and Broadis managed just two goals. With Ackerman moving on, Ivor was suddenly facing the prospect of playing a peripheral role at Brunton Park as younger players were drafted in.

The writing was on the wall, as the season progressed. Players with whom he had formed good relationships and footballing partnerships began to retire. First Jimmy Whitehouse, then Allan Ashman and then the long-standing Paddy Waters hung up their boots. Still Ivor stood firm and played on, until the end of the 1958/59 season. Then, in June 1959, for the second, and last, time he left the club. He had played a total of 250 games in all competitions for Carlisle United, scoring 84 goals, among them two hat-tricks.

BROADIS LEFT CARLISLE at the age of 37 and yet one can imagine that there would still have been no end of playing offers made to him. The draw of football continued to lure him. It was, after all, what he knew best. So it was that he made the move into the Scottish game, this time to show his wares at Palmerston Park, Dumfries, home of Scottish side Queen of the South. Life over the border invigorated fresh enthusiasm into Broadis and, after a few appearances, he agreed to act as club coach for a short time.

By 1962, now 40, he had effectively retired from the game. Unlike so many players of the time this intelligent and articulate man had options. His eloquence and ability to write about the game, matched with his outstanding knowledge of football, allowed him to pursue a second career. He became the north west's leading sports journalist, specialising in writing about football. It should be said that he was equally as successful on this front as he was as an inside-forward. Even today, nearly half a century later, Ivor Broadis is one of the most respected journalists covering the northern game.

Few footballers command such respect after their playing days are over, but Ivor is an exception to the rule. He is still to be found at almost every Carlisle home game, sitting in or around the press box area at the rear of the main stand. And still he enjoys nothing more than a good debate about football and his beloved United. The master indeed!

ALF ACKERMAN

1956-1959

UNITED CAREER

Games	96
Goals	62

MAGIC MOMENT

The Brunton Park crowd would roar – "Acker, Acker, Acker, Ackerman. He'll score a goal if anyone can!" Ask Birmingham City's defence who had no idea how to contain him

'ACK-ATTACK'

GOALS and goal scorers play a common theme in determining Cult Hero status at all football clubs. Perhaps more than any other position on the pitch, strikers are provided with the best opportunity to elevate themselves to hero level. At United there have been many such men, some coming very close to warranting a place within this work. Players like Frank Clarke (moustache and all), Billy Rafferty, Joe Laidlaw and David Reeves have all made their mark and left behind legacies of great goalscoring exploits and match-winning performances. Billy Rafferty indeed makes a spirited effort to gain access to the top twenty Carlisle Cult Heroes thanks to his ten minute hat-trick in the closing stages against Cardiff City in 1976, a feat which snatched victory from the jaws of defeat in comic book hero fashion. Billy still lives in the city and is best known for this performance. But one match does not maketh the man.

Likewise Frank Clarke, of 'six foot two, eyes of blue, Frankie Clarke is after you' fame came close to earning a place in the top twenty. Frank's incredible goal contribution during our promotion-winning season up to the First Division back in 1973/74 was nothing less than exhilarating. Four fantastic goals in one game against Swindon Town, then a brace against Orient ensured that the promotion push was kept on track. Sadly, Cult Hero status is not something that can be bestowed due solely to skill, quality or quantity. It comes down to much more than that; it is the unwritten affinity the individual has with the club's support, the eccentricities of those players that cause fans to love them or hate them. Whatever, it provides certain men with a status that can never be removed.

One such player who most definitely had a close relationship with the United fans of his era was Alf Ackerman, who joined the club in November 1956. A forward with a marvellous reputation wherever he served, Ackerman was an instant success at Brunton Park, a place he always recalled with extreme fondness later in his career.

Born in Pretoria (now known as Tshwane) South Africa in January 1929, Ackerman took to playing football at local colleges in the South African capital. Pretoria has a long established history in football and is a city synonymous with top professional football in the country. Clubs such as Mamelodi Sundowns, Mamelodi United, Berea Park and Arcadia have enhanced the status of the South African game worldwide, but it was for a lesser known outfit that Ackerman established his ablity. Signing for the now defunct Pretoria Municipals, he developed into a quick and fleet-of-foot attacker, blessed with a lethal shot. Those skills earned him a growing reputation, enhanced by his goals. Over a two year period he established himself as one of the top three goal-getters in the local leagues.

In 1947 he was selected to play for a South African XI which was to face a number of tourist club sides, amongst them Glasgow-based Clyde FC. The showpiece game against one of the then top sides in Scottish football turned into something of a farce as Ackerman show-boated his way through 90 blissful minutes that would make his name. He took the Scottish sides defence apart with sweeping runs, peppering the Bully Wee's goal at every opportunity.

At the end of the match he received a standing ovation from not only the fans on the terraces, but from some of the Clyde players.

After the game discussions were quickly commenceed to bring Ackerman to Scotland for trials and contractual options. The end product was that Ackerman arrived at Shawfield, home of Clyde FC, a few weeks later, with a big reputation as everyone discussed the young South African who had terrorised one of the toughest defences in Scottish football.

The route from South Africa to British football was to become an increasingly well-trodden route in the 1950s. Most famously Bill Perry arrived at Blackpool, after being similarly spotted on a close-season tour, to score the winning goal in the sensational 'Matthews Final' at the climax of the 1953 FA Cup. Other names followed suit, including Wolves' Eddie Stuart.

But Ackerman was one of the first. Quiet and unassuming, he settled into his new home in the autumn of 1947 and was soon making his mark in Scottish football. He became a regular scorer, but with that, he found, came consequences. Ackerman literally became a 'marked' man and was on the receiving end of some brutal tackling, which saw him suffer more than his fair share of injuries. Whilst with Clyde, the team reached the 1949 Scottish FA Cup final (losing 4-1 to Rangers) and he enhanced his already high profile through the side's consistent good quality football.

Word spread of his talents and Second Division Hull City, then managed by the legendary Raich Carter, visited Shawfield to take a look at the promising young forward. Carter was impressed by what he saw and at once opened negotiations for the signature of the South African player. £11,500, the same fee which had taken Stanley Matthews from Stoke City to Blackpool just three years earlier, was what it took to capture Ackerman.

Carter, it is said, told colleagues that he saw in Ackerman something of himself; a forward who could turn defences and score goals at will. 34 appearances later, with a return of 21 goals, and he was sold on, this time to Norwich City. Alf always cited the fact that he couldn't settle in the city as his reason for departure, but there were also behind-the-scenes issues which aroused much concern. Carter had spent a lot of money on transfers and was unable to keep a big playing squad satisfied. In an era well before 'squad rotation' became a known phenomenon, player unrest at not getting an opportunity spilt over and it is believed that 'imports' were not readily accepted by many home grown players, some whom refused to link with them during training sessions. Carter is believed to have turned his back on a frustrated Ackerman in an attempt to resolve the dressing room issues, so the South African nomad was sold on. Being a gentleman himself, Alf never discussed this publicly; he declared that he liked Hull City.

THE MOVE TO Carrow Road would prove a good one. Norwich were then managed by Scotsman Doug Lochhead, who had been tipped off about Ackerman's potential when he had first arrived at Clyde. Carter had beaten him to Alf's signature, but now at last he had got the player he wanted. The move suited Ackerman. He didn't have anything to prove and Norwich were a well respected football team, regarded as a football-playing side in Division Three (South).

The Norwich support took to him at once, as the goals just flowed from his boots and head. A total of 66 appearances, with another remarkable return of 31 goals in two seasons, means he is still revered as one of the all-time prolific centre-forwards at Carrow Road. Imagine then, the surprise when it was revealed in October 1953, that City had sold Ackerman; allowing him to return to Hull City! There was uproar. However, the club were in no financial position to withold the player from such a move.

The Hull return was bemusing to many, although it is explained by Ackerman's desire to complete unfinished business. Raich Carter had left Boothferry Park in 1951 after a dismal failure to get the Tigers promoted to the First Division. Indeed even over 50 years later Hull remains the largest city in these Isles never to have boasted a top flight football team. Carter had spent considerable amounts of money in recruiting stars to the club, including the young Don Revie, but had failed to achieve success. He was replaced as manager by Bob Jackson (who was to later sue Hull City), and the return of Ackerman was welcomed. It was under Jackson that Alf flourished, as he starred alongside Bobby Crosbie in attack, with the pair terrorising defences throughout the land, becoming known as the 'terrible twins'. But still Hull couldn't make it into the top flight.

In 1955, Ackerman was on the move again, this time in a double transfer which also saw fellow Tiger Ken Harrison switch to a rather unfashionable Derby County. There can be no denying that Alf's second coming at Hull had been much happier than his first, but, with no tangible success to speak of, his release more or less coincided with the dismissal of his British football mentor, Bob Jackson.

The move to the East Midlands did not prove a positive one, yet Rams followers still recall the days when Alf Ackerman wove his magic on the Baseball Ground pitch. One Third Division (North) game against Accrington Stanley at the Baseball Ground remains a firm favourite. Rams fanatic Damon Earl told me: "I still remember Alf Ackerman as one of the cleverest centre-forwards of his time. I think it was him who inspired the local press headline [*Derby Evening Telegraph*] 'Crack 'em in Ackerman.' I think this was when he scored four goals against Accrington Stanley. It was a top of the table clash [on 7 April 1956, before an atten-dance of 22,993]. Alf was sensational that day, he used to celebrate his goals with style, doing a little sort of jig for the crowd. He would entertain supporters with his ball-trickery, mocking the defender and winking at the crowd as he bamboozled players with his skill. He was really confident and one of the greatest characters we ever had at the club."

When Derby boss Jack Barker moved on, he was replaced by Harry Storer, a manager who wanted to rebuild the team and bring in his own players. Ackerman was in and out of the team and couldn't get a decent run of appearances to prove himself to the manager. Storer, it should be said, was odd. He would place his pet dog on guard outside his office to deter people from entering, thus excluding himself from social interaction. Certainly he was an arrogant man, who didn't listen to players desires or needs. As such he took a dislike to Ackerman's confidence and tended to ignore or undermine his influence during training sessions. Eventually matters came to a head when Alf, frustrated by his lack of first team opportunities and the treatment he received from the manager, burst into Storer's office one morning and demanded a transfer at the earliest opportunity. It isn't recorded what Storer's response was, although we can probably guess. What is for certain is that it benefited another set of fans as Alf Ackerman was sold to Carlisle United for a knock down fee of £2,250 in November 1956.

DURING THAT FIRST SEASON at Brunton Park, Ackerman burst into supporters' consciousness, scoring 26 goals in just 32 games. His total included a remarkable seven goals in four games in the FA Cup alone. In one match against Mansfield Town in December 1956 he scored four times in a 6-1 victory. Leaving the pitch he was mobbed by the Brunton Park support and said of his feat: "That's what you want me to do, so I do it. Please keep singing my name. It gives me the greatest thrill to know I am pleasing you. I like it here. You people are the best I have known since coming over here." Manna from heaven for Blues fans.

Ackerman certainly had the wow factor on the pitch, and he also had the perfect touch when it came to being a down to earth star. There are those around Carlisle who will tell you how he gave out gifts to children before games and always took time to discuss his perform-ances with anyone who wanted to speak with him. Combine footballing prowess with such geniality and care and you have the perfect Cult Hero in the making.

In more ways than one Ackerman launched United into the record books when, in 1957, a club record attendance was set at Brunton Park. Alf had scored both goals in an FA Cup second round victory over Darlington to put Blues into the third round proper. The draw paired United with First Division Birmingham City. The interest was immense. In those days of difficult away travel, Birmingham might only bring a few hundred fans to Carlisle, but in the city itself everyone wanted to attend the game. Temporary stands were built to house fans and extra turnstiles had to be constructed to ensure full gate receipts were taken. The media reported an attendance of 27,500, yet only 27,164 tickets had been sold! To make matters worse, Brunton Park wasn't infiltration proof and it is said that over 3,000 fans gained entry without tickets meaning that over 30,000 were inside the ground. Whatever, a new ground attendance figure was set that day. The record books say 27,500, the reality is that it was clearly over the 30,000 mark.

With such an attendance it was always going to be an intense affair on the pitch. City were expected to win comfortably, but they hadn't accounted for Alf Ackerman. In a spirited fight-back, United clawed back from certain defeat to claim a 3-3 draw; and Ackerman was the scorer of all three United goals. It was an outstanding performance not only by United, but by Ackerman, who was at his devastating best that day. In an interview later in his career he alluded to the Birmingham game as being the most outstanding of his career, claiming that if he had taken all the chances that had come his way, Carlisle could have won 7-3. Never one to shirk away from a belief, he also referred to Carlisle's Ivor Broadis and Allan Ashman as being the best two forwards he played with during his entire football career.

DURING THE 1957/58 season Ackerman continued his outstanding performances, scoring 40 goals in all competitions for Carlisle, including three against Accrington Stanley, who were clearly a club he enjoyed destroying! Gateshead were another side who found themselves on the receiving end of an Ackerman hat-trick. By now he was the terrace favourite and the cry 'Attack them Ackerman' or 'Ack–Attack–Ackerman' often resounded around the Brunton Park terraces.

The bond between star striker and adoring public appeared unbreakable. But then everything changed.

The arrival of Andy Beattie, a manager who undoubtedly used Carlisle United to his own ends and whose name continues to appear in some of the clubs more 'interesting' historical pieces, saw the break up of the Ackerman/Carlisle relationship. Beattie arrived in May 1958 and took an instant dislike to Ackerman whom he felt, for want of a better expression, was too big for his boots. The pair failed to bond and soon it became clear that the manager was not one to succumb to a player's demands. Beattie, it is said, offered Ackerman a move out of Brunton Park, but the player refused to budge, claiming he enjoyed it so much in Carlisle he wanted to stay.

Beattie took matters into his own hands, placed Ackerman on the transfer list and played him in the first team only occasionally, much to the disbelief of the supporters. By January 1959, he would be gone, sold to Millwall. Beattie it has to be said, did little or nothing for Carlisle United. In fact he was an extremely fortunate man to have managed at the level he did with Nottingham Forest, Wolves and Huddersfield Town. He is remembered at most clubs as an autocrat, who saw himself as the man fans should revere, forgetting that those accolades should be left for the men on the pitch, not in the dugout. Certainly Beattie is not remembered with any great fondness at Brunton Park, albeit he did ensure that the club purchased houses as an incentive to attract players. Without doubt, he forced Ackerman out for egotistic al, rather than footballing reasons. Those who knew Alf during the period after Carlisle say that he flatly refused to discuss Beattie or Harry Storer in any form. One cannot suggest that Ackerman was at fault for these 'bust ups' as his on the pitch discipline was exemplary and there is no record of him being dismissed or punished anywhere in Football League records.

AT MILLWALL FURTHER ADULATION fell at the player's feet as, alongside the youthful Joe Broadfoot, Ackerman forged a brilliant strikeforce. In one Third Division (South) game against Chester, with the Lions leading 1-0 with 20 minutes remaining, Ackerman and Broadfoot cut loose. Chester were eventually defeated 7-1, six goals coming in that closing 20-minute period.

At the end of his first season at Millwall the team just missed out on promotion, but Alf finished the season with 18 goals to his credit. Once again, although now adjudged to be a veteran at the age of 30, he was held in high regard as one of the best strikers outside the First Division.

Recently the question was asked as to who the most prolific foreigner in the history of the Football League is? To my surprise the name Alf Ackerman, with 405 appearances and 217 goals for Hull, Norwich, Derby, Carlisle and Millwall cropped up. Certainly compared to the likes of other foreign imports, Alf stands proud. He was consistent and devastatingly lethal wherever he played, and importantly to us Blues fans, many of his career performances came for Carlisle United.

After leaving Millwall in June 1961, Alf joined Dartford FC as player/manager. During his first season he guided the Darts to reasonable success in the FA Cup competition and to promotion. He naturally continued to score goals himself and built a solid foundation from which the Dartford club would thrive. For two consecutive years under his guidance Dartford won the Kent floodlit league and were regarded as the county's top side, despite the existence of the rapidly improving Gillingham.

In 1966, he received his first and only managerial dismissal in the game, after the club found itself struggling and were eventually relegated. It was a sad blow, but one which wasn't to prove devastating. Ackerman was held in high regard throughout football and as a result he wasn't to go short of work within the game. Within days of his dismissal he was offered scouting positions at various London clubs including Charlton Athletic, Millwall and Queen's Park Rangers.

Contacts back home in South Africa were by now feeding some of the larger, more aspiring clubs throughout Europe. Thus Ackerman tried to influence a greater input from South Africa into the London football scene. Success never followed, but he did possess an incredible knowledge of football in the south east and was soon feeding these clubs with young stars. Having settled in north Kent he opened a newsagents in Dartford and looked to have drifted out of a front line role in the game, when, in 1968, Gravesend and Northfleet offered him a managerial position. He knew the local football scene like no-one else and soon had acquired a number of shrewd signings for the Stonebridge Road outfit.

Again success followed and promotion was achieved in 1970/71, but Gravesend was a distant cry from the great days of Carlisle United and the 30,000 plus fans who packed Brunton Park to witness Ackerman at his best. In quiet moments he told friends in Dartford that he felt Gravesend and Northfleet signalled the end of his career in the British game. The club had a decrepit stadium without any hope of improvement, and, with relatively successful neighbours Gillingham in the Football League, the club had been left with a tiny fan base. The Gravesend years were aptly named. Alf did his best to motivate the entire club, but as he told his friends: "it had always been and was still regarded a dreary place football wise." Finally, in 1974, having struggled to get the backing of the board of directors to push for promotion, and with his heart now elsewhere, Alf stood down and turned his back on the game. Coincidentally, he was replaced as manager of Gravesend by Tony Sitford, a player who had scored the winning goal for Gravesend to painfully knock Carlisle out of the FA Cup in 1963.

A FEW YEARS LATER Alf Ackerman, suffering from ill health, returned to his native South Africa, where he died, in Johannesburg, on 10 July 1988, aged just 59. It was a great loss to football at a relatively young age.

More positively football supporters of greater and bigger league teams than Gravesend recall Alf Ackerman as a very special talent indeed. He was someone who cared for the fans and genuinely tried to succeed. At Clyde there remains a pride that it was they who first unearthed his prodigious talent and gave him the opportunity to showboat on British shores. At Derby County he is recalled solely for his goalscoring exploits and celebrations, at Hull City he is recalled for his cheek and impudence when on the ball, at Norwich and Millwall he is still respected enormously for achieving so much in so little time. At Carlisle United his goals and all-round contribution is still discussed in the clubs, pubs and bars throughout the city. The great debate as to just who is or was United's best striker will continue on. It is of course an unanswerable question. But be your own belief McConnell, Whitehouse, McIlmoyle or Poskett, one thing for certain is that Alf Ackerman will always be regarded as one of the very best to wear the Cumbrians' blue and white.

ALLAN ASHMAN

'THE BOSS'

1951-1959
63-7 & 72-5

UNITED CAREER

as player

Games	207
Goals	98

as manager

Games	349
Wins	150

MAGIC MOMENT

Firing a lethal hat-trick on his debut against Rochdale in a 4-0 romp

THERE is a saying in football that advises players and managers against returning to old football haunts and successes. Thankfully not all conform to this advice. The case of George Allan Ashman certainly disproves the theory that failure awaits second time round as the expectancy is so high.

A true Yorkshireman, Ashman was yet another United Cult Hero born into a mining community, this time in Rotherham, South Yorkshire. He arrived in this world on 30 May 1928, around the same time that Carlisle United first entered into the adventure that is the Football League.

Playing local football, Ashman was spotted by Sheffield United, who offered him amateur terms playing in their Central League side. Nottingham Forest then signed him up to their 'A' team when he was aged just 16. Twelve months later Ashman signed on professional terms. Whilst his career was put on hold for national service, he was soon back at Forest and making a name for himself, scoring six times in one reserve game against an RAF XI. Unbeknown to him at the time, this was a game which was to map out his future in football. Watching from the sidelines was Bradford boss, Fred Emery. A man as knowledgeable as anyone in the strengths and weaknesses of the northern game, he was on the lookout for new talent. He noted the name of Ashman and closely monitored his progress.

Meanwhile, in Carlisle, with Bill Shankly having moved to Grimsby Town, United found themselves managerless. The board of directors were looking for a solid and dependable replacement for the charismatic Shankly, someone who would take the club forward without looking to move on too quickly. It was no surprise that in July 1951 they turned to the ex-Doncaster Rovers stalwart, Frederick David Emery. Moving into the Brunton Park hot-seat, Emery knew exactly what was required of him. He wanted out-and-out goal scorers at the club to bolster a bid for promotion and seized the opportunity to make contact with Nottingham Forest to enquire about Ashman. The striker had scored three times in 13 league starts for Forest, but had not been able to make a first-team spot his own. The two clubs agreed a transfer fee (a then sizeable £5,500) and Forest allowed Ashman to visit Brunton Park for talks. "I remember talking with Fred Emery, he really sold the club well," Ashman recalled. "He told me he could make me into a first rate centre-forward and that he would play me every week as long as I was fit enough to meet that demand. I told him I was up to the challenge and signed."

IN HIS FIRST GAME for United, Ashman netted a hat-trick in a 4-0 win at Rochdale. He scored twice on his Brunton Park debut and added a further two in a 4-1 home victory over Accrington Stanley. Seven goals in his first three games, a remarkable return and a start which catapulted the youngster into the realms of folklore. He fired home 19 goals that season and appeared in all 46 league games. Ashman remembered: "It was great playing alongside footballers like Jimmy Whitehouse and Billy Hogan. The delivery is all important for a centre-forward and I certainly was never starved of the ball and good crosses. I like to think I could score goals with my head and both my feet, but it now seems like the majority of my goals came from head. It just shows the quality of the crossing though. I learned an awful lot about football from the likes of Hogan, McIntosh and Whitehouse, they were decent players with a lot of experience. I don't think any of us were outstanding as players, but we were solid and reliable. I cannot recall any United player of that era ever giving less than 100% in every game, that's friendly matches included.

I remember when Grimsby, managed by a certain Bill Shankly, came to Brunton Park and the fans were desperate for us to beat them. So was Fred. He came into our dressing room and told us to use our pace on the wings and to get behind them all the time. We knew we had the beating of Grimsby in us and as usual we were raring to get out onto the pitch and play football. Minutes before we were due out, who should walk into our dressing room but Shanks. He laughingly apologised and told us he had forgotten that this wasn't his dressing room any longer, but wished us well. As he was about to leave he turned and announced: 'I don't recognise some of the faces here, hope you won't be overawed by my players.' He then winked at us all and walked out. That was Shanks at his psychological best, upsetting our rhythm and being very gentlemanly about telling us his team were bigger and better.

Fred was really unhappy about it all and told us to forget what he had said and to get out there and make our names known to the Grimsby players. 'Remember, run at them and get behind them at every opportunity,' he said. We tried, but from the kick-off Grimsby flew into us. They weren't a dirty team, but let's just say they weren't playing in the true spirit of the game. They went 2-0 up before half-time. We came back and scored in the second half, but Shanks had outwitted us."

Shankly wasn't alone in doing so, as another old boy came back to haunt the club. John (Jackie) Lindsay, who had been released and moved to Southport, scored the Sandgrounders' winner over United at Brunton Park.

"One of the games which will always stand out in my career at Carlisle was that against Scunthorpe and Lindsey United [as Scunthorpe United were then known]. It was Christmas Day 1952. They had knocked us out of the FA Cup a few weeks earlier and we were desperately disappointed by our display there. At Brunton Park we wanted revenge, and certainly got it. It was one of those games that happen once, maybe twice, in a lifetime, everything we did came off, Jimmy Whitehouse was incredible; every time he touched the ball he would shoot and it went in. He scored five that day. I scored two and I think Bobby Harrison got one as well [Carlisle won 8-0]. We marched off the field like gladiators, our chests puffed out and smiling profusely. For weeks afterwards the supporters would come up to us and shake our hands in the street. It was a great feeling to know we had equalled the club's record victory."

Three months later the euphoria of that victory disappeared. Tuesday 10 March 1953 had seen Falkirk visit Brunton Park in a friendly fixture. After the game the players went home as usual and the ground was locked up. During the night the old wooden grandstand mysteriously burnt down, destroying all the club records, complete with playing kit and players boots.

"It was the craziest time I can remember in the game," recalled Ashman. "We had nothing; no footballs, no kit, no boots. Newcastle United came to our rescue and loaned us some of their black and white striped kit and some old boots. We had to get changed at James Street swimming baths and get a bus to the ground."

ASHMAN PROVED A CONSISTENT and frequent goal scorer, continually reaching double figures. His best season without doubt was 1953/54, when he scored 30 goals, then a post-war club record, although it was to last just four seasons. In total he played seven seasons for United before he was forced into retirement through a knee injury which first came to light in 1954 and progressively deteriorated over the following seasons. Ashman eventually had a cartilage removed from one knee but then cruciate ligament problems took hold in his other and a promising, but ultimately unfulfilled career was over.

His last ever game for United came on 30 November 1957, a 4-1 defeat at Stockport County, and his last goals had been scored nine games earlier, a brace in a 3-1 home win over Tranmere Rovers. "It's not something I recall, my last ever goals, as I didn't believe they would be. As a player you tend to think you will just bounce back from injury time and again," he later recalled. "The 1957/58 season was a tough one for me personally. I was in a lot of pain during games and sometimes couldn't walk out of the ground afterwards. I do remember the Stockport game very well, I felt okay before the kick off and did my usual warm up routine. Early doors I went up for a header and came down heavily on my feet. I felt my back judder with the impact. My knees just turned to jelly and there was a searing pain surging through both of them. I didn't want to let the team down, so carried on playing, but I was finished, I knew I was. I had an awful sick feeling throughout the game. Worse still I missed a couple of chances which normally I would have scored. We were thrashed that day, 4-1, I think. In the dressing room afterwards I spoke to some of the players and told them how I felt. They knew something was wrong. The manager told me to go home and not to do anything hasty, to consider everything before making a decision as to my future.

Realistically I knew it was over. I was unable to walk for a week after that game. Training was out and I needed more operations to try to sort the problem. My own doctor told me to pack football in and get a proper job! I didn't want to leave Carlisle United behind because they had been so good to me, giving me a break in the game and the supporters were really the best, so it was with a weary heart that I had to tell the board of directors that my playing days were over."

SUCH WAS THE RELATIONSHIP that Ashman took a 'proper job' working for United director, Jim Monkhouse, looking after chickens on his farm at Langwathby. "It was a strange and often difficult job, but I was grateful for still being able to somehow earn a living," Ashman said. "There was more to it than just throwing them a few bits of corn. I had plenty of time to think and contemplate my future. Penrith asked me if I fancied helping them out as manager in my spare time. I spoke with Jim and he told me to go for it. It was a poor standard really. We were in the Northern League, at the bottom in fact. I managed to get a bit of team spirit going and we got up and running. We moved on from being strugglers to a top three side in the Northern League in four seasons, so I think I repaid their decision to employ me."

All the time, though, Ashman was thinking about Carlisle United. He had watched a couple of managers come and go without any improvement to the club's position. Then, in late January 1963, Jim Monkhouse asked to have a chat with him, away from the farm and away from Brunton Park. "I was worried a bit, I wondered what Jim was going to say, it was all cloak and dagger. Then he told me that the club weren't satisfied with manager Ivor Powell. He had become too settled in the role, comfortable. He asked if I would consider taking over if Powell was to suddenly leave. I was naturally stunned, but at once said that I would. The next thing I knew, Gravesend and Northfleet had knocked Carlisle out of the FA Cup and Powell was sacked directly after the game!

I never heard anything for a day or two, then came the call I had been waiting for. It was Jim asking if I would pop down to Brunton Park for a quick chat. I asked him when and was told straight away. I wasn't even dressed for the occasion. When I got there I had a chat to some of the directors and was offered the job. My smile was broader than Eden Bridge. I was so proud to be manager of the club."

It was in February 1963 that Ashman took over as manager of Carlisle, but due to the 'big freeze' of that winter, strangely no games were played under Ashman's reign for a full month. Despite an upturn in results, relegation to the Fourth Division was already a certainty. So it was that, in an inauspicious start in management for Ashman, the club was relegated.

The following season, however, was different in the extreme. Ashman went about his business swiftly, signing Hugh McIlmoyle from Rotherham United. It proved to be an inspired acquisition, the centre-forward scoring a club record 44 goals that season. With such a prolific marksman on board, the team was successful and won promotion back to the Third Division at the first time of asking, losing out on the championship by goal average to Gillingham.

The team that then took the Third Division by storm during the 1964/65 season was dramatically revamped with a big change in personnel. McIlmoyle left to be replaced by Frank Large. In, amongst others, came such hugely influential figures as Tommy Passmoor, Stan Harland, Willie Carlin and Johnny Evans. United went up as Champions, beating Mansfield Town 3-0 at Brunton Park in the final league game of the season in front of 18,764 spectators. "It was a great result because Mansfield could have pipped us to promotion, it was that close. The support that night was incredible. They made more noise than I have ever heard at a football match anywhere, and I've managed at Wembley in a Cup Final! I was nervous, but Frank [Large] and Johnny [Evans] settled it for us. We were magnificent in that game. I was in the dugout and Dick Young said to me: 'boss, was it as noisy as this on the chicken farm?' Dick had the knack of defusing tense situations with a moment of humour. I told him the chickens were a noisy lot when they got going. All this while my players were winning the Third Division Championship in the biggest league game the club had ever took part in!"

THE FOLLOWING SEASON THE Ashman army continued to advance, only just missing out on promotion to the First Division, finishing the season in third place at a time when only the top two clubs went up. "I really was disappointed that we didn't manage to win the Second Division in 1967, we were so close. We had the smallest squad in the league and had definitely spent much less than the teams around us, but we matched them all the way. I think, during our run, it was the time I realised that we weren't quite ready for the big time. That goes for me as manager and not just the players. More experience was needed."

But then came a crushing blow for all Blues fans, expectant of another sustained promotion push. In the summer of 1967, after the sudden departure of Jimmy Hagan, Ashman was installed as new manager of West Bromwich Albion. It was a move which stunned the support of Carlisle United, yet no-one blamed him for moving on. He had done more for United than any other manager up to that time. It came as no surprise that Ashman was an instant success at the Hawthorns. In the four years he had in charge of the Throstles he took them to the European Cup Winners' Cup quarter-finals, and Wembley finals in 1968 (FA Cup) and 1970 (League Cup). He actually won the FA Cup in the 1968 final.

Even so it was a little disheartening when he returned to Brunton Park to face United in the semi-finals of the Football League Cup competition in 1970. United won the first leg 1-0, but fell away in the second leg, losing 4-1 on the night and 4-2 on aggregate. "I didn't really want us to face Carlisle in the semi-final, but it was always going to happen," he recalled. "They had been having a good run, beating some quality First Division sides on the way. I watched them beat Oxford United in the quarter-final and felt ill at the thought of coming up against them, not because I feared them, but because I knew it would be emotional for me. At Carlisle they should have beaten us by three or four goals. I told my players afterwards: 'You lot have got out of jail here, take the initiative and let's beat them at our place.' Thankfully we did, but only just. The final score didn't tell the true story."

BY NOW, JUST ABOUT everyone knew of the humble beginnings of the successful West Bromwich Albion manager. Perhaps he, more than anyone else, had put the name of Carlisle United on the football map. He certainly missed no opportunity to mention the club in interviews. But it still came as something of a shock when, in May 1971, he was dismissed as manager of Albion. For Ashman it was more the manner in which this happened that caused him issues, as opposed to the reality of it all. "I was out of England on holiday, in Greece. We hadn't had a great season in 1970/71 and I needed the break to ready myself for a real challenge the following season. Suddenly, I had this journalist come up to me and ask if I was Allan Ashman, the ex-manager of West Bromwich Albion. I laughed and told him: 'not the ex-, the current manager.' He laughed and said: 'Haven't you been told, you're sacked.' I was stunned and made my way to a phone and rang the club. Sure enough they confirmed it. At least the lady on the switchboard did, as to this day I still haven't been told by the chairman!

What a pile of shit it all turned into, I tell you. I gave West Brom some good times. More success than they deserved, I think. The players were good, Jeff Astle in particular. He called and apologised for the way I had been treated by the club. Don Howe came in after me. He must have been laughing as he inherited a bloody good side, but he won fuck all with them.

I thought then: 'What goes round comes round.' It happened to me with Ivor Powell, now I was on the receiving end of disgusting management. The management game in football is a cut-throat place. You are always looking for some other manager to fail before making your move, it's like a game of chess. The West Brom board really soured me against the English game. I needed some space. I felt embarrassed and very angry about what had happened."

Not one to rest on his laurels, Ashman took the opportunity to look outside the English game for work opportunities. Stoke City's manager Tony Waddington made an approach, asking him to scout for them, but the badly bruised Ashman declined, without giving the option any thought. It wasn't too long before he was offered a position as coach of Greek club side Olympiacos Piraeus, a far cry from the miserable grey skies often found in the Black Country, and in particular West Bromwich.

Success in Greece soon followed, as Ashman lifted Olympiacos from mid-table obscurity to the runners-up position in the Greek league by the end of the 1971/72 season. He may have felt alienated and unwanted in England, but the reality was different. Carlisle had never wanted to lose him and sought an opportunity to bring him home. Ian MacFarlane, a colossus of a man, was at the helm at Brunton Park and doing very well with the team having finished mid-table in Division Two, the third best finish in their history. He had brought the talented Stanley Bowles to Carlisle and was very much a tough and forward-thinking manager. Much to his dismay, in July 1972, MacFarlane received the news that he had been dismissed by the club, leaving the manager's chair, rather suspiciously, vacant.

IT WAS FOOTBALL'S worst kept secret, Allan Ashman was soon back in office at Brunton Park, desperate to prove himself to his doubters in the game and bring success to Carlisle United. In essence, he was a man on a mission. He inherited the basics of a very good side that had been put together by MacFarlane. In fairness he had a little tinkering to do, but even he could not have expected what was to follow. Within two years he took Carlisle to the very pinnacle of football in England, the top of the First Division (the equivalent of the Premiership). It was an incredible feat. "I couldn't believe we had done it. Dick Young and myself had worked hard at getting things right. The players we were after all signed and others that we already had, like Joe Laidlaw and Bobby Owen, just kept getting better. Dennis Martin in particular raised his game and proved himself a quality player. Then there were the likes of little Les O'Neill and Ray 'Puffer' Train. It was a great time to be at the club. People like John Gorman will never forget something like that. Carlisle United in the First Division... phew!

That first game at Chelsea typified everything the club aspired to, guts and determination and a sheer will to succeed. I admit I shed a few tears after the game. I never expected us to beat them 2-0 at Stamford Bridge. It was like being in a dream."

The dream continued for three games, putting United top of the league. Then the bubble, as opposed to bursting, began to slowly deflate. "It was tough once the results started going against us. It was like all the players were Cinderella, at 4.38pm every Saturday they would turn into pumpkins and the opposition would snatch late goals. It happened so often that we thought some curse may have been placed on Brunton Park. Dick had them in doing extra training, but it didn't work. We were relegated at the end of the season, but for me, if we had managed to bring in a couple of extra players we would have stood a better chance of surviving."

Relegation followed at the end of that 1974/75 season. Ashman was blamed by some areas of the media for hastening this by his failure to buy a proven goalscorer. He became conspicuous by his absence and failure to defend his best efforts.

The following season started woefully as United suddenly became the team everyone wanted to beat, a situation they were unused to. They slid down the league table, sinking close to the bottom. In October 1975, Ashman offered his resignation and walked out of the club, leaving his old friend and colleague Dick Young to take the flack. "Looking back, I didn't handle the situation well," he later admitted. "It seemed clear to me that I was going to be sacked. I had lost a lot of the players in the dressing room. It's one of those things you just know. It was time to go. I should really have talked it over with those who mattered at the club, but I just wanted to get away, get out of football for a while."

The club's support still held Ashman in great esteem. No-one had truly expected Carlisle to survive in the First Division and every Carlisle fan was proud of what had been achieved, even Bill Shankly, who declared it the greatest feat in football. Ashman, though, found failure difficult to deal with. "I was ashamed of myself. I felt as though I had let the whole city down," he said. "I didn't like going out in public. It was an awful feeling."

Moving words, which will arouse emotion in even the most hardened Carlisle supporter. Ashman clearly was, at this time, a man who was questioning his own professional ability. What happened next did not do him any favours in the eyes of the support of Carlisle United.

Two months after his resignation from the Brunton Park hot seat Ashman joined Workington as their boss. It was a bad move, not simply from a personal perspective, but from a professional angle too. Workington were a Fourth Division side, who were struggling to make ends meet. There was little optimism at Borough Park. The procurement of Ashman as their manager appeased Reds fans, but did little else but paper over the ever-widening cracks of a football club in freefall. In February 1977 Ashman reached the lowest point of his football career, when he was sacked by a club who sat bottom of Division Four.

"My time at Workington was not by any standards a good one," he remembered. "There were some really good people there, people who gave everything to the football club, working 24 hours a day in the hope of success. The simple fact of things, though, is that there was no money available for transfers, hardly enough for wages sometimes, but even if there was, there was little I could offer to players in the way of selling the potential of the club or offering financial reward. The club had been down and out for a few seasons, continually fighting for survival, looking over their shoulder at non-league football. Despite this, I saw it as a real challenge and I liked the place and the people. To be fair their supporters really made me feel very welcome. I admit I was shocked when they sacked me, but things like this happen in football. It was similar to the West Bromwich Albion situation, in as much as people who should know better went out of their way to ostracise me. The press were onto it quickly, I think someone must have leaked it out from the club before it was formal. I remember it wasn't long after I knew that I received a telephone call. It was Dick Young. As always he was the perfect gentleman. He told me he was sorry to hear the news and wished me every success in the future. Dick was a great man. I think I let him down more than anyone at Carlisle. He deserved more from me.

A few weeks later I was out shopping in Carlisle when I was approached by a man who looked worse for wear through drink. He was wearing a Carlisle United scarf. I thought to myself: 'Here we go, trouble'. I couldn't have been more wrong had I tried. The man told me he had been sacked from his job a couple of weeks earlier for not hitting monthly targets. He was out looking for work, any kind of work. He told me not to let things get me down and to persevere, as something would eventually come along to help me move on. He told me that supporters of Carlisle United would always be grateful to me for what I did for their club and the fantastic memories I provided. I never knew his name, but he was a man who had a real impact on me. He was someone who actually made me realise that life in football was a merry-go-round and how lucky I was to have had such a wonderful career at a wonderful club. Even if it meant being relegated, we bloody well achieved the impossible."

ALLAN ASHMAN BECAME something of a football nomad after the Workington experience. Although he received many offers of work he turned most of them down. One offer he couldn't refuse was that of scouting for Manchester United. He became well known as a scout and with the right contacts was eventually appointed manager of Walsall in August 1978. For Ashman, it was a mistake of Workington proportions. Within a full season at Fellows Park, during which time Walsall (who were relegation fodder when he joined them) were relegated. With the fans of the club permanently on his back, he had no option but to stand down.

Within months he was appointed chief scout for Derby County, later moving up to assistant manager at the Baseball Ground under John Newman. Derby, however, was another club in turmoil. They were in the threws of a takeover. Typically, the new owners wanted to make changes and first to go was the managerial team. In November 1982 both Newman and Ashman were shown the door.

The following March (1983) the same pairing took over as a management team at Hereford United. It was a difficult time at Edgar Street, but the pair experienced a modicum of success, turning Hereford from a club which propped up the table at the end of 1982/83 into promotion contenders just two seasons later. But in July 1987 they were both released from their contracts. By now, all the perils of what had happened at Carlisle and then Workington had been forgotten. Demons exorcised, Ashman could be remembered as the man who succeeded at West Bromwich Albion and had taken lowly Carlisle United to the top of the First Division. His endeavours in the game had earned him an excellent reputation and he was never without work for long. He was to later scout for Plymouth Argyle and then Mansfield Town.

"I know I have won the FA Cup and led my teams out at Wembley, but my fondest memories in the game are all associated with Carlisle, first as a player and then later as a manager. It was a real honour to be able to manage the club twice. I don't have many regrets in football, but if I was to choose one, it would have been to commit myself longer to the club after we came down from the First Division. I have never been one to moan or complain about things, but I can honestly say that I have never had anything but the utmost support from the directors and officials at Carlisle United. They are among the best I ever worked with; genuine, honest and dedicated. I always relish going back there to see everyone and still watch out for Carlisle's result when they are playing."

In December 2002 Ashman passed away after suffering a stroke and later a heart attack in hospital. He will always be remembered at Brunton Park as a true blue and the man who fulfilled our ambitions and dreams.

JIMMY WHITEHOUSE

'WHAM'

1951-1957

UNITED CAREER

Games 205
Goals 101

MAGIC MOMENT

He wasn't called 'Wham' for nothing. Poor old Halifax Town took a battering as Jimmy looted three goals for himself in 1955

> **'Wham was one of the best strikers of a ball in football. He could trap a ball, turn and shoot in one movement. That takes some doing.'**
>
> **Allan Ashman**

BELIEVE it or not it isn't easy in a book of this sort to pick 20 genuine Cult Heroes in the entire history of the football club. I'm not particularly certain that it would be an easy task at any football club. What I will say, though, is that as soon as I discussed it with Simon (my publisher) some names immediately signed themselves up as potential contenders without any further thought. Jimmy 'Wham' Whitehouse was one of the first names on the list. Wherever I go on my travels and the history of Carlisle United comes up, a few names get bandied about. McConnell, Broadis and Whitehouse are generally the first three to get a mention by football supporters of a certain age group. Though I doubt few still alive today can say they witnessed Jimmy McConnell's heroics, he is still recalled with great fondness.

However, when it comes to recollections of football in the 1950s this is when the tales of Broadis and Whitehouse crop up. Time and again it's the goals of Jimmy Whitehouse that bring smiles to people's faces. Without doubt, he is the one player in the club's history who, when recalled by supporters, can still stop them mid-sentence as they remember his predatory fashion on the football pitch. Phrases such as "Jimmy Whitehouse, oh he was the best" or "Wham Whitehouse, a warrior on the pitch, a gentleman off it" litter my research of this wonderful footballer. Although I met Jimmy several times, my one regret was never being able to see him play a competitive game for the club.

Out of sheer respect for every player to don the shirt of Carlisle United (except Jim Tolmie) I would regard them all as gentlemen of the highest order; hand-picked gods sent to Brunton Park for a purpose. In the case of Jim Tolmie it was to relegate us and to therefore effectively end his football career on these shores. In the case of Jimmy McConnell it was to launch us into the Football League. In the case of Jimmy Whitehouse it was to simply thrill supporters and create lifelong memories which still make supporters happy.

I confess, I have met with and interviewed hundreds of footballers, almost all of whom have had a direct link with Carlisle United. Why on earth would I want to interview them otherwise? Believe me when I tell you that in person, it's fair to say, not all are the gods I or other supporters would like them to be! Jimmy Whitehouse, though, was different. Each time I met him I was left with a feeling of euphoria. Some people have the ability to make people happy no matter what the situation is. Jimmy Whitehouse was, in my opinion, one such individual. He made you smile by simply greeting you. When recalling his football days at Carlisle United he could, in a flash, have the listener laughing at some of his and his peers' antics, then crying as he told of his more disappointing times.

James Edward Whitehouse was born in the Black Country, West Bromwich to be precise, on 19 September 1924. During his adolescence he played local football in the Birmingham and West Midland leagues, earning a decent reputation as a strong and forceful attacker, who could annihilate defences with his power. There is no doubt that he would have realised an opportunity within the game much sooner had it not been for world events of the early 1940s, as war rightly pushed football to the back of most British people's minds.

Reputations are often difficult to live up to, but in the working class area of West Bromwich, Jimmy Whitehouse had created his own as an amateur footballer and continued to live up to it. The war over, and with Britain trying to return to some normality, football was again on the agenda, a perfect distraction to the regeneration efforts across cities and towns up and down the United Kingdom. Fred Everiss, a lifelong employee and then manager of West Bromwich Albion (later to become a club director, until his death) was a man who wanted the very best for the Throstles. He learned of the Whitehouse reputation through his local league contacts and had the player watched. In March 1948 Jimmy was invited along to Albion for a trial. It went well enough that this one-off opportunity turned into a few games. Jimmy recalled to me: "West Bromwich were regarded as a big club. It was my local team and, of course, who wouldn't want the chance to represent your local side? I was asked down for a couple of trial games, one against Aston Villa. I remember as we took to the pitch looking up and seeing the selection committee stood around on the side of the pitch. I never once thought they were there to look at me. I was proud to be given the chance. Well, after about ten minutes this Villa player, I still don't know who it was, probably a trialist like me, comes up to me on the pitch, pushes his fist or something into the small of my back and tells me that he'll chop me off at the knees if I show him up. He must have thought I was soft or something. First chance I got that was it. I went straight for goal. I looked up and saw the goalie looking confused, so I hit the ball into the far corner of his goal. Running back to kick off again this player reminded me that next time he would have me. I never saw or heard of him again.

Afterwards, this chap in a suit came up to me. He seemed a real businessman and asked me to come to register with Fred Everiss. I asked what he meant by 'register' and was told it was to offer me amateur terms. Naturally I was delighted. Fair enough it was amateur, but it was a chance to prove myself."

Prove himself he did, signing professional terms in May 1948, at the age of 24. Within a couple of months, though, Whitehouse found himself left out in the wilderness as Fred Everiss stood down as team manager/secretary and took up a place in the board room, being replaced by John Arthur (Jack) Smith in July 1948. The ex-Wolverhampton Wanderers trainer had his own ideas about playing style and the future of the club and Whitehouse simply didn't fit in with those plans. So it was that, after a frustrating first full professional season, he moved on a free transfer to neighbouring Walsall in June 1949. Fellows Park was much more receptive to Jimmy's talents and Saddlers boss Harry Hibbs motivated Jimmy and made him work harder than most in training sessions to invigorate enthusiasm inside the player. "I thought Harry Hibbs would be terrible. He was an ex-goalkeeper. 'What would he know about scoring goals?' I first thought. As it worked out he was a great manager and motivator. I really enjoyed my time at Walsall. It was only a little club by comparison to Albion, but it was a genuine club and the support was fabulous for a club of its size.

My initiation into football at Walsall was a tough one. On the pitch during a game you would end up getting kicked, punched, slapped, shoved and the referee's just ignored it. When you complained, they would tell you to shut up and get on with it, and you had to without a second thought."

Twenty league games and eight goals later and the inside-forward was on his travels yet again. Desperately keen to make a career out of football and to fulfil his ambitions, Jimmy agreed a move to Rochdale in July 1950. His transfer this time commanded a fee of around £750.

"Walsall was great, but I didn't think I was being given the opportunities I deserved. It was great to be involved, but footballers want to play football every week. When I got the chance to speak with manager Ted Goodier at Rochdale, I was thrilled. Ted had been involved in Birmingham football during the war. He knew that side of the game well and he was a man of great repute. It was known that he was trying to turn Rochdale into a good footballing side, so I was keen to listen to what he had to say. Not long before I went there they had won the Lancashire Senior Cup. That may not sound anything today, but it was then a real achievement. They beat the great Blackpool team in the final, a marvellous feat.

Ted was the man who put the 'Wham' into Whitehouse, I believe. He really seemed to believe in me and was always pushing me and urging me to shoot at every opportunity. To be honest, I think he treated me worse than he did all the other players as he wanted the very best out of me and expected me to score in every game. Now I realise that he was building my psychological resilience. He believed that if you believed in yourself then you would achieve your beliefs. It worked. I started to think I could score every time I got the ball. It didn't always please my team-mates, though, and I was often accused at Rochdale of being greedy and selfish with the ball."

GOODIER'S ROCHDALE DIDN'T really make a great deal of headway to match that ambition. Jimmy fired 13 league goals during the 1950/51 season, which again made him a marked man. By marked, I don't mean on the pitch, this time he was being marked by managers of many northern clubs. Professionally, Carlisle United could offer more to Jimmy than Rochdale and when United boss Fred Emery offered a handsome fee for the player, Rochdale accepted. Thus Jimmy Whitehouse was persuaded to come to Brunton Park, signing for a fee of £3,500 in October 1951.

The United boss was thrilled by his new acquisition and was quick to entertain the fact that the club had got itself a real bargain. In order to substantiate the manager's claims, Jimmy stole the show on his debut at Bradford City. It was a 2-1 victory away from home and both goals came courtesy of United's new inside forward. A week later and Whitehouse scored another two, this time at Brunton Park against York City. United fans took to his bustling and arrogant style at once. Joining the club well into the season meant he could only achieve 24 appearances in that first campaign, 1951/52, but he still managed to score 11 goals, and his pairing with striker Allan Ashman was clearly something special. Both players' goals undoubtedly helped United to salvage something from a very average season and achieve a very decent final league position of seventh in Division Three (North).

It was only the beginning of the Ashman/Whitehouse partnership, which was to grow stronger as both players matured in a very decent side. Ashman told me: "Wham was one of the best strikers of a ball in football. He could trap a ball, turn and shoot in one movement. That takes some doing. I don't think I know of a stronger, more capable forward in my time in football. Jimmy had everything, class, strength, and more importantly, he instinctively knew where the goal was, no matter where he was on the pitch. If Billy Hogan, Wham and me were able to play now [the interview was conducted in the 1990s] we would make up the best forward line in the country I think."

Whilst the Brunton Park faithful loved Ashman's 'swan-like' aerial ability, they fell in love with Whitehouse, who proved to be a goal scorer who was without doubt a very determined and single-minded player. Jimmy always added an edge of excitement to the game, especially in the front line, a discipline previously missing from the Blues' line up. Jimmy just wanted to score goals, nothing else; goals were his sole aim on the pitch.

The following 1952/53 season was to be regarded as Jimmy's most successful, not only at Carlisle, but in his entire football career. In 45 games he missed just two matches through injury all season. During that season he scored 29 scintillating goals for the club. These were dream times for Carlisle supporters. Goals flowed throughout the team in abundance, mainly through Whitehouse. He notched five against Scunthorpe on Christmas Day. But it wasn't only goals that day that made him a notable player, it was his all round game. Jim Baty recalls: "Jimmy Whitehouse was really outstanding. He battered Scunthorpe on Christmas Day 1952. He was at their defence all game, him and Allan Ashman. It was great to watch. It seemed that every time he got the ball he would burst through the defenders and shoot. The poor Scunthorpe goalkeeper must have wondered what had happened to him. It wasn't really just that game that made him a favourite, it was everything about him. Even long after he retired, around Carlisle he was approachable and kind, and I think he enjoyed reminiscing about his football days. Our age group worshipped him really and there was nothing better than going home on a Friday night having shared a pint with 'Wham' and discussed everything to do with the club."

Another ex-player, now gone, was Paddy Waters, who, for countless years ran a newsagency in London Road, which was where I first interviewed him. Paddy was something of a joker in the pack. He told me: "Of all the players I recall as being great Jimmy Whitehouse would have to be there with the best. He was fantastic for our club, a workaholic and a truly nice man. He would share his tea or piece of orange with anyone who asked in the dressing room. I don't know anyone at the football club during his time with us who didn't like Wham. Sure he was from Birmingham, I think, but that's not a bad thing really, is it? He would often tell us tales of how life was in a big city, and how it was in Walsall or West Bromwich. Ashman would then talk of Nottingham and how great it was there. Then we would agree how bloody marvellous it was at Carlisle, best place ever, and we all really thought that too.

Wham could be infuriating because he was so committed, whereas some of us just wanted to get home and have a few beers. It's good because we all stayed in touch and remained in the city. I think Ash [Ashman] was the only one to move away, but he didn't do too badly as a manager, so I can't blame him for that. Jimmy and I often bump into each other up town and that starts a long chat and, of course, a few beers as we tell each other how wonderful we were. If you ask me when it was that Jimmy Whitehouse first fell in love with Carlisle United I would have to say Christmas Day 1952, 8-0 against Scunthorpe. He was spectacular."

The result itself remains the club's record home win. One could say that it is a suitable legacy to Jimmy Whitehouse as a goalscorer. It didn't cease there, however. A fortnight later he was scoring goals again. This time United beat Rochdale 5-0 with 'Wham' amazingly getting four of them. Nine goals in such a short space of time is, some would assume, sufficient for a player to be elevated to Cult Hero status. Yet Jimmy was equally highly regarded off the pitch. Mixing with supporters before and after games and greeting them heartily when he met them in the city centre ensured that he was creating his own unique place in United folklore. That season an incredible 82 league goals were scored by United, a fantastic achievement. But still they could only manage a rather disappointing ninth place finish.

The following 1953/54 season saw 47 games played by the striker who was now on top of his game and bursting with enthusiasm and confidence. A further 22 goals were scored during this campaign, which included another 5-0 home win. This time the victims were Halifax Town with Whitehouse helping himself to four goals. Press reports record that: 'Whitehouse was United's man of the match' and by all accounts both he and Blues could have won by a greater margin. But despite the individual glory, the season was again disappointing for the club. Thirteenth position didn't seem to equate with the incredible front line of Whitehouse, Ashman, Atkinson and Bond, who were at times nothing short of breathtaking.

"We always seemed to keep the fans happy no matter what the results were" said Jimmy. "Memory is a funny thing. I don't really recall us losing many games at all. We had a lot of out-standing footballers coming through the club. Geoff Twentyman was in charge at the back and in Jimmy McLaren we had one of the best goalkeepers of all time in my reckoning. No matter how loud the crowd was, you could always hear Jim yelling out instructions to us. You would hardly believe how relaxed he was off the pitch, totally different. Bill Shankly, whenever I bumped into him, which was fairly rarely as he went onto bigger and better things, would tell me how good Jim was in goal and how much he admired our front line. That says a lot about how decent a club Carlisle was. You don't get many top people admiring forwards of lower league clubs nowadays."

The 1954/55 season was to prove Wham's last full campaign in football and at Carlisle. He maintained his outstanding goal scoring record, this time 25 goals, one of which was his only FA Cup goal for the club in a 2-2 home draw with Watford in the second round. Sadly with players reaching an age where injuries took their toll and stamina wasn't as long lasting, the team really struggled, finishing 20th in Division Three (North). A nail-biting finish to the season meant just three points separated Blues and the dreaded bottom place in the league. That aside, 'Wham' still managed two hat-tricks in the campaign, a sign that he would never give up the fight to make United successful.

1955/56 WAS TO SIGNAL the end of Wham's playing career. Picking up a nasty and long-lasting knee injury early in the season, he was forced to miss most of the early games in the campaign. The injury took its toll and, although he returned to the first team in October, Whitehouse lacked the pace and speed he showed in previous seasons. He managed 37 games, but his goal return fell. This time he scored only 13 goals, a perfectly respectable total, but by his own standards, disappointing. "I knew when my knee collapsed on me that my career could be over," he recalled. "I worked hard with the doctors and trainer and managed to break back into the first team, but I always knew that my knee could give way at any time. I lost confidence in my physical ability and that reflected in my game."

Keen to play on for as long as he could, Whitehouse worked hard during the pre-season of 1956/57. Inside he realised his career was over, but he still fought pain to turn out for the side. As laudable as that was, he wasn't really bringing any value to the side in that last season as his knee condition worsened. He played just five more games for Blues, scoring his last ever goal for the club in a draw at Boundary Park against Oldham Athletic in December 1956.

In what was then deemed a local derby against Barrow, played at their Holker Street ground on Boxing Day 1956, Jimmy Whitehouse wore the United shirt for the last time in a competitive match. He was to bow out of the game having been administered treatment and physiotherapy for over five months. Back then such treatment wasn't as advanced, and despite the best efforts of the medical profession there was no sign of improvement in the joint. So it was that Jimmy 'Wham' Whitehouse, at the young age of 32, retired from professional football. He remained in Carlisle, working for local companies, taking early retirement in 1987. A year later he returned to Carlisle United for the club's centenary celebrations, and for one last time inside the stadium proudly wore the shirt in a guest game.

Whitehouse, who was once described by the late Bill Shankly as being 'absolutely lethal' finished his football career with a more than enviable record; 101 goals from 205 appearances. Little wonder football people like Shanks regarded him so highly. My old school teacher Billy Graham, himself an ex-United full-back, always raved about Wham and told me during my Kingmoor school years that I should try to emulate the master of shooting, passing and goalscoring.

Wham was an exceptional player, an exceptional person and a true Cult Hero. Sadly, he passed away in 2005, but, I gather, the mention of Carlisle United always put a smile on his face. Much as the memory of his great goals and performances still does today to those who can recall his wonderful talent.

DICK YOUNG

1955-1975
1975-1982

UNITED CAREER

as manager

Games	45
Wins	13

MAGIC MOMENT

Dick stood crying in absolute happiness on the side of the pitch when, after three games, his beloved Carlisle topped the First Division

'MR CARLISLE UNITED'

IN the entire history of Carlisle United FC just one man stands out among all others for his honour, integrity and loyalty. Unlike so many of his peers, this determined man stuck it out when the going was tough. He gave his all for the club and always stood proud when discussing his beloved Carlisle United. He would never have a bad word said against them. This was a football man through and through. A man who served loyally over a period of four decades. He maintained the status quo while so many managers moved on to what they believed were greener pastures. In my opinion few men in football warrant adulation and admiration as much as Dick Young.

In my previous book about the club, I bestowed upon Dick Young the title of Mr Carlisle United. I stand by that declaration to this very day, a close second being current club chairman Andrew Jenkins, who is, I believe, the most passionate and loyal chairman or club director in our history. The reason I mention Andrew is because a previous incumbent of the chairman's position at the club tried to tell me that he deserved the title Mr Carlisle United for all he had done for the club. I will not waste time on the fact that this particular man led us into administration and the darkest hours this football club has ever witnessed. That person is thankfully no longer associated with the club. My personal response to his assertion that he was Mr Carlisle United was a negative one. I told him straight, he wasn't fit to be mentioned in the same sentence as the great Dick Young, which is why his name does not appear here.

IT'S EXTREMELY HARD to put into print just why and how one falls in love with a football club. It's very much a personal and emotional affair.

For me, I fell in love with the whole match day experience long before it became the vogue to class it as any form of entertainment. Back in 1968 there were no television rights or electronic scoreboards. Programmes were bland – full of adverts selling Vauxhall Vivas or dodgy haircuts at Clive's. The Brunton Park pre-match music consisted of Herb Alpert songs and seats in what we called the grandstands were for the rich or infirm only. The smell of Oxo (Bovril wasn't sold inside Brunton Park back then) and the shingle-filled railway sleeper terracing of the scratcher or the Waterworks End was the domain which aroused my passion for the lads in blue. That and Dick Young!

Richard Harker Young was born in Gateshead in April 1918. A strapping young man, he was every bit the athlete, standing at over six feet tall. He was obviously made for the position of centre-half. Like so many of his Carlisle United Cult Hero peers, Dick was raised within a mining community, those in the north east of England being regarded as some of the toughest around. His football days began with Bolden Colliery, before he moved on to represent Wardley Colliery Welfare. He soon earned a reputation as being a solid and reliable defender and one of the top local sides, Hebburn St Cuthbert, were attracted by his defensive skills and work-rate and Young was signed up by the club to play in the Tyneside Catholic League. Other local sides in this competition included Jarrow St Bede's, Hebburn St Aloysius, Jarrow Rangers and North

Shields Victory. Sadly, St Bede's apart, all these clubs now survive only in memory. Countless players from this league have been plucked from obscurity into the limelight of the professional game, with the likes of Chris Duffy and Pat Woods playing for Newcastle United, while Pat McLarney moved to Manchester United.

Add to that the name Dick Young, who, in November 1935, aged just 17, signed for Sheffield United after their boss John 'Teddy' Davison, a devoutly religious man who also hailed from Gateshead, saw the potential in him. The Blades had been relegated from Division One the previous year and Davison was trying to assemble a promotion-winning side, with the youthful Dick Young being viewed as a future asset.

It wasn't long before Young broke into the first team at Bramall Lane, and success was waiting just around the corner. At the end of the 1937/38 season United missed out on promotion back to the First Division on goal average only. The following season, 1938/39 saw them promoted as runners-up behind Blackburn Rovers, but a point ahead of city rivals Wednesday. During his spell at Bramall Lane, Dick made 74 appearances before the outbreak of World War II stopped all first class football activities.

Signing up for the Royal Air Force, Dick quickly found himself posted around the United Kingdom on wartime duties. As a professional footballer he was allowed privileges which included time away from service to be allowed to play football. The game was seen by the authorities as a way of entertaining the populace during extremely tough times as the first few years of the conflict saw Nazi domination spread to the shores of the British Isles, with special wartime regional leagues and cup competitions being introduced. While Sheffield United still held Young's official Football League registration, special dispensation was granted through the league for players to make guest appearances for clubs which were situated closer to the base where they actively served. Between 1939 and 1945 Dick managed to make just 42 wartime appearances for his formal club Sheffield United, scoring three goals. Guest appearances were made for Luton Town, where he appeared 52 times, scoring twice, and at Northampton Town, six appearances without scoring; at one time featuring in the same side as Bill Shankly. During this spell, Young found himself turning into what we would today regard as a utility player. He could be found at both left and right-back positions as well as at centre-half. On one occasion he even played up front for Luton .

Football took its toll on him physically and he found himself injured during the last season of wartime competition, a situation which jeopardised his place at Sheffield United.

In March 1949, now aged 31, Young moved to Lincoln City as player/coach, working with another north easterner in the form of manager Bill Anderson. Dick worked hard to deliver results, as a centre-half he was inspirational and the team won promotion to Division Two in 1948, beating Rotherham United to the championship. As a coach he was extremely serious and was one of the first of his era to get players building muscle tissue through intensive gym work and weights. Sadly, injuries took their toll and he was forced to retire from playing in 1954, but not before he had again won a Third Division (North) championship medal and promotion in 1952 with the Imps, following relegation in 1949.

Soon afterwards Young received notification that Fred Emery, then manager of Carlisle United, wanted him as trainer. Dick didn't think twice about it. He met with Emery and visited Brunton Park and could see the opportunity for development and the flexibility to introduce his own training methods and quickly agreed terms. The rest, as they say, is history.

IT WAS IN 1969 that I first met Dick Young. I, along with my brother, had moved my terrace positioning to beside the players' tunnel and we found ourselves chatting to the players and officials as they came in and out. Dick had got to know us through our regular presence there and often talked (more to my older brother) to us. I remember him asking who my favourite player was. I instantly told him Alan Ross because of the full-length, flying save I had witnessed him make against Huddersfield Town the previous season. He asked me if I would like to meet him. Astounded I said 'yes'. Expecting a brief encounter by the tunnel I was disappointed when Rossy passed by me several times before and after the game. Then I was told that, before the next home game, my brother was to bring me down to Brunton Park early so I could meet Alan Ross. Excited doesn't begin to describe my emotion.

When the day arrived I walked through the narrow officials entrance of Brunton Park, which was situated behind the main stand. My brother asked to see Dick Young and told the young lady behind the counter that Paul Harrison was here to see him. As a mere ten year-old you can imagine how overawed I was at seeing footballer after footballer walking around. Manager Bob Stokoe came out and spoke to another waiting man, handing him two complimentary tickets and giving him a wink before disappearing back into the club corridors. Suddenly there standing in front of me was Dick Young. He held out his hand and told me he was pleased to meet me and informed me that I should be polite and courteous to everyone I met on my tour.

Within seconds I was walking inside the official club area. The smell of liniment and lots of excited voices filled the air. I was ushered down a narrow corridor towards one of the offices. Dick knocked on the door and opened it and there sat a beaming Bob Stokoe. I was terrified. To me Bob Stokoe was famous and here I was in his office. I remember him asking me lots of questions and giving me his autograph before we again moved on. Next it was Herbert Nicholson, the club physiotherapist; he was very friendly too and allowed me to sit on the treatment bed where so many stars had previously sat. My anxiety must have been showing as Dick reassuringly told me that the Carlisle dressing room was next. I could hear from a nearby room the chatter of footballers laughing and joking. I recognised several of the voices as those of the players I had heard shouting instructions to one another on the pitch.

I honestly didn't know what to expect as we walked into the dressing room. I wondered if the players would ignore and dismiss me, or if they would simply nod their heads in acknowledgement. As we walked to the centre of the room, Dick called for quiet and told them that I was a very important visitor, Carlisle's biggest fan, who stood next to the tunnel at each game. Nervously I smiled, then without warning the players swarmed round me and asked dozens of questions. Each seemed to be based around who my favourite player was. I forget how many times I said 'Alan Ross'. Then there he was, dressed in his green top and white shorts; Rossy. Dick pushed me towards the keeper's outstretched hand, which was ready to shake mine. It was quite an incredible and unforgettable few minutes – and all thanks to Dick Young. He introduced me to the referee, took me down the players' tunnel to the side of the pitch and even allowed me to sit where the man who played the pre-match music resided each game!

At the end I couldn't thank him enough. He'd had the humility and understanding to make a young boy's dream come true. It had cost him nothing but his time and for that I am eternally grateful for I saw a side to football that many kids never see. I am certain that my bond with Carlisle United was permanently forged by Dick Young that day. I was made to feel special. I was made to feel part of it. I was given memories that will never fail to inspire me.

Later in my life, as a postman, I moved onto a round which covered Dick Young's house. Quite incredibly, as I walked up the garden path towards the front door of his home, I felt nervous knowing that this was the private residence of the great man, who at the time was also manager of Carlisle United football club. There was no grand reunion or encounter. I think he may once have picked up the mail as I pushed it through his letter box, but that was it.

Genuine football ambassadors are few and far between, but Dick Young stands among the very best the sport can offer as my own personal experience of meeting with him shows. I have shared it with countless football people who knew him and they all share the same opinion; he was the best thing to happen to Carlisle United. The late Bill Shankly said of him: "Dick Young was unique. His unassuming character was a cover for his determined personality and desire for Carlisle United to succeed. Some of my players often ask me who I believe are the top trainers I have known in the game. Let me tell you Dick Young is among the elite few who I respect. What he has achieved for Carlisle United on a shoestring is incredible. He puts players through hell, but they love him for it. Dick would live inside Brunton Park if he could. He could have moved to bigger clubs and earned much more money and kudos for himself, but he loves Carlisle too much."

The ex-Leeds United and England manager Don Revie told me how his coach/trainer in both positions, Les Cocker, would often speak with Dick Young to determine positive ways of player motivation and to ask advice. I am aware that another England international coach, Harold Shepherdson, who was Sir Alf Ramsey's coach in England's glorious 1966 World Cup campaign would also speak with the Carlisle trainer on motivational and player fitness matters.

Few outside or inside Brunton Park realised just how high the regard for Dick Young actually was. Players like the late Chris Balderstone revered him, respecting his every word or opinion over and above many of the managers.

He told me: "Dick was a very special person. He had an incredible sense of priority where the club was concerned. He had the knack of knowing when to talk with a player privately or in the open area of the dressing room. He worked us relentlessly, but made training and work-outs fun. Skinburness was his favourite place for the team to train. He would have us running on the beaches, up and down sand dunes. Press-ups in soft sand aren't easy, but anything we did, Dick would match and often beat himself. He loved the competitiveness of it all. He was a natural character in the dressing room. In all my time in the game Dick would have to be the most influential man I ever knew.

I know it's not a good thing to admit, but he had the respect of every Carlisle United player I knew or know. If Dick Young said 'Jump', players would ask 'How high?' Whereas some managers would tell us to do this to do that, but it wouldn't happen. The players would be telling him where to go when his back was turned. It wasn't like that with Dick. We all realised that he knew what he was talking about, he knew how it felt as a player. We would bend over backwards to help him.

Honestly, sometimes when we lost games, it would be awful walking back into the dressing room and seeing how disappointed in us Dick was. He could you make you feel guilty without saying a word. Players would apologise to him for their poor performance or for missing a goalscoring opportunity. That just didn't happen with certain managers. Every time someone mentions Carlisle United I always think of Dick Young, says it all really."

The late Alan Ross was another who could find no criticism of his training mentor. He said: "Truth was Dick Young was the boss. We [the players] always referred to him as 'the gaffer'. He didn't like it, so out of respect we only did it when there was no-one around. In training he was like a teenager. He loved running us along beaches, round Rickerby and Bitts Park and generally anywhere there was any hills. Silloth and Skinburness beaches were great fun, but hey, did you feel the muscle pain the next day? One of his favourite tasks was working with the medicine ball. Those things are really heavy, full of sand, but he threw it around as though it was a table tennis ball. He would tie it from a beam and ask players to jump up and head it aggressively. They did and it would leave you with a bad head for days after!"

Young was Carlisle through and through and many players felt he should have been given a crack at the manager's position long before he did get a chance. The team he inherited wasn't his. Allan Ashman was a good manager, but it seemed he didn't listen to Dick in the end (1975), which is perhaps why it went wrong. The club then dumped the responsibility onto Dick. Naturally he jumped at the opportunity to manage the team, but he was always fighting a losing battle. When he stood down the players went mad. Not one of us wanted him to go. A few of the directors wanted him to stay on too, but others had already earmarked someone else for the position he held. You can't treat someone as loyal as Dick so poorly and hope that he will continually accept it. He was so professional and dignified in all he did. He was the perfect role model for a trainer/coach. He was the best.

IN 1975 WHEN TAKING over as team manager from a deserting Allan Ashman, Dick moved to resolve obvious goalscoring problems, signing Billy Rafferty from Plymouth Argyle for £30,000. Rafferty himself went on to become a Carlisle Cult Hero in his own right, scoring four goals against Cardiff City in a legendary 15-minute spell. Defensively he brought in a centre-half in his own image in the form of Iain McDonald from St Johnstone. Both signings made their mark and earned an excellent reputation for their consistently reliable performances. It was also a measure of the manager's eye for talent and filling first team gaps.

Twelve months later, with the team still languishing in the nether regions of Division Two, Dick resigned as first team manager, handing over the reins to Bobby Moncur, who got the team relegated and whose only claim to fame at Carlisle was the capture of Peter Beardsley, albeit that was actually down to the efforts and work of scout Brian Watson!

Essentially that was the end of Dick's football career, he was offered the assistant manager's position, and later given a coaching job at the club. However, the reality was that he was playing a backroom staff role, moving further away from first team activity. Finally in 1982 he announced his retirement from football.

Bob Stokoe was a great admirer of the work of Dick Young. In his final few interviews with me he spoke honestly and openly about the man who he referred to as 'Mr Carlisle United'.

"Dick Young was my rock during my time with Carlisle," Bob said. "I never needed to ask him to do anything. Dick knew instinctively what was required. Opposition dossiers were unnecessary. He could tell you player by player the opposition's weaknesses and strengths. He had a huge network of contacts and could also tell you what player was unhappy at what club and how much it would cost to bring him in. He was passionate about Carlisle and I would love to have taken him with me to other clubs, but it was pointless asking. If you cut him in half I swear he would have Carlisle United printed through his body. I don't know anyone in the game who remained as loyal to one club. That in itself says a lot about the man.

I always believed I had an excellent working relationship with my staff and players, but my skill in that area pales into insignificance when compared to Dick's. He could turn any negative into a positive. He never left a player feeling unwanted when we dropped him or bad about a performance. Even though defeat hurt him, he would thank every player for giving their best for the club.

As a trainer he was innovative, but, whatever he did, it worked. Players would jump through hoops for him, give that extra yard to satisfy his appetite for match fitness. When he stood up from the dug out, cupped his hands round his mouth and shouted instructions to players on the pitch, they listened and responded immediately. That's respect, that's what Dick Young deserved."

DICK YOUNG PASSED AWAY on 31 January 1989. It was a sad day for everyone connected with the club. The following home game four days later saw a crowd of just 2,627 inside Brunton Park for an abysmal team performance and a 3-0 home defeat to Scunthorpe United, totally representative of the mood of the city of Carlisle with the passing of the greatest man ever connected to the football club.

It is entirely appropiate that Dick Young's memory lives on at Carlisle United, not only in the form of a bar named after him, but by virtue of the fact that his son, Dick Young, is a serving director of the club, a fitting and lasting commemoration.

ALAN ROSS

1963 - 1979

UNITED CAREER

Games   465+1
Clean Sheets 149

MAGIC MOMENT

Tommy Smith strode up to slam the penalty home at Anfield. Rossy proved his match, flying full length across his goal to turn the scouse warrior's effort away. So good was the save that the Kop saluted him!

'SCOTLAND'S NUMBER ONE (ALMOST)'

'The supporters are what you play for really. It wasn't the money at Carlisle. It was a love of the game.'

Alan Ross

TO be a goalkeeper, it was once speculated, one had to possess an air of insanity. After all, who would dive head-first at the feet or flying boots of opposing strikers and centre-forwards? Who else would often endure the loneliness of being the last man, of standing alone and being an on-the-field spectator for most of a game, being called into action only sporadically? Or standing in what are often the most inclement weather conditions imaginable, including blizzards of driving snow, torrential rain and gale force winds? Who else, but a goalkeeper.

The position of goalkeeper is, without doubt, the most exposed in any football team. One mistake and there is the grim reality that it will result in a goal. One missed punch or dropped catch or fumble and the spectators, who are perilously close and within earshot, are straight on your back. Terrace cries of 'dodgy keeper' or the age-old taunt of 'What's your name keeper? Dracula. You're scared of crosses' get slung at the poor old keeper throughout the 90 minutes; not always only by opposing fans. It goes without saying then, that goalkeepers have to be thick-skinned and incredibly confident. Throughout the years, we at Carlisle have had our share of quality keepers and, I'm afraid to say, duck eggs!

Older supporters may recall the supremely agile Scotsman, Jim McLaren, who fiercely guarded the United goal in the seasons between 1948 and 1955. Highly regarded for his shot-stopping prowess, he would often acrobatically throw himself full length across his goal to repel opposition attacks. Another Scot, Dave McKellar was an outstanding guardian of the Carlisle goal. One suspects that had it not been for a back injury, then McKellar could have gone on to prove himself worthy as being one of the United greats covered in this book. Trevor Swinburne in the late 1970s and early 1980s was another colossus between the sticks, dependable and strong, rarely putting a foot wrong in the sticks. Tony Caig was another in the mould of Swinburne; nothing exceptional about him, but he was reliable.

At the opposite end of the spectrum, sadly we have had more than our fair share of calamitous keepers. John Blott made his Carlisle debut at Maine Road, Manchester in front of the *Match of the Day* cameras. Not the tallest of keepers, he actually conceded just one goal in his two sole appearances. But awkward in his handling and woeful on crosses, he left United and later followed a career in the police force. He hit the headlines a few years later when he was jailed for rape! Steve Crompton in the 1980s was simply nervous. In the 1960s Joe Dean lacked match concentration and was slow, terribly slow. Ex-Newcastle great Kevin Carr simply had one accident after another, while Martin Burleigh in the mid-1970s was Captain Spectacular, making a sensational save from the simplest of back passes (which were then allowed).

One man stands head and shoulders above all these contenders as a real Cult Hero and goalkeeper of exceptional quality; another Scotsman built like a racing snake, but with a heart as big as Brunton Park and courage to match any hero. Ross went on to become United's record appearance holder and was very much a footballer who supported and loved the team he played for.

Alan Ross began his football career at Petershill Juniors in Glasgow. Petershill were a well respected club and their stadium, Petershill Park, often held crowds of well over 19,000, the largest recorded being 19,800, which gives some idea of how big a junior club this actually was. Ross was a regular in the first XI. Agile and courageous, with a touch of the lunatic about him, as all good goalkeepers should have, his progress was closely monitored by a number of clubs in both Scotland and England. Celtic had at one time taken a close look at him and at one particular fixture, over a dozen scouts are said to have been on the vast terracing of Petershill Park, all watching Alan Ross.

In something of a melée to take him from Petershill, it was ex-Charlton Athletic goalkeeping legend, Sam Bartram, then managing Luton Town, who won the fight to take a closer look at the young Ross. What Bartram didn't know about goalkeeping wasn't worth knowing and he recognised the real potential in the rookie keeper. So it was that young Alan Ross made his way from Glasgow to Luton Town's ill-built Kenilworth Road ground for a brief trial period. Taking part in training sessions with the first team, he shone like a lighthouse beacon. In a friendly fixture against the first team, he was outstanding, causing Bartram to move quickly to sign the keeper on a permanent deal. It was March 1962, just a few months before Carlisle United signed what they thought was a quality goalkeeper in the form of Joe Dean from Bolton Wanderers.

Dean was in fact an England youth international, who had made his way through local football to sign for Wanderers. He made his First Division debut on 19 October 1957 against Tottenham Hotspur and had gone on to make a further 11 appearances for the Burnden Park side. At Bolton it was never going to be easy for Dean, he was under-study to the legendary Eddie Hopkinson, a keeper who himself is a Cult Hero in Bolton. So, with Carlisle not looking for a keeper, the link with Alan Ross was extremely tenuous. It was to get more tenuous as time went by. At Luton Town, Ross was second choice to ex-England International keeper and fans' favourite, Ron Baynham. It was never going to be easy to oust such a player from his position. Despite this, Ross gave everything he could to prove his worth. One day, in December 1962, the Luton boss, Bill Harvey, called Ross in and told him that due to Baynham attending his father's funeral, he would be turning out for the first team.

Sadly, the opportunity was whisked away from Ross by a bizarre situation. The Luton team had left the dressing room and were about to make their way down the players' tunnel and onto the pitch, when suddenly manager Harvey bellowed out for them to stay where they were. Everyone was mystified. Harvey summoned Ross back to the dressing room where he was told that Ron Baynham had without warning turned up and would now be playing in his place. Mass confusion surrounded the incident, as Baynham rushed out to take his place in the starting line up, while poor Ross was left to change back into his day clothes and sit on the bench. It was a harsh lesson the keeper never forgot. "Some things in football you can't legislate for. Being selected for the first team at Luton was a proud moment for me, but then to be told at the very last minute it wasn't happening was devastating. It made me realise that I shouldn't take anything for granted, by that I mean in my life as well as football. Bill Harvey apologised to me after, but it was a hollow apology. I vowed there and then to leave Luton and to prove him wrong. He laughed off the suggestion and reminded me that he was the manager and he was experienced enough to know who was the best goalkeeper to play. It was the worst piece of management I suffered throughout my career."

The transfer that released Ross from his Kenilworth Road hell and set up his move to Brunton Park was fortuitous, in United's favour, to say the least. The Luton manager desperately wanted to shore up his leaky defence and saw United full-back Alex McBain as an ideal candidate for the job. Contacting Allan Ashman, Harvey discussed the player's availability and offered winger Jackie Lornie as an exchange. Ashman wanted money as part of the deal and told his Luton counterpart to come back with a better offer. Hours later, Ashman received another call from Luton, this time not only offering Lornie, but allowing him the choice of any of the reserve team players too. The United boss wasn't impressed, so the two clubs were at an impasse and transfer discussions cooled down for a few weeks.

Luton's problem was money. Due to financial restrictions at Kenilworth Road, which were caused mainly by an increase in players' wages, Bill Harvey was struggling to find any cash to support transfers. On the field the Hatters were awful, plummeting to the depths of Division Two in 1962/63 and ultimately being relegated with a total of just 29 points. Ashman hadn't forgotten the Luton offer. He liked the look of Lornie and saw his potential to get at defences. However he had now been alerted to the potential of young goalkeeper, Alan Ross, who had been outstanding for Luton reserves. Carlisle weren't alone in their admiration of the Luton reserve keeper, both Leeds United and Liverpool were also monitoring his performances.

Heavily influenced by the United trainer, Dick Young, Ashman pounced in an attempt to bring both Lornie and Ross to the club. It wasn't that straightforward. By now Harvey was aware that other clubs were sniffing around the keeper and saw the chance to bring in some vital money by selling him to the highest bidder. He was reluctant to let Ross go as part of the deal and told Ashman so. Dick Young, forever the ambassador, made the trip to Kenilworth Road and spoke with Harvey. Discussions were simple as the United man left Harvey with no other option but to include Ross as part of the McBain transfer deal. It was in fact Dick Young who had been to watch the Luton reserves and seen what talent was available. It took him just half a game to realise that the young goalkeeper was the man for Carlisle. Alan Ross signed in a permanent deal in June 1963.

IT WASN'T TOO LONG before Ross made his United and Football League debut at Brunton Park on the 27 September 1963 in a 4-0 victory over Aldershot. He was virtually an ever present for the remainder of that campaign. Over the following three seasons he shared the number one spot with Joe Dean. From 1966/67 it was Ross who took control as the custodian of the Carlisle United goal.

He said: "When I first came to Carlisle I fell in love with the place, Dick Young really influenced me to join. He was a straight-talking and honest man and told me that the club was looking to progress in the right direction. He made it clear that it would be hard work, but that my career would flourish if I was prepared to get stuck in. My first job was sweeping out the dressing room and sorting out Joe Dean's playing kit. I knew of Joe from his days at Bolton. He had a great reputation as a solid professional.

When I first met him [Dean], he asked who I was. I told him and he told me to: "fuck off back to wherever I came from." He was the United goalie and he wouldn't be giving up that position lightly. I told him he would have to make sure he didn't mess up otherwise I would take his place and he wouldn't easily get the jersey back from me. We shook hands and, from that day on, got on really well. Joe was, in my opinion, underestimated as a goalkeeper. I learnt good technique from him. But he was a real wind-up merchant, constantly making jibes as to him being the boss's favourite. It was all good humoured but sometimes, with Joe, you weren't quite sure.

When the chance came along for me to make my debut, I couldn't believe it. Joe took a knock, against Oxford I think it was, and was out for a few weeks. As I came out onto the pitch I was as nervous as anything, half expecting that voice to bellow out and someone to again snatch away my chance to play a league game. It didn't happen, the fans were great and gave me a really good reception. I had to make a diving save at the feet of one of the Aldershot attackers early on and that set me up for virtually the next 20 years really!

Although we won 4-0 it wasn't an easy game, they obviously knew that I had been called in to replace Joe and were having a go at every opportunity they got. It was mostly crosses, but I had to pull off a few stops. Big Joe Kirkup and Hughie Mac took them apart up front and, when we took the lead, I leapt in the air, punching upwards in joy. The fans behind the goal loved it and that was it, I was a part of Carlisle United. I still remember that game. At the end, Dick Young came up to me, shook my hand and said that he thought it was the best goalkeeping performance he had seen for a long time. That comment made me feel brilliant about myself. The rest of the team were equally as complimentary and even Joe Dean nodded and gave me a wink of support."

THE RELATIONSHIP BETWEEN Alan Ross and the United supporters is best described as unique. Before the game he would stand in the main club car park, chatting to fans and signing countless autographs, before disappearing into a tiny door in the stand, marked Players and Officials. Few players were as popular during those days back in the 1960s as the United stopper. He proved his commitment time and again, but also the slightly eccentric side of his personality, which all goalkeepers possess.

"I remember one game against Bolton Wanderers. It was a warm sunny day and the team were stroking the ball about and were in complete control. I hadn't touched the ball since kick-off when Terry Caldwell, in time honoured tradition, passed it back to me. I hoofed it upfield and that was the last I saw of it for about half an hour. I was trying to keep myself agile by doing the usual running around the penalty area routine. The Carlisle fans in the Waterworks End were ribbing me, asking for a piece of the Wrigley's chewing gum I had in my cap in the goal. It was a bit of a ritual for me, throwing in my cap, gloves and Wrigley's as we came out. I looked into the crowd and saw this chap reading a newspaper. I was astounded. Why wasn't he watching the game? By now I was oblivious to what was actually going on in the match. I walked up to him. He was stood at the front of the Waterworks, just to the right of my goal. In a bit of fun, I took the paper off him, walked back onto the pitch, leaned against the post and pretended to read it. The fans were hysterical, I loved it.

Suddenly, one of my defenders, Hughie Neil, yelled out at me to "stop messing around" and get on with the game. "Miserable sod," I thought, only to look up and see the ball coming towards me in mid-air. I caught it comfortably and sent it back towards the Warwick Road End. At half-time I was expecting some stern words from the boss, but nothing was mentioned. Dick Young, though, whispered in my ear not to be too cocky, but followed this by joking, did I

Jimmy McConnell, the first man to score a century of goals for Carlisle, heads home one of them against New Brighton in a 3-1 win in the FA Cup first round on 29 November 1931.

Jimmy McConnell (front row with ball between feet) poses with Bethlehem FC, for whom he played while scoring over a hundred goals during his jaunt in the USA.

A cartoon hails Jimmy McConnell's achievement at reaching a century of goals for Carlisle and shows the strength of feeling amongst the people of the city for their hero's feats

The final resting place of the man who scored Carlisle's first ever goal in the Football League, back in 1928 at Accrington. United were elected to Division Three (North), replacing Durham City, at the end of the 1927/28 season.

The incomparable Bill Shankly; a man who began his path to greatness at Liverpool by becoming a legendary manager at Carlisle.

Shankly took over the reigns at Brunton Park after retiring from playing in March 1949 and brought both grit and panache to Carlisle; most notably with his pre-match communiqués across the booming Tannoy system at the ground.

'Twinkletoes' the Carlisle mascot (aka George Baxter, a road sweeper) and Olga the fox. The pair were regularly to be found at Brunton Park, and around the city, shouting 'C'Mon Ye Blues!'. The name Olga came about as it is an anagram of the word 'goal'.

Billy Hogan (front row, extreme left) poses with his Carlisle United team-mates during the 1950/51 season.

Goalscorer, captain and manager: Ivor Broadis (right) was the perfect ambassador for Carlisle United throughout both his spells at the club.

Broadis scores England's equalising first goal past goalkeeper George Farm in a 4-2 win over Scotland at a packed Hampden Park on 3 April 1954. The result meant England qualified for the 1954 World Cup finals in Switzerland and Broadis was one of the squad selected to take on the world.

During the 1954 World Cup finals, Ivor (standing) relaxes on a paddle steamer on a Swiss lake while colleagues Gil Merrick (left) and captain Billy Wright soak up some sunshine.

Alf Ackerman, the South African who made Carlisle his home, had a remarkable goalscoring ratio; netting 62 goals in just 96 games.

Ackerman scores for Carlisle against Birmingham City at Brunton Park. This third round FA Cup tie finished in a 3-3 draw. Birmingham, who finished 13th in the First Division that season, won the replay 4-0 at St Andrew's.

Another Ackerman goal. The Brunton Park crowd would roar: "Acker, Acker, Acker, Ackerman. He'll score a goal if anyone can!". They were generally right!

His biggest achievement in football may have been to lift the FA Cup at Wembley with West Bromwich Albion, but Allan Ashman cut his managerial teeth at Brunton Park and returned to Carlisle to lift the club into the top flight of English football for the only time in history: arguably an even greater feat than winning the Cup.

Jimmy 'Wham' Whitehouse became only the second man to score over
100 goals for Carlisle, reaching 101 in 205 games between 1951 and 1957.
His nickname came from his thunderbolt shot.

The legendary Dick Young; (above on left) with manager Allan Ashman and (below on left) sprucing up the smart-looking Ivor Broadis before the striker went on England duty. Dick was involved as trainer at the club for 27 years from 1955. The monicker 'Mr Carlisle United' was never more aptly given than to this kindly soul.

Dick Young (on right) in his playing days; on this occasion for Lincoln City.

Legendary goalkeeper Alan Ross keeps his eye on the ball to make yet another save;
although his concentration would sometimes wander as he entertained fans by reading
a newspaper during a game!

Alan Ross (above, second from left) still holds Carlisle's appearance record, after playing in 466 games for Blues, but he will be best remembered for saving a Tommy Smith penalty during the famous goalless FA Cup tie at Anfield in 1974 (below).

One of the most talented and classy footballers ever to grace Brunton Park, remarkably Chris Balderstone combined being the heartbeat of one of the best United teams in the club's history with being a professional cricketer good enough to win two Test caps for England against the fearsome 1976 West Indies tourists.

The smiling BobStokoe. Bob managed the club on three separate occasions, totalling 349 games.

Hugh McIlmoyle scores in the 1-1 draw at Filbert Street early in Carlisle's season in the First Division, 1974/75.

Hugh McIlmoyle in full flight, taking on and beating Chelsea's Ron 'Chopper' Harris during Carlisle's wonderful debut in the top flight of English football. The 2-0 win set Carlisle up for that most splendid of moments: sitting atop the First Division after three games.

Dick Young and Allan Ashman survey the scene from the summit of English football during training in August 1974.

Kenny Wilson is perhaps the unlikeliest Cult Hero included in this book. After starring for Beith Juniors, he arrived at Brunton Park with the ambition to score hatfuls of goals for Carlisle. Sadly he managed just one in his entire stay at the club, a statistic which has turned him into a legendary figure in his own right amongst Blues fans. He is pictured here (above) during his days at Beith; front row, third from right with trophy.
And below, front row, centre, behind mascot.

Stan the Man. Stan Bowles enjoying a nightcap of, er, milk!

Carlisle boys we are here! Stan Bowles celebrates his call up to the England squad in April 1974 on the shoulders of Ipswich defender Kevin Beattie, himself born in Carlisle. The impish winger played in three consecutive games, scoring against Wales in a 2-0 win in Cardiff. Stan won five full caps in all.

Bowles in action against Holland in a game which proved to be his last for his country.

Everyone's favourite son, Peter Beardsley (front row, second from right),
in the 1980/81 team group photo. Fellow Cult Hero Malcolm Poskett is in
the back row, second from left.

Peter Beardsley went on to a glittering career, winning the League title with Liverpool and
59 caps for England (left). He also won a Merit award from the PFA in 1995 (right), but the
football world should not forget that it all began for the wee man at Carlisle United.

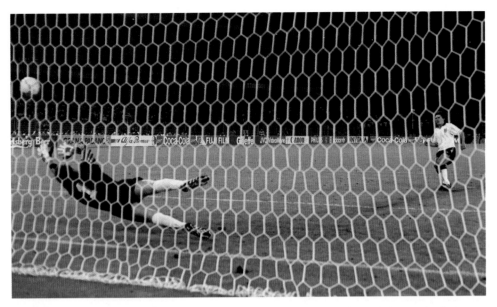

Beardsley slots his penalty home in the shoot out against West Germany in the semi-final of the Italia 90 World Cup. Sadly others missed and the former Carlisle man would miss the chance to appear in a World Cup final.

Malcolm Poskett winds up to shoot. The big man slammed in 60 goals in 186 games for the Cumbrians.

Malcolm Poskett's wonderful 'tash was one of the main reasons for his cult following; to the point that this author grew one too!

John Halpin secured cult status in Carlisle by scoring arguably the greatest goal ever seen at Brunton Park against Blackburn Rovers in January 1986. John set off from the half way line (above), weaving his way through half the Blackburn team before slotting the ball past the Rovers keeper to complete a truly magical moment (below).

Stephane Pounewatchy shows his brute strength in a titanic League Cup tie at White Hart Lane, in which the Premiership club just sneaked home, 3-2. Above, Pounewatchy tackles Spurs' Jose Dominguez, while below he sees off Chris Armstrong.

The Gallic Giant in full, menacing stride.

One of the sweetest moments in the club's history. Jimmy Glass, the goalkeeper on loan from Swindon Town, has just scored the goal against Plymouth Argyle which kept Blues in the Football League, to the utter delight of everyone present.

The celebrations both on and off the pitch after Glass's last gasp goal were long, loud and memorable. Above, Jimmy savours his big moment, while, below, the team rejoice after one of football's most magical episodes. Jimmy was doing interviews for weeks afterwards about his wonder goal which made him the ultimate in footballing one hit wonders.

The battling warrior that is Kev Gray. Here he leaps like the proverbial salmon
to clear his lines, while opposing forwards keep well clear.

Above, Kev Gray puts his body on the line once again, this time blocking a shot at Gravesend & Northfleet during a 3-1 victory in the Vauxhall Conference promotion season.

Below, manager Paul Simpson and captain Kev Gray celebrate with the spoils after winning the 2005 Conference Play-off final against Stevenage.

Kev Gray lifts the Division Two trophy into the Cumbrian sky as Carlisle's remarkable rebirth continues with a second successive promotion in April 2006.

The author (left) and Kev Gray after writing the foreword to the book.

happen to read what had won the three thirty at Doncaster! They were great days and I loved the banter with the fans."

Ross's style was vastly different from the often sullen but wholly professional performances of Joe Dean. United supporters had never seen such a character in their goal before. Rossy was very much an earlier version of Bruce Grobbelaar. He enjoyed nothing more in those relatively early days of his career than playing to an audience. But behind this apparent supreme confidence was a footballer who was determined to succeed and give his all for the club. In training sessions he continually worked on his agility, handling a medicine ball in an attempt to build up his muscle strength. Others followed suit as the medicine ball became something of a regular feature in the training sessions for other players too under coach Dick Young.

Young never allowed the keeper an opportunity to slacken during training. "With Alan Ross you got the complete bundle. As agile as any keeper I knew, he could match them all, but there was also a side to him which sometimes left me despairing. He sometimes had a real showman attitude. In training he would be laughing and joking with others, but eagerly working towards delivering the product we wanted. At times he could take your breath away with a fantastic save, the next he was rolling about on the floor feigning injury, just to wind me up. He certainly knew how to do that! So I would take out my revenge on him by making him do extra circuits, getting him to sprint round the cinder track surrounding the pitch. Every time he would do as he was told with a beaming smile on his face. Alan, despite his antics, was a genuine professional. Chris Balderstone wouldn't have a bad word said about him, but at times in the dressing room, the pair of them would be at each other. They truly enjoyed playing for the club and would give everything they had until the final whistle."

Managers came and went in the 1960s. Allan Ashman, Tim Ward, Bob Stokoe, all had nothing but good words to say about the Carlisle keeper, who within his first full season between the sticks had already become a Cult Hero. I was a young fan in the 1960s and Ross was my first football hero. My first visit to Brunton Park for a game saw my brother, before a game, introduce me to the rangy-looking keeper. Dressed in a suit and tie, he looked every bit a footballer. I remember at the time that he towered above me like some huge giant. Appearances can be deceptive. Gently he shook my hand, asked my name and signed my programme. He then took time to chat to us as though he knew us both personally. I felt very proud to have met him and his kind persona was something that had a real impact upon me.

Foolishly I thought all footballers would be the same, only to have Everton keeper, Gordon West, a couple of years later, in similar circumstances in the main club car park, tell me to: "fuck off and stop bothering me" after I approached for him for an autograph. Rossy would never have been so callous and cruel. He respected the fans and as I grew older and got to speak to him more, I realised that he respected them as much as they did him. He told me: "The supporters are what you play for really. It wasn't the money at Carlisle. It was a love of the game and a real need to do well for the loyal fans that paid to come to watch us as a team. There were a few footballers who tended to forget that fact and some would look down on us as poor country cousins when we played against them. That only spurred us on to beat them on the pitch."

Ross was to suffer the highs and lows of football during the 1966/67 season. United were pushing hard for promotion from Division Two, along with Coventry City and Wolverhampton Wanderers. The keeper proved a consistent shot-stopper and a resilient leader of the United rearguard, a defence which had pushed the Blues into the top three of the division. Football was at last taking notice of Carlisle United and with that came the attention of scouts from bigger clubs. A procession of managers appeared in the United main stand, checking out the stars on show, the most consistent of which was Ross. Leeds boss Don Revie was himself known to be keeping a watchful eye on the keeper, as too were Newcastle United. Despite the attention, Ross stood firm and never once did he ask for a move or show any dissent to his employers. Then, in February 1967, came a real low point of his football career. In a vital game at leaders Coventry the United keeper was kicked and punched in what resembled a scrum down in the United penalty area. The referee struggled to control the incident as players pushed and confronted one another. In a fit of temper, Ross, who believed he recognised the player who kicked him, lashed out at Coventry's Bobby Gould. Gould in absolute melodramatic fashion, dropped as though he had been hit by a steamroller, thrashing around on the floor feigning agony. The end result was the sending off of Alan Ross. "I felt wretched afterwards," he said. "But he definitely kicked me and tried to injure me. It was unnecessary. Then he wanted to get me sent off. Unbelievable really. The referee got it all wrong."

The keeper's status as a hero developed further when, out through a finger injury, he came on as an outfield substitute in a league game against Portsmouth. And it wasn't a token appearance either. At one point Ross skipped past a couple of players before crossing the ball, sadly with no end result.

As disappointing as it was, United missed out on promotion that season, but soon the accolades were winging their way towards the Carlisle keeper. The 1969/70 season was a memorable one for United fans. The team again excelled themselves, this time progressing to the semi-final of the Football League Cup competition. The feat was in no small way down to the heroic performances of Ross. In particular there were some incredible saves made against Chelsea at Brunton Park, when he threw himself across the goalmouth to stop certain goals from the likes of Osgood and Cooke. In the first leg of the semi-final against West Bromwich Albion at Carlisle, he stopped England striker Jeff Astle from scoring several times as United won 1-0. In the second leg he was again in outstanding form. Sadly as his defence collapsed through exhaustion, he leaked four goals as the team crashed out of the competition, having been just 37 minutes from a Wembley final. After the game, Jeff Astle commented to a reporter: "The difference between the two teams was Alan Ross. I didn't think we would ever get the ball past him. He really didn't deserve to be on the losing side tonight."

Those performances saw him called into the final 16 of the Scotland full international squad for the 1969 Home International Championships. He never managed to break into the Scotland national team, however, being kept out by Birmingham's Jim Herriot, but Rossy was as close as you could get to such recognition.

BACK AT BRUNTON PARK, the eccentricity continued, as Ross grew closer to the ever-increasing crowds. It seemed that at every opportunity he enjoyed having a chat with the fans behind his goal. As someone who was privy to such scenes myself, I can remember him turning to face the fans and talk to them. Some would mock him, which made him laugh, others would simply enjoy witnessing acts of supreme confidence, or professional lunacy. If the opposing team moved into the United half, the crowd wouldn't be slow in letting him know.

Sadly, as the seasons progressed, as is the case with all goalkeepers, Ross became susceptible to the odd blunder and made more than a few mistakes. In general these occurred not when he was fooling around, but when he was heavily involved in the game. Against Queen's Park Rangers, for example, a long range effort by Mick Leach, which lacked any real power seemed a comfortable save. Yet somehow the ball squirmed beneath Ross and into the net. On another occasion he came out to collect a cross and the ball went straight through his hands and into the net. The mistakes caused a section of the crowd to get on his back. For a time, Ross didn't seem to be the goalkeeper he had been. A loss of confidence had really affected him. Rumours abounded that he took nerve pills before every game, apparently to calm himself down. Such talk didn't remain in Carlisle, it travelled with him to away games, where opposing fans would continually taunt in an effort to unnerve him. Despite this, Ross was as solid a goalkeeper as there was in Division Two, potentially as good as any in Division One. At Anfield in September 1972 his nerve was really put to the test, when, in a League Cup replay, he faced a penalty from Liverpool captain and tough guy, Tommy Smith. The defender had an outstanding record from the penalty spot and hammered his spot-kick goal wards. It looked a certain goal as the ball sped to the keeper's right at a terrific pace. Ross launched himself full-length across the goal and somehow managed to repel it. It was an incredible save, which earned Ross a standing ovation from the Liverpool Kop, as well as looks of incredulity from Messrs Smith, Toshack and Keegan. Nervous during a game? Alan Ross? Don't think so!

During the 1973/74 promotion season Ross was immaculate in his handling and management of the United defence. After an early blip at Luton, where he conceded six in the first half, he produced some incredible form and kept 18 clean sheets in all competitions throughout the season. The absolute high point of his United career came in the 1974/75 season when he appeared for United in the First Division. Despite relegation, Ross still managed to keep seven clean sheets. At Chelsea in the opening fixture, he looked calm and collected, though Chris Balderstone inferred something rather different. "The opening First Division game at Chelsea was the pinnacle of most of our football careers. None of us really expected to get that far, yet there we were, playing in the same league as the country's biggest club sides. In the dressing room before the game we were quiet, contemplating what might be. I turned to Rossy and asked him how he felt about it all. He said he felt sick and felt uneasy in an excited sort of way. He looked a bit pale to be truthful and I really thought he was going to be sick. I never said anything to the others, but he was putting himself under immense pressure. Then when he got out there he turned to me at half-time and told me that he didn't want the euphoria to ever end."

Ross never really put a foot out of place in the First Division, despite the club ultimately finishing in last place, though he was made the scapegoat for a number of last minute defeats when his concentration came into question and he appeared to dither instead of coming to collect crosses, some of which found an opposition striker and ended up in the back of his net. Injuries, rather than a lack of confidence in him by the management team, allegedly kept him out of a number of games, when Tom Clarke deputised for him.

"The First Division was a great time for us all," he remembers. "I still have to pinch myself to believe it all happened. I remember the civic reception in Carlisle when we won promotion. Tens of thousands of supporters turned out to cheer us on. I felt on top of the world. I was feeling a bit dodgy before the Chelsea game at Stamford Bridge. Nerves had really got hold of me. Dick Young told me to focus and concentrate on the game for 90 minutes, no talking to the fans. It would have been hard at Stamford Bridge, they were miles behind the goal. All I could hear throughout the game was Carlisle fans singing. It was wonderful, I made a couple of difficult saves and took the sting out of other shots, dropping one, but I always felt in control of my game there.

The boss had a bit of a go at me a few times throughout that season. He reckoned I was switching off after about 80 minutes. It wasn't that, it was down to the fact that in most games we were so far on top that I didn't have a lot to do. We couldn't finish games and didn't score the amount of goals we should have. When we tired, the other teams would snatch it, coming at us in the closing stages and laying siege to my goal. Eventually a few chances are going to go in. Maybe I was a bit slow to react at times, but then we were playing against the very best footballers in the land, so we shouldn't kick ourselves about it."

Relegation followed and another pretender to Ross's throne emerged, a younger more energetic keeper in the form of Martin Burleigh. He couldn't oust the King of the Brunton Park goal for long; 17 games later and Rossy was back in goal as first choice. Then came the arrival of Trevor Swinburne, a goalkeeper who Ross described as being among the top ten in the English game. Ross was now ready to stand down, handing over the mantle of Carlisle's number one to a much younger man. Even then, though, he didn't hang up his gloves. Ross was called up to play one last game, a 2-0 win over Swindon Town on the 28 October 1978.

ROSS PLAYED OVER 500 games for Carlisle United, appearing in every division; an achievement enough in itself. After his retirement he worked on the commercial side of the club for a short time, before taking up a job with Carlisle City Council, where he worked in the housing department, primarily as a rent collector. It was in this role that I got to know him a lot better. He was a kind and caring man who always made time to talk about football and I am delighted to say that I took advantage of that fact to speak with him as much as I could. So it was indeed a shock when Alan Ross passed away in 1999 at the age of just 57. No-one can or ever will replace his presence, passion and eccentricity on the pitch. He was and will always be number one.

CHRIS BALDERSTONE

1965-1975

UNITED CAREER

Games	369+7
Goals	68

MAGIC MOMENT

The Liverpool midfield had no anwer to him. He strutted around the Anfield pitch as if he owned it; in fact he did that day in 1973

'MR MAJESTIC'

WITHOUT doubt, the question I am most frequently asked as a journalist, author and historian of Carlisle United, has to be: "Who is the best footballer you have ever seen play?" It's an almost impossible one to answer. How do you define 'best' after all? But Chris Balderstone was, most definitely, the most graceful, talented and skilful player I have ever clapped my eyes upon. Quite simply, he was magic. Don't just take my word for it either; other members of the Baldy fan club include the late Emlyn Hughes and Manchester United legend Denis Law. Emlyn, who was himself a Cumbrian by birth, once said of Chris: "He was quite exquisite in the way he could stop the game, look around him and spray a pass with pinpoint accuracy well over 80 yards. For a bloke as big as he is, he is so quick-footed and nimble. We faced Carlisle a few times in my time at Liverpool, but never once did we manage to stop him playing his wonderful football. I would say he is possibly the best player in the history of the game never to have realised national team recognition in football."

Denis Law proclaimed him as a "wonderful player at every club he has represented. He wasn't bad at cricket either!"

There can be no doubting that Balderstone possessed supreme ball control and at times appeared more agile than a ballet dancer. He could score goals too, 68 of them in 376 games in all domestic competitions for Carlisle United. His solitary weakness was perhaps his pace, but that didn't prevent him from hip-swerving his way past full-backs, feigning to go one way with a sharp move of his head and a drop of the shoulder, before slipping the ball past them in the other direction. The late Bill Shankly once described him as: "a master of football deception". That's not in any derogatory sense, but more in the way he made the ball do the work. Baldy simply used his brain to deceive the opponent.

It is somewhat disappointing to those who recall his talent whilst wearing the shirt of his beloved Carlisle United, that he is more commonly remembered for one day in September 1975. It was 15 September to be precise, the day Baldy made a piece of sporting history, which has become an oft-asked trivia question. In the second day of the contest, as third man in, he took to the cricket crease at Chesterfield representing Leicestershire against Derbyshire. It was an important fixture. Leicestershire, who had been revitalised under the guidance of ex-Yorkshire star Ray Illingworth, went into their final game in search of the seven points which would guarantee them a first ever County Championship title. The pressure dropped when, in mid-afternoon, news broke that results elsewhere meant that Leicestershire couldn't be caught at the top of the table and so were champions.

Chris Balderstone, the ultimate professional, finished the day on 51 not out. It was now 6.30pm and waiting in the stand at Chesterfield was Doncaster Rovers boss Stan Anderson. Rovers had signed Baldy from Carlisle in the summer of 1975, following United's relegation from the top flight. As Chris left the field in full cricket whites, Anderson whisked him off in his Triumph Stag to dash 30 miles up the motorway to Rovers' Belle Vue stadium, where Chris turned out for Rovers against Brentford in a league match. The game ended 1-1. Balderstone did not score, but created history by being the first footballer/cricketer to play both sports in first class competition on the same day.

He returned to the crease at Chesterfield the following day to finish with 116 as Leicestershire's title celebrations continued, but Baldy's began. He also took three wickets later in the afternoon. It was an incredible sporting achievement, which in reality will never again be repeated. But at Carlisle, we remember him for being much more than a piece of sporting trivia. He was our captain, our leader, our ultimate football hero and legend.

CHRISTOPHER JOHN BALDERSTONE was born on 16 November 1940 at Longwood, Huddersfield. He attended Paddock County School where cricket was the favoured sport and football regarded as a secondary subject in games lessons. He played in Paddock's cricket team in the Huddersfield League before his 15th birthday. His passion for active participation of sports of any sort was satiated in the winter by his appearance in local level football. As a local amateur he was picked up by Huddersfield Town, then managed by Bill Shankly. Chris recalled: "I had been told that Huddersfield Town were looking at me. I just enjoyed playing really. I knew the scouts had been out at a few of the games, but no approach was made until one day I saw Shankly himself at a game. He came up to me afterwards and asked if I fancied a trial at Leeds Road. I jumped at the chance, but never thought I would make the grade."

Make the grade he did and Balderstone was quickly offered professional terms in May 1958. It was to be some time before he broke into the first team, mainly due to the form of another of Shankly's acquisitions, one Denis Law. Eventually Law was sold on and Chris stepped up, making his debut in March 1959 at Ninian Park, Cardiff, where he scored the Terriers' only goal in a 2-1 defeat.

In 1961, whilst now a fully-fledged professional footballer, Balderstone made his first-class debut for Yorkshire County Cricket Club against Glamorgan at Headingley, scoring 23 runs in what was his only innings that summer.

The emerging talent of Balderstone the footballer was being monitored by scouts who were keen to pick up other potential stars in the mould of Denis Law from a Huddersfield side who had lost their way since the departure of Bill Shankly, who had moved on to take over at Liverpool in December 1959. He had been replaced by Eddie Boot and then Tom Johnston, who had a different perception to his illustrious predecessor. Rumours of unrest in the Huddersfield dressing room spread through the game and to the ears of the then manager of Carlisle United, Allan Ashman. The Carlisle boss hailed from South Yorkshire and had an excellent network of scouts covering the region. Rumours that Huddersfield were open to offers for the cultured midfielder who Johnston didn't rate were confirmed and so Ashman picked up the telephone and made the call to his counterpart at Leeds Road. Ashman offered to pay £7,000 for the player. Johnston accepted and in June 1965 Chris Balderstone became a Carlisle United player. During his time at Huddersfield he had made a total of 131 appearances, scoring 25 goals. Ashman didn't quite realise it then, but he had got himself a genuine bargain.

BALDERSTONE GOT OFF TO the perfect start to life at Brunton Park, scoring on his debut in a 4-1 home win over Norwich City. "As soon as I arrived at Carlisle I felt settled," he later recalled. "People depict it as being removed from civilisation, but nothing could be farther from the truth. Granted it used to be a long haul to get to by road especially, but with the advent of improved road networks and motorways it became much better to get to. Allan Ashman was a good manager. We didn't always agree on football matters, but overall I think he was one of the best managers I played for. When I left Huddersfield, the boss there, Tom Johnston never really gave me much inclination to wish him well or say goodbye, but later, after I had gone, I heard he regretted selling me to Carlisle.

There were rumours that Bill Shankly wanted to take me to Liverpool, but missed out as he delayed getting in touch. I was never sure whether it was true or not. I got the chance to ask him when we played Liverpool at Anfield one evening. He laughed off the suggestion and asked me why he would want to sign Chris Balderstone? I didn't know what to say, so he said "See, if you don't know why, then how the hell do you expect me to know?" As I turned to leave, he quipped: "You looking for a move then?" Shanks, was like that. You were never sure whether he was taking the piss out of you. He really shook things up at Huddersfield. It needed it. When he brought in Denis Law, he looked a bit on the weak side, but he improved no end with Shanks on his case all the time. I saw him grow in stature and confidence and you could tell he was going to be world class. People say I was in his [Law] shadow, but I don't think that was the case. Sure he performed consistently, but we were two different types of footballer. I reckon I was better!"

IN HIS FIRST SEASON at Carlisle, Balderstone gelled with his colleagues. Allan Ashman was building a team capable of sustaining Second Division status following promotion in 1964/65. Despite having a few problems at centre-forward, United enjoyed high-scoring victories against Bristol City (5-1) and Bury (4-0), with Balderstone scoring in both these fixtures. "We really needed a reliable centre-forward who could finish for us," he said. "Willie Carlin and I were working our socks off supplying balls, but time and again there was no-one to finish. When Davy Wilson came in from Nottingham Forest it was a relief. He was a clinical finisher and did okay for us, but we lacked consistency really. The boss was always telling us to get the ball forward, so in frustration I asked him: 'to who?' He barked back: 'Listen Balderstone. You are on the field playing, not me. If you can't get the players forward then don't expect me to do it from the sideline. Use your bloody head and think football. Not who to apportion blame to!' He was right too, I never forgot those words."

Behind the scenes, Ashman and his right hand man, Dick Young, were busy putting together a squad of players who lived, breathed and worked for one another. Players like Terry Caldwell and Peter McConnell were viewed as integral parts of Carlisle's set up as much as the very stadium itself. No wonder that many fans to this day still cite Messrs Caldwell, McConnell and Passmoor in their all time great Carlisle United XI. Dick Young, in particular, recognised just what they had in Balderstone.

He told me: "Chris was a good man and a great footballer. I was fascinated by the way he strolled round the pitch during a game. Yet he was always in control, always a pass or a move ahead of anyone else. He was a powerful individual, morally committed to Carlisle United. He was the cornerstone of the dressing room. He held it together when others around him were falling apart. In his early days at the club, I took him to one side and asked if he wanted to come in for extra training to help improve his game. He said 'yes' and do you know, for years after, he always stayed beyond the allotted time. He hated the runs at Silloth and Skinburness, but once he got into it he was like a little boy on his holidays. That goes for all the players then. They loved nothing more than running along the sandy beach. It was something that really caught on in football, I think we were the first to do it, to strengthen leg muscles. Next thing the press are onto it and photographing the players running up and down sand dunes. I had a few coaches asking me about it. Les Cocker came up to watch us once. The coverage of it made the players feel part of something new, it all helped towards team building.

I used to rib Baldy telling him that I could beat him up and down the dunes three times in succession. One day he said: 'Dick, okay. Ten bob on it.' Off we went with all the players cheering us on. He was winning and so he should, he was younger than me, but I wanted the ten bob, so as we passed, him coming down and me going up, I tripped him up and off he went rolling down to the bottom. Hastily I finished my three climbs and won. Everyone was laughing, but not Chris. He hated to lose at anything! I never took the ten bob off him."

Balderstone enjoyed a marvellous working relationship with the United coach and some of his peers. People like goalkeeper Alan Ross matured alongside Balderstone, with them graduating into fine players in the Dick Young mould for the biggest part of their careers. It's no surprise that these two players are Blues' longest playing servants. They truly enjoyed being part of the Carlisle United experience, despite the fact that during his spell at Brunton Park, Balderstone played for four different managers, two of which, Ashman and Stokoe, returned to the managerial chair whilst he was there.

"The managers were all good in their own way," he recalled. "Allan Ashman was relatively quiet on the surface, but he could let blast when he wanted to. I always felt as though I had let him down if we lost. That's probably the sign of a good manager, to get you feeling like that and making sure you don't feel like it too often. Bob Stokoe was a different kettle of fish. Boy did he sulk if you upset him. I've had more than a few bollockings off him in my time. The thing about both these men is that they were committed to Carlisle United; they knew what was expected of them and expected the players to respond accordingly. I remember someone once put some rubbish in Bob's coat pockets, nothing bad, just screwed up pieces of paper. He went mad and interrogated us all to try to find out who had done it. I reckon if he had found out who it was they would have been sold, thankfully he didn't find out it was me!

Tim Ward was different again. He was quiet and level headed. We always joked at how relaxed he used to seem to be. He got some stick when he was with us, for some reason he seemed desperate to change things. It didn't work like that then at Carlisle. He didn't seem to cope very well with pressure and it wasn't really a surprise when he left. When asked to make him a cup of tea, we always made it with luke warm (almost cold really) water. He never once said anything about it.

Then there was Ian MacFarlane. A lot of people didn't like his way, but I thought he was excellent as a manager. A big, gruff Scotsman he wouldn't accept 'no' for an answer. He knew what he wanted and was intent on getting it. Players like Stan Bowles, though I don't suppose they would admit it, were scared of him, but he really did Stan a favour in trying to get him to focus on playing and not on gambling and being sexy. I remember Mac telling another player that he would ride him to the gates of hell if he didn't change his ways. That was the way he had been brought up in football. He used to say how tough it was at Aberdeen and Bath City and to be grateful as to how lucky we were to be at Carlisle!

There were rumours for a time that he had mouthed off at one of the directors, not long after he was gone. I wouldn't like to say it was right or wrong, but I do know he left pretty sharpish and it surely can't have been because of football reasons as we were doing alright for him. When the boss [Allan Ashman] came back, things really began to happen."

Ashman realised the club needed an injection of some new blood, not least a goal-scorer, a player who could get him 30 plus goals a season. A number of offers were coming in for Stan Bowles and it was clear that the player knew of these. Ashman didn't want to stand in the way of ambition, so reluctantly allowed the player to leave, ensuring a good financial deal for Carlisle. In came Kenny Wilson, a legend at his previous club, Dumbarton, destined to be a flop at Brunton Park, but Second Division status was eventually secured, with Balderstone performing at his very best in midfield.

All this while Balderstone's cricket ambitions were being realised too and, after scoring 1,332 runs in eight seasons for Yorkshire, he followed his mentor Ray Illingworth to Leicestershire in 1971. Here, his cricket career took off with the United favourite winning Gold Awards in both the 1971 and 1972 seasons as Leicestershire won its first ever trophy, the Benson and Hedges Cup, at Lord's in 1972.

THE 1973/74 SEASON was to be one dreams are made of, yet for Chris Balderstone it started oh so badly. "The cricket season wasn't over and we (Leicestershire) were doing well," he recalled. "I couldn't just walk away and return to football at such a crucial time. I contacted the club and asked for permission to miss training for a short time until the cricket season was over; it seemed a reasonable enough request."

Whether Balderstone thought it was a reasonable request or not, the simple fact of the matter was that he was under contract to play football for Carlisle United during the football season and that included attending pre-season training sessions. There was real conflict between player, manager and clubs as Balderstone elected to see out the cricket season during August 1973. Ashman was furious and immediately suspended the player and relieved him of the captaincy. As captain of the side he was expected to set an example to the playing squad. No matter what, the damage had been done. Chris Balderstone played his first full season of cricket during 1973, making 1,222 runs. He went on to pass the 1,000-run mark in ten of the next 12 seasons, batting either in the middle order or as an opener.

It seemed that there was a big decision necessary where Balderstone was concerned. For a start, the Carlisle boss decided not to lift the suspension until a full disciplinary enquiry had been completed. In an out-of-character act of defiance, Balderstone asked for a transfer. It was that great football gentleman Dick Young who eventually pacified all parties and talked Balderstone and the club down from their positions on high.

Despite the rift, Balderstone eventually worked his way back into the first team as the Second Division table was ascended. By May 1974, United sat in third position and had won promotion to the First Division, the equivalent of today's Premier League. "It was sensational, a truly historic occasion," Balderstone rhapsodised. "I had withdrawn my transfer request mid-season and I was thankful I did. I apologised to the boss and to the fans for my lack of loyalty, but to be honest, the fans never thought it was too bad an indiscretion. It was a great place to be and everyone at the club was focusing on First Division football. When the fixtures came out and we saw Chelsea at Stamford Bridge as our first game it was unbelievable.

I remember looking around Stamford Bridge before the game, that massive stand over-shadowed the pitch. Rossy said to me he felt nervous and worried that we might not be able to cope with it as players. When we came out onto the pitch for the game it was the greatest, most proud moment of my career in all sport. The noise was deafening. All I could hear was the Carlisle fans chanting. I thoroughly enjoyed that game. I reckon it was one of my best for Carlisle. As for when Bill Green scored early on, I didn't know what to do, I wanted to scream, but I wanted to cry as well. Rossy told me at half-time that when the goal was scored he wanted the referee to blow for full-time! We played as one that day, and really messed up the Chelsea game plan. Peter Carr and John Gorman were exceptional in our defence, and Rossy didn't put a foot wrong, he was confident and commanding.

When, in the second half, Les [O'Neill] scored our second goal, I just lost it. I was trem-bling with excitement and disbelief really. When we came off at the end we received a standing ovation from part of the Chelsea crowd. Who would ever have believed it? We stuffed Middlesbrough away 2-0 too, before Spurs came to Carlisle for our first home game. We really outplayed them all match, I thought. As for my penalty, well, I had to retake it, but wasn't fazed by Pat Jennings' antics and I just belted it past him. That was three wins out of three; we were on top of the league, at the very top of football. That night was all about us and Carlisle United. No-one can ever take that away from us. We topped the First Division."

The excitement didn't last too long as the team slid down the table, gradually hitting rock bottom where they stayed until relegated back to the Second Division at the first time of asking. "It was an awful feeling being relegated after all the euphoria of getting promoted," Balderstone continued. "I figured that my football days were numbered at Carlisle. The boss didn't like me doubling up with cricket, but I was still fit enough to do it and wasn't about to give it up now. I left Carlisle after Doncaster Rovers came in for me and it had been made clear that as far as Allan Ashman was concerned there was no negotiations to be had: if I stayed it was as a footballer only. So I left." Chris had been at Brunton Park for eleven years. His record of helping the team win promotion from the Third Division to the First Division will be forever etched in the football history books.

"Carlisle United getting promoted to the First Division was the highlight of my football career," he recalled. "It was a pleasure to serve the club for as long as I did. I know a lot of the players of that era feel the same. Alan Ross, in particular, loved the place. He couldn't get enough of Brunton Park. Alan and I trained very hard to keep ourselves fit. I think he was probably the one other player I truly looked up to and respected. He was a bit of a joker as well, but didn't like jokes being played on him. He used to wear a baseball hat during games when it was sunny. Once somebody swapped it for a children's hat. It was much smaller, and when he went to slip it on his head in goal one game, it wouldn't fit. He went daft at half-time. Thankfully we had a proper-size replacement to give him!"

CONCENTRATING MORE AND MORE upon cricket, Chris was able to consolidate himself as a top performer, his runs being an important factor in securing Leicestershire's first County Championship success in 1975. As an all-rounder he chipped in with 43 useful wickets during that season too. In 1976, he received the ultimate accolade for his cricketing prowess when he was called into the England Test team to face the rampaging West Indies touring team, featuring the likes of Viv Richards, Clive Lloyd and Michael Holding. He played in two matches and at number four produced a stubborn display of batting, scoring 35 runs in the first innings at Headingley as the Windies flattened England in a series which proved seminal in beginning the Caribbean domination of the game that was to last 15 years. Balderstone's technique was supported by a bagful of courage and his confidence ensured that he kept his place for the Oval Test. Sadly this wasn't his most inspired performance as he picked up a pair, being bowled on both occasions by Michael Holding during his record 14 wicket haul. Baldy was also an outstanding fielder, though he will never forget dropping Viv Richards, then on 151, at the Oval off Derek Underwood's bowling.

"I don't think 'Deadly' ever forgave me for that."

Typically, Balderstone, when reminiscing about those times, would never discuss the fact that he held an incredible catch at cover to dismiss Roy Fredericks during the same game. It should not be forgotten either, that he batted for almost three and a half hours at Headingley against what can only be described as a wickedly ferocious West Indies attack.

Back in football, his Doncaster experience wasn't the best, and it seemed that the juggling of the two sports was now becoming more of a toilsome task than a pleasure. Despite this, he made 39 appearances, scoring just once for Rovers. In 1977 he moved on, this time to Queen of the South, where he made 34 appearances for the Dumfries and Galloway side. One crowning moment of his career in Scotland was when he played against a Celtic team which had amongst its ranks, Kenny Dalglish. The Celts ran out easy 5-1 winners, albeit three of their goals came in the last 12 minutes when Queens had begun to tire. One report reads: 'the elegant midfield player Chris Balderstone bossed the game at his commanding best'. After the game, Celtic boss, Jock Stein, had a chat with Man of the Match Balderstone and advised him: "If you were ten years younger, I'd sign you". Moving home to Leicester, no doubt to support his cricketing roots, his final football days were played out at non-league Enderby Town.

In 1986, Chris retired from playing cricket of any sort to become, two years later, a first-class umpire, standing in two one-day internationals in the mid-1990s. His Leicestershire cricketing career had seen him make 17,627 runs for the Foxes. Further, he took some 310 wickets in his career. Without doubt, his best performance as a bowler was 6 for 25 against Hampshire at Southampton in 1978. He also took a hat-trick against Sussex at Eastbourne in 1976. To this day he shares the county's second-wicket partnership record of an unbroken 289 with David Gower against Essex at Grace Road in 1981. This book though, isn't about his cricketing exploits. Chris Balderstone will be revered elsewhere for those achievements. These pages are about a young footballer who developed into the most exquisite player in the game at the time and whose loyalty to Carlisle United remained. Despite being courted by several bigger First Division clubs he remained a blue through and through.

Chris Balderstone is a legend. He was for countless years the first name on the United team sheet. He was also, by a country mile, the first name on my list of Cult Heroes for this work. He was a footballer who provided so much pleasure, his ability to control a game and his football vision have never been replicated at Carlisle United since. Baldy passed away due to cancer on 6 March 2000 in the city he loved so much, Carlisle, aged just 59 years and 111 days.

BOB STOKOE

1968-1970
1980-1985
1985-1986

UNITED CAREER

as manager

Games	349
Wins	130

MAGIC MOMENT

So nearly taking Carlisle to Wembley for the first time in history in the 1970 League Cup semi-final

'NORTHERN & PROUD'

MANY of life's defining moments have a real and lasting impact upon us. Where Carlisle United are concerned I have had several defining moments. However, above all, Sunday 1 February 2004 is a date which will forever stick in my mind. It is the date that I received the telephone call from a nurse at the University Hospital of Hartlepool, advising me that Robert Stokoe, ex-manager of Carlisle United had passed away. He had been admitted the previous Tuesday, suffering from a severe form of dementia. I didn't know whether to thank the caller or rebuke her in disbelief. I don't actually think I replied with any words. My heart sank as I stood in the study of my home and stared blankly at a 1980s photograph of a Carlisle United line-up, with a sprightly-looking Bob as manager. I had been due to go see him the following week, surely it had to be some mistake? I replaced the phone on its cradle and sat down. I didn't cry, I just felt completely saddened and empty; for that day football and Carlisle United lost one of its greatest managers and a man who genuinely loved the football club and all it stood for, and I had lost a good friend.

I WAS FIRST INTRODUCED to Bob Stokoe in 1980 and maintained a Carlisle United-related friendship until he passed away. In later years, together, we were planning a book on his life in football; no garish revelations, outside of accusing Leeds United boss Don Revie of attempted cheating and attempted football match-fixing, telling a pain-stricken Sunderland centre-forward called Brian Clough that he was cheating and to get up and play on, and telling Chris Balderstone he was a dreamer if he thought he would ever enjoy more success at cricket than football!

Over the years I spent hundreds of pleasurable hours with one of the most sincere and knowledgeable men in football discussing his outstanding career as a player and later as a manager. Although Bob had a real and genuine affection for potentially his most successful club side, Sunderland, deep inside he held a true fondness for a team in the north west of England. Publicly he could never admit it, but his team was Carlisle United; a football club to which he dedicated around 11 years of his life as a manager and, later, scout. It seems that when Carlisle United called, Bob always responded positively and quickly. On one occasion when Bob was out on the golf course, enjoying a stress free absence from the game on his doctor's instruction, United called and, yet again, he dropped everything to come to the club's aid.

Anyone meeting the smiling and gentle Geordie for the first time could be forgiven for thinking that he was the epitome of calmness and serenity. Those who got to know him could tell a completely different story, for behind the almost pastoral image that pervaded was a deeply passionate football manager and a man who would take no nonsense from his players or staff. He could be volatile and was more than capable of throwing tea cups or anything he could lay his hands on in the dressing room if he was displeased with a team performance or that of an individual. He was a man of strong and strict principles and expected others in his employment to abide by his rules. If they didn't, then let them beware.

The son of a miner, Robert Stokoe was born in Mickley, Northumberland on the 21 September 1930. An athletically built young man, he grew into a strong footballer, standing 6ft tall. His football career started at well-respected local amateur side, Spen Juniors. By September 1947, aged just 17, he made the move to the professional game signing for Newcastle United, making his debut on Christmas Day 1950 at Ayresome Park, then home to Middlesbrough. It was a dream start for him personally, as he scored for the Magpies, though the team disappointingly lost the game 2-1. Unusually, Stokoe was playing at centre-forward that day. Making a huge impact, he went on to become a regular first team player at Newcastle, but not until he switched to the position of centre-half, playing 287 games and scoring five goals during that time.

When discussing the Magpies, Bob would speak of how he regarded his finest hour as a player as coming in 1955, when he starred at Wembley in the FA Cup Final. Newcastle's opponents that day were Manchester City. The Blues were reduced to ten men through injury after just 20 minutes of play, and with no substitutes in those days it was always going to be a difficult task facing a fiercely competitive Newcastle side, who had taken the liberty of scoring in the opening minute through a flying Jackie Milburn header. It was the Geordies who took complete advantage of the situation and went on to win the game 3-1.

Despite the deficit of scoreline and players, City threw everything at Newcastle, but Bob Stokoe was a colossus. He marshalled and patrolled throughout the Newcastle defence, battling for every ball with a never-say-die spirit. It was his performance that day which broke City's hearts, for they could get nothing past him. It is something of travesty that he never went on to play for England, but then he always said that he believed the winners' medal was worth more than any international cap or appearance. "Playing in the final and winning the FA Cup with Newcastle was something special, but there were low points as well," he told me. "I remember squaring up to my Newcastle team-mate Jimmy Scoular during a game. Jim could be a really obnoxious, arrogant bastard at the best of times, who was always upsetting players in the Newcastle dressing room with his selfish ways. During one particular game he had been fannying about with the ball instead of passing it and we missed a couple of good goal-scoring opportunities. I couldn't hold it in any longer. I marched up to him and I told him to his face what I thought of him: he was a fucking prima donna. I told him that he was greedy with the ball and didn't read the game well. Anyway he called me "a tosser", so I returned the insult. It ended up in a flurry of pushes and abuse. Very unprofessional, but it needed to be said to him. It happens, so what can you do?"

Whether the incident played any part in Stokoe's future at the club will never truly be known, but what is known is that in January 1961, Scoular left for Bradford Park Avenue. But then, after 14 happy years at St James' Park, Bob Stokoe was released on 10 April 1961 as part of a £24,000 deal which saw him move to Bury in exchange for the Shakers' centre-half John McGrath. "Naturally I was disappointed to be leaving Newcastle," said Stokoe. "But I honestly wasn't too upset to be moving on. I must have been one of the few players then to sign for a new club and become captain for the very next game. Before my arrival, John

McGrath had been the team captain, so to be signed up and directly replace him I saw as a huge compliment."

The new Bury skipper led his team to a 17 game unbeaten run, as a result of which they won the Third Division Championship. It came as something of a surprise when the Bury manager, Dave Russell, unexpectedly left the club in December 1961. "It was a difficult time," recalled Bob. "We were struggling in one of the relegation spots in Division Two most of the season and were playing poorly. I was called in by the board and told that Dave had left the club. Before I could say anything, they asked if I would be interested in taking over as manager. I told them I didn't want to give up playing yet, but would see it as a great privilege to be player-manager." The end result was that, at the age of 31, Bob Stokoe became one of the League's youngest ever managers.

"I was ready for a change and a challenge because I'd been a player for so long," he said. "I can never thank the board of directors of Bury enough, for it was they who gave me the opportunity to prove that I could make it as a manager; great people." Stokoe the manager guided the Shakers away from the relegation zone, finally finishing the season above the likes of Leeds United and Swansea Town, and so avoiding the drop back into the Third Division. "I remember the closing stages of that season well, we played Leeds twice over Easter. We were expected to go down and Leeds were not expected to be down there with us, but they were. Don Revie, who was the new Leeds boss back then, was keen to prove his ability as a manager. They weren't a good team at the time. They knew we had the beating of them if we performed well on the day. Revie came in to see me before a game and was acting furtively. I asked what was wrong. It was then that he offered me £500 if we would lose one of the games against Leeds. I was furious and told him so. He was trying to cheat. I told him that I was disgusted with him for stooping so low. He was an absolute disgrace as a professional manager. He wouldn't take no for an answer and still wanted to go to my players to offer them the chance to forfeit the game. I told him, whilst I was in the game, I would never do business with him and that I would make sure everyone knew he was cheating his way through the game. I never did forgive him for what he did. He was nothing but a bloody cheat. I told our chairman and a couple of other people in the game, they advised me not to say anything as it could do more to us than it would to him or Leeds. I wasn't alone either, others were offered bribes. It still angers me to think that he thought he could buy me and my players.

We never really said a great deal to each after that, but what goes round comes round and I tend to think justice was finally served upon him in 1973 FA Cup final. I couldn't resist telling him at Wembley what a wanker he was. When we won the Cup I told him: 'no amount of money can take away the emotion of knowing you have won something fair and square.' He dropped his head and didn't respond."

It is curious to note that whilst Revie did successfully sue for libel (not Stokoe, but the newspaper who published these and other such revelations in 1977), he never made any effort to go to court to clear his name, which has subsequently left something of a stained image. In desperation to sprint to Revie's defence, some authors have tried to stain Stokoe's character, saying that when he did reveal all, it was for a sum of £14,000, thus implying that he made it all up and sold his soul for money. These same people also questioned why he waited fully 15 years to bring it to light. The reality was that such rumours and information had been doing the rounds in football circles for many years, not only against Revie, but others too. Stokoe reported it at the time to his chairman, but was told to leave it. He obeyed orders, but was more than happy to reveal the truth when the shackles were removed.

THE 1962/63 SEASON WAS Stokoe's first full season in charge at Gigg Lane and it has to be said it was a truly fantastic one for Bury supporters. Incredibly, they reached the semi-finals of the League Cup, and were unfortunate to lose out (4-3 on aggregate) on a Wembley final appearance to a very tough Birmingham City team. As well as this, the Shakers turned football form on its head. For once this was not to be a season of struggle, but one which saw them flirt with promotion, finally settling for eighth position, not too far behind Newcastle, Middlesbrough and Sunderland.

That season also saw the end of the playing career of Sunderland and England striker Brian Clough, through a severe tear to a cruciate ligament during a game against Stokoe's Bury. It was Boxing Day and the Roker Park pitch had a covering of slush on its surface. Elsewhere in the north east matches had been called off due to the heavy snowfall and cold spell. But in Sunderland forecast rain had fallen half-an-hour before kick-off, somewhat thawing the pitch and clearing much of the snow. After a gruesome-looking collision between Bury goalkeeper Chris Harker and Clough, the striker lay in a crumpled heap on the floor. The challenge on the keeper by Clough, who slid into the advancing Harker, looked clumsy, but was typical of incidents seen regularly in games. It incensed some of the Bury players, who felt that Clough had deliberately gone in hard to hurt the keeper. Stokoe ran over to the injured Clough, tapped him with the toe of his boot and said: "Come on, ref. He's only codding, get him up."

Stokoe recalls the incident: "I honestly felt it was a daft challenge from Clough. He could really have hurt our keeper. He was one of those players who would give as good as he got, always nudging and pulling at you in the challenge on and off the ball. He had been going on and on from the kick-off, moaning and complaining to the referee about every ball he didn't win. I admit the way he went into our keeper upset me. I went over and saw him laying there with his trainer looking at him and told him to his face I thought he was a cheat. The look on his face told me he was in pain, but I never thought it was that bad. He mouthed some disgusting obscenity back at me, so I told him to: 'get up and to get on with the game.'

He was carried off and didn't come back on the pitch. I never thought any more of it. It was just one of those confrontations you have on the pitch. It was a bit of a surprise when I found out his career was over, but still I didn't think a lot about it as he was nothing to do with me. Months later I learnt from other players that Clough had proclaimed his hatred for me and would never forget the comments I made. We did occasionally meet up and he would ignore me. The times we did have to speak we did so, but I always saw malice in his eyes when he looked at me. It's sad that people feel that way and hold grudges, but that's life I suppose.

A few years later I was sat watching television and Brian Clough was on there, talking about his life. At one point he said that when his children were young and misbehaved he would threaten them by showing them a photograph of me, as though I was something bad and evil or to be scared of. That did upset me as it wasn't necessary. I think it's fair to say we had a clash of personalities. To be honest, the Brian Clough event meant nothing to me."

It certainly did to Clough, who was never to forgive Stokoe. His version of events is similar to that of Stokoe's, but when I interviewed him a few years ago and mentioned the name of Bob Stokoe, he told me never to say the name again to him. I was never certain if he was joking or serious, but the occasions I did meet Clough thereafter and discussed Carlisle United, he never once uttered Stokoe's name.

IN THE SUMMER OF 1965, Stokoe left to manage Charlton Athletic. There he remained from 1965 until 1967, though his time at the south London club was less than memorable. He would still often turn out for the reserves and take part in training sessions. Ultimately he would win only a quarter of his games during his two-year spell in SE7 and the side finished just clear of the relegation zone in both of his seasons. Finally, Stokoe attempted to change the format of the team, selling Billy Bonds, Len Glover and Mike Bailey (all of whom went on to make good names for themselves elsewhere). The 1967/68 season started disastrously as Charlton failed to win any of their opening five games, with a 3-0 defeat at Crystal Palace resulting in Stokoe resigning from his position. There followed a year in charge of Rochdale, where he rebuilt his managerial reputation before taking over in October 1968 as manager of Carlisle United, then bottom of Division Two.

Stokoe transformed Carlisle into a strong and stable Second Division side, steering them to a League Cup semi-final in 1969/70 which they agonisingly lost to Allan Ashman's West Bromwich Albion side.

"I didn't quite know what to make of things at Brunton Park when I first arrived; it was a club with a very good reputation and everyone was so welcoming. The club trainer, Dick Young, was the driving force behind a lot of the success, I learned a lot from him. His knowledge of players was the best I have known anywhere. I tried to take him with me to other clubs, but he wanted success for Carlisle only. After one training session I was having a bit of banter with a couple of the players, including Chris Balderstone. Chris was a marvellous footballer. He was settled in Carlisle and highly regarded by the fans. He was a good man who was excellent at whatever he turned his hand to. I watched him one day tossing a tennis ball in the club car park. He was fake bowling it like a cricketer against the grandstand wall. As I walked out into the car park I went over to him and told him to stick to football, because from what I could see, he couldn't throw the ball straight, let alone catch it! He went on to represent England at cricket and took every opportunity to remind me of what I said to him back in 1969.

I always felt we should have got through to the League Cup final that year. We were better than West Bromwich, it was Dennis Martin [who later signed for Carlisle], who destroyed us. Bob Hatton had an effort that clipped the inside of both posts. If that bugger had gone in we would have won.

One of the best deals I did at Carlisle was bringing in Bobby Hatton from Northampton. I knew the Cobblers were always looking for money, so offered them a silly price for the player. He was then regarded as being a hard-working and industrious striker with real finishing prowess. I couldn't believe it when they came back accepting my offer. I knew we could make money on him, but also that he would score goals for me. It was a good deal all round."

Sadly, the relationship between Stokoe and the Carlisle board of directors took a turn for the worse when, in December 1970, newly-promoted First Division club Blackpool approached them asking to release Stokoe in order that he could take over as their manager after Les Shannon had paid the price for a dreadful start. Carlisle asked for an £8,500 compensation fee; Blackpool refused to pay. "I was offered £7,000 a year salary plus bonuses if we won trophies or promotion, but Carlisle wouldn't talk," Stokoe told me. "I was really bitter and resentful about the way they [the Carlisle board of directors] dealt with it. I felt as though they were treating me as a second rate citizen, almost like a little schoolboy. I requested to leave the club. Looking back now, they clearly didn't want me to leave. I became the second manager in Carlisle history to negotiate their own transfer, my old mate Ivor Broadis was the other."

FINALLY A DEAL WAS agreed and Stokoe took up the reins at Blackpool. Two years later he arrived at Sunderland where he will always be remembered for winning the FA Cup in 1973. "As good as it was at the time, it was all over too quickly. I desperately wanted to get one over Revie and a few words were exchanged between us in the Wembley tunnel, especially after we had beaten them. He was, I think, one of the most undignified and insecure people I have ever met in the game. It gave me great pleasure to ask him if he wanted £500 to drown his sorrows and mark another failure in his managerial career. I know it was wrong, but you don't get many chances like that, so when they come along you have to seize them."

Carlisle knocked Sunderland, and their former manager out of the competition when they defended the FA Cup the following season, winning 1-0 at Roker Park thanks to a Dennis Martin strike. "I just knew Martin was going to come back to haunt me," Stokoe told me. "Every manager has a player who always seems to do well against him. He seems to have been my nemesis. To be fair, Carlisle outplayed us and deserved to win that game. I hate losing and it was very disappointing to go out so early in the competition, especially as we were Cup holders, but personally now, it wasn't too unpalatable to go out to Carlisle."

By 1976 Stokoe had guided Sunderland to the Second Division title, but the new season started very badly as better quality opposition found out a Sunderland side which looked out of their depth, easy prey. With no victories in the opening nine games the tide of support turned against the once-revered Stokoe. Sunderland fans chanted for Brian Clough to replace him, [the ultimate insult] and the usually buoyant Stokoe found himself ostracised by the supporters and club officials who had hailed him as the Messiah less than three years earlier.

Feeling constantly tired and suffering from sleepless nights Stokoe resigned from his position at the club. "I won't forget how alone and low I felt when everyone turned against me at Sunderland. I needed a friendly face to offer me some support, instead I received abuse from supporters and was ignored by club officials. If I hadn't resigned I would have been sacked, I know that. Football club directors are among the strangest breed of people I know, fickle. I was disappointed by everything that happened at Sunderland, the glory of the FA Cup was lost amongst the vitriolic abuse and treatment, but I still hold them memories of success dearly. Not everyone there was shallow and I don't blame the supporters really."

Having spent a whole year out of the game the outspoken manager returned as boss of Bury in December 1977. It has to be said that it was potentially the worst and most disastrous six months in his managerial career. Results were poor and he got little in the way of support, financially or otherwise from his directors. This was followed by second spells at Blackpool and Rochdale. During the latter he fined his players for not trying hard enough in both training and matches. His hands were tied at Spotland as the club had no money to recruit new blood and he was constantly fighting off criticism of his style from players, supporters and the media. After one particular game at Crewe Alexandra, Stokoe told the press: "I would like to drop five or six players. But I can't drop anyone because I have no-one else to bring in. There isn't any money to buy. To buy we would need to sell and I haven't had any inquiries about players. On the game as a whole at Crewe, the lucky people were those who missed it."

He then retorted to some of the criticism he'd received from the clubs fans: "I feel that I am taking the stick for someone else. I inherited a situation that was none of my making. Doug Collins said the manager who followed him into the job had it made. He must have been joking. If the players haven't got it I can't put it there. In fact, some of them couldn't care less about Rochdale FC."

Despite everything, Stokoe still fought for the future of Rochdale. Altrincham were strong favourites to gain election to the Football League in 1980 in their place. As it was the Cheshire club lost out by one vote, all down to Bob Stokoe, who was instrumental in whipping up support for his team. Curiously, two directors of other clubs, who, it is said had promised votes for Altrincham, didn't get the opportunity to register their votes. The reason? In one case the director was in the wrong room and in the case of the other, he had somehow got the voting-time wrong! Despite this, Stokoe, having had enough of the poor treatment, resigned.

IT WAS ANOTHER OF his old clubs, Carlisle, who held out the olive branch offering their former manager work as a scout, a position he held until September 1980 when he took over once again as manager. He told me: "Carlisle United has in many ways been my best friend in football. They supported me when others doubted or questioned my ability. I could see when I came back that it was a club without huge financial resources, looking at bringing through youth and local talent. The supporters are second to none, always have been, I haven't a cruel word to say about them, they always backed me.

I like to think that the Carlisle side I built in the 1980s was my best ever. The promotion we won [from Division Three] in 1982 was sweet and just reward for a season's hard work. We wavered a bit towards the end, but eventually 'Pop' Robson delivered the goods at Sealand Road, Chester on a Tuesday night. I remember what seemed like thousands of Carlisle fans being on the pitch celebrating that night. It took me back to my FA Cup-winning success. There was a genuine look of happiness on the faces of our fans and players, I felt right at home.

I then brought players in from all over the leagues and Scotland. John Halpin from Celtic was quality with a capital Q. Then there was the likes of Alan Shoulder and Malcolm Poskett, who proved to be two wonderful signings. Superbly professional too, though I did have my moments with Malcolm, but I tend to think that overall he was a bloody good striker and I managed to get the best out of him. Probably, though, my biggest coup was getting Tommy Craig to sign. Everyone said he was past his best, but Tommy was the ultimate professional and kept himself very fit. I remember in particular a goal he scored against Bolton. His poise and skill allowed him to control and fire home a goal through a crowd of players. It wasn't luck, it was absolute pure skill. He was good in the dressing room too, strong and powerful in thought. He acted as my assistant for a couple of seasons and my one regret at Carlisle is that I recommended the wrong man to take over as manager from myself. 'Pop' Robson got the vote, but Tommy was all round a better tactician, strategist and motivator. He should have been the manager to replace me. As a result Carlisle lost out.

It was always a seesaw of emotion at Carlisle. Another memory I hold is the disappoint-ment of relegation in 1986. It still rankles with me that it was in our own hands that we could stay up. Charlton Athletic, one of my old clubs needed to beat us at Brunton Park to go up, and we needed to beat them to stay up. Big Wes Saunders put us 2-0 up and things looked great. Then it all went wrong. In all my time in football I have never seen a more spectacular, but more stupid own goal scored. Jim Tolmie, who I had brought in on loan, fired the damn ball back to Scott [Endersby] in our goal from the half-way line, for no reason. The ball drifted in the wind, looped over Scott and into our goal. What can you do when players do something daft like that? Tolmie was never going to start a game for Carlisle United again, not while I was there anyway.

Suddenly we were defending like our lives depended upon it. They kept coming at us and equalised, then went on to score the winner. We squandered a two goal lead. I was angry, very angry."

At the end of the 1985/86 season, Stokoe handed over the reins of club management to Harry Gregg. There was a brief return to Sunderland as caretaker-manager to help the club as it got itself into a mess and plummeted down the leagues, followed by a bit of scouting for Newcastle and Chelsea, but effectively, that was the end of Bob Stokoe's football career.

Devoutly loyal to the north of England, Stokoe always cherished his roots and in his later years could be regularly seen on the side of the park football pitches giving support to some local sides. One of my last ever conversations with him was not unnaturally about Carlisle United. He told me: "I'd love one day to come to thank all those wonderful fans who got behind my players and me, good old Carlisle. I really enjoyed it there, you know." Typical Bob; wearing his heart on his sleeve to the end.

HUGH McILMOYLE

1963-1964
1967-1969
1974-1975

UNITED CAREER

Games	171+3
Goals	76

MAGIC MOMENT

Hughie fired the ball into the Mansfield net from twenty, maybe thirty, possibly fifty yards. Whatever, it was an incredible goal

'THE ORIGINAL SUPERMAC'

FOOTBALL is littered with players and managers who have returned to scenes of former glories only to find that second time around things are somewhat different. Very few are capable of living the dream and winning over fans to such an extent that they are held in absolute adulation, not once, not twice, not three times, but four times. Hughie McIlmoyle is one such player, though it should be said that his fourth period at the club was his return as an ambassador. The truth of it is that Hugh McIlmoyle is adored and worshipped by the supporters of Carlisle United not only because he was absolutely brilliant and not only because he was one of the club's most famous players. No, it's because Supermac is a down-to-earth hero who genuinely loves Carlisle United and found the pull of the city and its football club too great to resist, to such an extent that he left rural Leicestershire to return to his Carlisle roots: a return which all supporters of the club truly welcomed.

THE FOOTBALL STORY OF Hughie McIlmoyle is anything but a real-life fairy tale. He was born and raised in working class Port Glasgow, a suburb of nearby Glasgow, an area commonly associated with ship building. Today derelict and gaunt-looking warehouses and abandoned, rusted dockside cranes unceremoniously line the route into Port Glasgow. I visited the area recently and was stunned when, totally out of the blue [pardon the pun], in conversation someone raised and still living in the area told me that he went to school with Hughie. In Port Glasgow it seems, Hugh McIlmoyle is held in almost as much adulation as he is in Carlisle.

One of 11 children, Hughie was born on 29 January 1940 and played his early football in the tiny back streets of the area, not with a ball but with any object that would suffice as a replacement for footballs which were a luxury few could afford. Hugh's father worked in the ship yards and did his best to provide for his family and made sure that their needs came first in all he did, a positive family trait inherited by Hugh himself. By 1952, Hugh had progressed to school football, playing in handed down, loaned or discarded football boots, which by today's slimline standards are more akin to ankle boots. Fixtures generally took place on ash-covered pitches. Hugh learned his trade the hard way, but he was clearly an exceptional talent.

Despite this, his football career came second to a more basic family function, that of earning money. From a young age he worked as a ship's painter, but still found time for the occasional game of football. With his obvious skill and pace he was soon in demand as local side Port Glasgow Rovers invited him to sign and play for them. It was the first football-related move he made and one which he was never to regret as it ultimately propelled him into the professional game.

After one game for Rovers, he was approached by a scout for Leicester City who invited him to Filbert Street for a two week trial. The trial turned into a permanent offer and on 3 April 1961 he made his Leicester City debut at home to West Ham United, scoring the fifth goal in a

5-1 rout of the Hammers. At Leicester he went on to make 22 appearances in all competitions including one in the European Cup Winners' Cup. His solitary appearance for the Foxes in the FA Cup came in the 1961 Wembley final, when he controversially replaced City's regular number nine Ken Leek, after playing just seven league games for the club. McIlmoyle took it in his stride and was not overawed by the importance of the situation, indeed, he was regarded by most Leicester supporters as the team's most dangerous forward on the day.

It was a difficult time for the player. Homesick and a long way from Glasgow, he missed his Glaswegian roots. Derek Dougan was brought into Filbert Street and replaced Supermac up front. By his own admission Dougan wasn't half the player Hughie McIlmoyle was. He once told me: "I was brought into Leicester to do a job, score goals. It was hard as everyone I met and spoke with referred to Hugh McIlmoyle, who had left to join Rotherham. I had heard about him through different players who had come up against him. They said he could leap higher than any other player they had seen, and he was quick. I always fancied myself as a bit of decent header of the ball, but having seen Hughie in action I couldn't match him. He had the knack of heading accurately and with power. He could head a ball as hard as many players could kick it. I never was quite able to shrug off the Hugh McIlmoyle tag at Leicester. I think because of that I watched his career closely."

IN JULY 1962, ROTHERHAM United, aware that he may be open to a move north, signed McIlmoyle. He was an instant success at Millmoor, scoring twice in the opening seven games of the 1962/63 season. There followed a spell of inconsistency and an absence from the first team, but Hughie returned with a bang later in the season and, as it transpired, scored in his last two games for the club. The first of those goals came in a 2-2 draw with Derby County, then in his final appearance he added the second goal in the 4-1 victory over Newcastle United.

In March 1963, United boss Allan Ashman brought the player to Brunton Park for a fee of around £7,000. It was the beginning of a wonderful relationship between club, player and fans. So far as the football was concerned the signing was a last ditch attempt by the manager to save United from relegation from Division Three. Despite scoring on his debut and firing seven league goals that season, Hugh couldn't save the team from relegation at the end of that season.

The 1963/64 season however, was one dreams are made of. Partnering big Joe Livingstone up front, Hughie was simply irresistible. After scoring five goals in the opening three league games, he went on to notch an incredible 44 goals in all competitions, making him the leading goalscorer in the entire Football League. The goals came mainly through his incredible anticipation of where the ball was going to fall in the opposition penalty area. But for many that season the best remembered goals from Hughie came from his head.

The late Geoff Twentyman, who later went on to make a name for himself at Liverpool, told me how highly he rated the striker. "Hugh was an incredible player, ahead of his era really in that he tried things others would never dream of. His greatest skill, which went relatively unnoticed by many, was that of dropping off the ball and running round the back of defences creating openings for himself. Bill Shankly believed he was one of the best in the game at doing this. It's something he tried to indoctrinate into the Liverpool attack, Mac was a master of it.

I recall the boss at the time, Allan Ashman, telling some of us just how good he thought Hugh was and what an asset he was for the club."

Now McIlmoyle was recognised as one of the top strikers in the game, it came as no surprise when United received a bid from a bigger club for Hughie too good to turn down.

Ex-Carlisle boss Andy Beattie had not long taken over at Wolverhampton Wanderers. Beattie was a genuine football man with a vast network of contacts and aides. His Carlisle connections alerted him to the prowess of the lean marksman and an offer of £30,000 was soon received to take him to Molineux. So, despite his wanting to settle into a role at Carlisle, and loving the city, Hughie was sold and went on his travels again.

At Wolves he was a success and the goals continued to flow; 35 in the league in just 90 appearances. It was this goalscoring return that generally aroused much in the way of interest within the game. Bill Shankly was one such manager who envied Supermac. He wasn't alone. "Looking back on his early playing days you could see that he had a hell of a lot of skill and a determination to succeed," Shankly said. "Matt Busby was a big admirer of him, as was I. It was fantastic to see a fellow Scot doing so well. I really think if it wasn't for the likes of Denis Law and George Best, Matt would have take a gamble on taking him to Manchester. Every time I took a look, someone else seemed to pop up and sign him. It was like that back in the 1960s. Hugh seemed to spend a great deal of his time in the Second Division, but he was a footballer who merited much higher than that."

After two seasons in the Black Country region, Hugh was on the move again, this time south to Bristol City. In March 1967 manager Fred Ford signed Hughie (one of his last signings as a manager before he was sacked by the City board) as a successor to City legend John Atyeo. He wasn't at the club long, seven months to be precise, managing four league goals before Carlisle United came calling in September 1967.

A fee of £22,500 was the price United paid for the return of the Mac, financially some astute business with the Blues making a £7,500 profit overall from transfers involving the player. There is an old standing joke at the club that Hugh McIlmoyle was worth more to Carlisle than goals. In fact he was literally worth more than the main grandstand.

Tim Ward was the boss who brought about the player's return. He recognised the passion Hugh held for the club and he had players on his books like Tommy Murray and George McVitie who could provide the ammunition for Hughie to fill the opposition net. Sadly for Ward, he wasn't at the club too long before he was moved out to pastures new. In came the much-revered Bob Stokoe, who did his best to get the maximum out of his players. The Stokoe team of that era was very much in a transitional state. With little or no money, the manager was forced to wheel and deal. He remained a firm believer in the ability of McIlmoyle and was desperate to build a team around him.

By September 1969 rumours were rife that Supermac was again to be on the move. Frantically at many games fans gathered in the main car park asking any club official or player if it was true that their hero was leaving. No-one, it seemed, knew anything. But the player's absence from the team to play Blackburn Rovers in a League Cup tie signalled the reality. Hughie McIlmoyle was being transferred once again; this time to Middlesbrough for a fee of £55,000. Hugh himself didn't want to leave and was never offered an option to stay. He claims that he would have accepted anything to stay as he wanted to end his playing career at Brunton Park. Sadly this went unheeded or unnoticed as the cash injection was once again simply too good an offer to reject. Middlesborough manager Stan Anderson said of the signing, "This is the final piece of my jigsaw, with McIlmoyle and Hickton we will be set for real progress."

McIlmoyle's spell at Middlesbrough was to last two epic seasons. He made 82 appearances for Boro, scoring 22 goals. He even made a return to Brunton Park in an FA Cup tie which attracted a record attendance. Blues lost 2-1.

There can be no doubting that at Ayresome Park Hugh was highly respected, he is still fondly remembered by the club's support, who often discuss the 'McIlmoyle match', so called after an incredible personal performance against QPR in 1970. Trailing 2-0, Supermac inspired a fight back to a remarkable 6-2 victory. According to sources, Hughie was outstanding and not only scored two goals (bullet headers) himself, he made three more for John Hickton. It is said that he ran the QPR defence ragged, upsetting one defender so much that he felt the only way to stop the striker was to punch him in the mouth. Even then Hugh didn't react, he took the blow and tried to play on!

The forward pairing of Hickton and McIlmoyle paid dividends and in the season that followed the pair bagged 38 goals between them. Anderson, though, became critical of his strikers, blaming them when Boro failed to score or perform. And soon McIlmoyle would be on the move again. This time, in the summer of 1971, to another of Blues' arch foes, Preston North End.

It wasn't the greatest of transfers in Hughie's career, but it provided him with more experience as he worked at Preston under Alan Ball senior and then later for Bobby Charlton. After a typical McIlmoyle spell of goalscoring, he was loaned out to Greenock Morton, literally his hometown club, located yards from Port Glasgow.

THEN, WITHOUT WARNING, and with McIlmoyle expecting to remain in the Scottish game until he retired, came the call he yearned for. Carlisle United, recently promoted to football's top flight, the old First Division, wanted him back. There was no contract discussion, no worries about money, Hugh accepted and made his way to Carlisle for the third time.

This return of the Mac was greeted with great enthusiasm in Carlisle. As a teenager I can still recall when the news broke. I was a pupil at Eden School in Rickerby Park and it was announced in assembly by headmaster Joe Rawlings that Hughie McIlmoyle was returning to Carlisle. Even more exciting was the news that his children would be coming to our school. Later that day, when sat in a lesson, a couple of us glanced up to look out of the classroom window and saw walking into the front reception area of the school, Hughie McIlmoyle. Instantly a whisper sped round the room and within seconds the entire class was out of its seats staring at Carlisle's most recent acquisition. If I can at all equate this to the modern day game, this to us would be like David Beckham putting his children into a local school and arriving to look round.

Naturally, the games teacher just had to rush out to greet him and was joined by some of the other teachers, whilst we were all told to get back into our seats and continue with our work. It remains one of my claims to fame; for a short time I went to the same school as Hugh McIlmoyle's children.

Undoubtedly, had the move transpired a few years earlier, Hughie would have been regularly among the goals in the First Division. Now in his mid-thirties he had lost a bit of pace, albeit he could still hang in the air while the ball travelled through the ether to him. A cracking goal, a volley against one of his ex-clubs, Leicester City, at Filbert Street early in the season looked like a continuation of his goalscoring trend. Sadly it was one of only two strikes he managed all season. Though, to be fair to the striker, instability was created by Allan Ashman persistently changing his front line in an attempt to find a regular goalscorer as Carlisle slid down the table following their dreamlike start to the campaign. The lack of consistency meant Hughie was often omitted from the team and so was never given the opportunity to develop an on-field relationship with his fellow forwards. Despite this, he was still regarded by the club's support as a diamond and whenever he did make a first team start he received a rapturous welcome.

After just one season with United, he left, returning for a very brief spell to Greenock Morton. Despite it being his home town, he never really settled into the Scottish game and after just seven appearances and one goal he retired from the professional game. He eventually moved to Leicestershire before returning to his spiritual home of Carlisle. Within weeks of his return he was back at Brunton Park watching the Blues and like all other supporters cheering them on. It was a natural progression for him to move into the field of ambassador for the club, and now he is to be found welcoming corporate guests and visitors and thrilling support-ers with whom he poses for photographs and recounts some of his greatest football moments. There can't be a more pertinent ex-United footballer to take on this role, Hugh con-stantly walks around with a smile on his face, an indication as to how happy and content he is to be back involved in Carlisle United, the club he fell in love with.

IN TOTAL HUGHIE MCILMOYLE graced eight different football clubs, making 481 appearances in total, scoring a remarkable 162 goals into the bargain. For Carlisle United his goals are legendary. Some talk of the amazing effort against Mansfield Town as being his best ever. Personally I recall the brace he fired against Bristol City in 1968 as being classic McIlmoyle goals. I think it fair to say that each and every goal Hugh scored for Carlisle was special. Not many players can list a record for one club that includes four hat-tricks, a brace on more than a dozen occasions, plus one unforgettable four-goal haul!

As a permanent reminder of how great and in how much adulation the football club holds him, a bronze statue of Hughie stands at the Brunton Park entrance on Warwick Road. The life size replica aptly displays him as so many supporters recall him, leaping like a salmon and hanging in the air. Supplementing this is the fact that he has topped so many polls when fans are asked to vote for their greatest United player of all time.

Of his times in football Hughie is open and honest. He told a group of local reporters when he returned to Carlisle a few years ago: "I never really wanted to leave Carlisle ever. Each time I just seemed to be moved on without any care as to what I wanted. I understood that the transfer income was important to the football club, but if I'd had my way I wouldn't have left. It's a great place and I feel the same coming back now as I did all those other times, this is my fourth and definitely the last time. I'm here to stay and don't want to live anywhere else. I love the place and I love the people. Carlisle felt right from the first time I set foot in the place. I feel this is my home."

Recollections of just how professional Hughie was and still is continue to flow throughout football. Revered icons, such as Ivor Broadis, claim that he was one of the best players of his time. Ivor often tells of how he enjoyed reporting and watching Hughie in the United team. Alan Ross always said that Hugh was the best header of a ball in the game and possibly the most clinical centre-forward he saw. Chris Balderstone simply called him: "Fantastic. An incredible footballer." Allan Ashman yearned for a strikeforce of Hughie McIlmoyles at every club he managed: "I don't think players of the calibre of Hugh McIlmoyle come round very often. Some players are simply made for one club. Hugh was made for Carlisle and vice versa. It was no secret in football that he was always likely to be a Carlisle player. I fancied him at West Brom, but the truth was that whether he wore gold and black or red and white, inside Hugh wore the blue and white of Carlisle United. I think that says everything about him as a person. As a footballer he was totally professional and worked hard for the full game. I can rarely recall him missing sitters; if it fell to Hugh in the penalty area it was a goal; it was as simple as that ."

I don't think there is anything I or anyone else can add that can relate to the absolute Cult Hero status retained to this very day by Hugh McIlmoyle. He left the club three times, each time against his wishes. Each time he returned and further cemented his status among the elite United players who without any effort built relationships with the club's support, respecting them as much as the fans worshipped them.

KENNY WILSON

1972-1973

UNITED CAREER

Games	14+6
Goals	1

MAGIC MOMENT

Kenny was a workhorse, although some would say carthorse. But the goal, that goal, no matter how it went in, was his only moment in a Carlisle shirt

'THE REAL KING KENNY'

IT'S always a cause for excitement and eager anticipation when clubs splash money on record-breaking transfers. Be they club records or national records, generally speaking the players themselves are good at a specific part of their profession. They can't be all things to all people. Just occasionally players display that flash of brilliance or that finesse – that swagger on the ball or the clinical eye of goalscorer supreme. If they are consistent in this skill then undoubtedly they progress in their career and can command, in the modern era at least, ridiculous salaries. Carlisle United have, over the years, played their own small part in record-breaking transfers. For example in June 1968 striker Allan Clarke (whose brother Frank played for Carlisle in the 1970s) was transferred from Fulham to Leicester City for a record-breaking total fee of £150,000. The deal was agreed and incorporated £110,000 cash exchanging hands plus ex-Carlisle United striker Frank Large. Almost 19 years later, ex-Carlisle United man Peter Beardsley moved from Newcastle to Liverpool for £1.9 million.

Having said that, more locally, we have broken our club transfer record several times since those long distant times of 1928 when we first entered the Football League. The club have continually dug deep into its financial resources to bring such quality players to Brunton Park as Billy Hogan, Ivor Broadis, Hugh McIlmoyle, Stan Bowles, Bobby Parker, Kenny Wilson, Gordon Staniforth, David Reeves et al. All excellent at what they did with a ball at their feet or alternatively, on their head. Hogan was a supreme dribbler, running at defenders week after week. Broadis, Reeves and McIlmoyle were goal scorers of undoubted quality, whilst Staniforth was a dynamo who wouldn't stop running for 90 minutes and weighed in with a few goals too. Bowles was simply a showman extraordinaire. His control and skill during his time at Brunton Park were awesome. Bobby Parker was solidly reliable and hardly ever put a foot wrong. He was also a great motivator of his colleagues. At this point I can hear some of you thinking: 'Hang on a minute, you haven't said anything about Kenny Wilson.' Some may even be thinking: 'who the hell was Kenny Wilson?'

THE STORY OF KENNY WILSON and why he simply must be included in this work is anything but straightforward. There are, from my perspective, a thousand and one reasons why Kenny must be included in this book; not least the fact that he was, without doubt, the crappest striker ever to play for Carlisle United. So bad was our Kenny that he is remembered, not for his football talent, but for how bad he was!

He was also the costliest (on the pitch) signing the club has ever made, costing roughly £3,272.72p per game started. Some of you are probably now thinking, well that's not a lot in comparison to the financial expenditure of the game in modern times. Yet back in 1972, Workington Reds hit the local newspaper headlines as they were losing somewhere in the region of £700-£800 a week and in football expenditure terms that was real cause for concern. I don't suppose anyone at Carlisle United has ever really worked out the cost of our one time record signing, who arrived at Brunton Park in what could never be described as a blaze of glory, more of a glow of hope and anticipation.

Kenny Wilson's football career began at St Johnstone in 1970. Originally from Dumbarton, as a youngster, and without the droopy moustache for which he would become famous, he was picked up by Scottish amateur side, Beith. The North Ayrshire town counts as one of its only claims to fame a resident by the name of Reverend John Witherspoon, who signed the American Declaration of Independence. Football, though, does count for much in Beith. Albeit in more recent times, the local side have been known to attract crowds of around 600 to their woodchip-laden Bellsdale Park stadium. Known as Beith Juniors, they are a semi-professional club and have had some success in the Scottish non-league game over the years, with the North Ayrshire Cup among their more recent trophies. However, they don't hit the football headlines too often. Indeed, more recent successes aside, other than a three season period in the mid-1920s when they were part of the Scottish League Division Three, oh, and winning the Scottish Qualifying Cup (Southern Region) three times in the early 1930s, there is little else to shout about. That is to say, other than when Kenny Wilson would strut his funky stuff across Bellsdale Park. Also, before I forget, there was a certain Carlisle United goalkeeper playing for Beith around the same time as our Kenny, one Tom Clarke.

There can be no doubting that Kenny Wilson prospered as a player at Beith, his regular goalscoring feats attracting much attention locally. Team photographs of the era show a youthful looking Ken, still minus tash, with trophies between his feet. Furthermore, when one speaks with supporters of the Juniors, Kenny Wilson is a name that frequently crops up. It shows how much esteem he is held in when he is one of the first names on the team sheet for supporters (old enough to remember him) when it comes to determining the greatest all-time Beith Juniors XI. Whilst it would be very easy to knock such respect, after all it comes from the supporters of a Scottish non-league side, I find myself unusually complimentary as to Kenny's undoubted ability in these, the formative years of his football career. When I commenced the research into Kenny I fully expected to uncover calamity following calamity. No such thing seemed obvious at Beith, where he continues to be regarded as a true legend.

With a host of Scottish league club scouts flocking to Bellsdale Park to look at not only Kenny, but Tom Clarke too, it came as little surprise when the club was approached by St Johnstone, inviting the centre-forward along for a trial at Muirton Park. One of the managers who had opted to take a look at the player was their manager Willie Ormond, who had joined St Johnstone in 1968. Kenny Wilson was high on his shopping list and joined permanently a short time later. Ormond is perhaps more renowned for moving into the manager's position of the Scotland national team in 1973 and taking the team to the following year's World Cup finals in Germany. He was also part of the 'Famous Five' attacking line-up at Easter Road in the 1950s alongside team-mates Bobby Johnstone, Lawrie Reilly, Eddie Turnbull and Gordon Smith. Like the rest of the Famous Five, Willie was also picked to play for Scotland. In 1954 he was the only Hibernian representative in the Scottish squad for the World Cup Finals in Switzerland. As well as winning six full international caps, Ormond collected other representative honours at the highest level of the Scottish game, including nine representative appearances for the Scottish League and a Scotland B cap. An extremely loyal man, Ormond was the last member of the Famous Five to leave the Easter Road side, when he signed for Falkirk in 1961, where he eventually became their assistant trainer. From there he arrived at St

Johnstone and built a very respectable side, steering the Muirton Park club into Europe for the first time.

There can no doubting Ormond's experience and credentials for identifying a footballer of great skill and ability in the Scottish leagues. He liked what he saw in Kenny Wilson. A part-timer at Beith, Wilson was also working as a joiner. But it was football where his heart lay and he worked hard and trained vigorously in order to impress his manager with his case for first team football. It worked for too, as Ormond noted Wilson's goals in second string encounters and gradually blooded him into the first team. It's fair to say that the best spell Kenny had at the club came in March and April 1970. It was during those weeks that he made a massive impact, scoring in three games out of four in which he appeared. The first of these came against Raith Rovers in late March. In early April, this was followed by a goal of particular quality, when his control and agility allowed him to trick the Dundee defence and give him the space to fire home a goal which had Ormond punching the air with delight from the sidelines. He then managed to snaffle a real poacher's goal in the penalty box against St Mirren a week or so later. He was the toast of Muirton Park. Supporters sang his name and he was beginning to look every bit the sharp striker he had shown himself to be during his days at Beith Juniors.

But, despite his obvious goal scoring prowess and form Wilson found himself frozen out of the first team. Ormond believed that the striker's problem was that he wasn't consistent enough. For every goal he was scoring, he was missing four or five easier chances. To be fair to the player, it was never going to be easy for him to sustain any period in the St Johnstone first team which included players such as Henry Hall and John Connolly, both of whom were consistent goalscorers and firm fans' favourites. Hall in particular is regarded as one of the most talented strikers never to have played for Scotland, bagging 114 goals in his Saints career, while Connolly was a virtual ever present in the front line during Ormond's tenure. He was a player of absolute quality and was to later successfully make the transition from the Scottish to the English game, first with Everton, then with Newcastle United.

IN THE SUMMER OF 1970 with first team opportunities at St Johnstone at a minimum, Wilson opted to move on. Ormond wasn't the sort of man to beat about the bush and one can only believe that he was honest with Wilson and informed him that Messrs Hall and Connolly would always be his preferred options up front. Now, with the bit firmly between his teeth, Wilson was desperate for regular first team football. He knew from his performances in the Scottish First Division with St Johnstone that he had the ability to do well. When the opportunity to return to his home town club emerged he seized the chance and signed for Jackie Stewart's Scottish Division Two side, Dumbarton.

It was a fantastic period for the club and Stewart was a shrewd man and manager. Readers should note, however, that this is not the famous Formula One racing driver Sir Jackie Stewart, who, coincidentally, was also born in Dumbarton.

In June 1970 Stewart brought in ex-Celtic inside-forward Charlie Gallagher, who was followed a few months later by Jack Bolton from Raith Rovers. These were additions to a squad which already consisted of talent such as Lawrie Williams, Johnny Graham, Kenny Wilson and Roy McCormack. Wilson settled in immediately with Stewart providing him with the confidence and support to go out and get goals. In September of that year, they were paired against Celtic in the Scottish League Cup semi-final. A truly memorable effort at Parkhead had seen Wilson and his colleagues defend sternly to fight out a 0-0 draw (after extra-time) against Celtic; a team which had, in fact, a few months earlier narrowly lost the European Cup final to Dutch side Feyenoord. The efforts in Glasgow were matched at Boghead Park, where Dumbarton frustrated their more famous opponents (which included the likes of Lennox, Dalglish and Auld) all over the park. Finally, in extra-time, with fitness a telling factor, Dumbarton succumbed, but only by the odd goal in seven [3-4].

Elsewhere, in all competitions, the goals were flying in from all over the place as Kenny Wilson and Dumbarton narrowly missed out on promotion, finishing fourth behind the two promoted sides Partick Thistle and East Fife. As for Kenny Wilson, he had already made himself virutally indispensable and a terrace hero, wading in with 41 goals in all competitions in the campaign. The boy had returned to his home town and was finally rewarding his supporters with some scintillating performances and goals. One reporter of the time said of the striker: "Wilson, it would appear, has the world of football at his feet. A few of those who have witnessed his gritty and determined performances of this season will think they have a genuine centre-forward. He is much more than that; strong and determined, he worries defences with his power and shooting skills. I cannot remember witnessing a striker who could shoot on goal on sight with such accuracy. He is fearless too and has put his head where the boots fly, all to score a goal. I can't remember being excited by a player as much as I have by Kenny Wilson."

The following season proved to be even more spectacular for Kenny. Indeed this was the season which would be the high point of his football career, although at the time no-one was to realise. Dumbarton secured promotion by beating Berwick Rangers 4–2 in the final fixture of the season. After what can only be regarded as a poor start after the performances of the previous season, it was all down to a run of ten victories from the last 11 league fixtures to ensure that the championship trophy came to Boghead. For the Dumbarton centre-forward it proved to be an even better return than the previous season, as Wilson scored an amazing 42 goals, a club record, and the highest in Scottish football that year. Tom Neil, a lifelong Dumbarton supporter, remembers Wilson fondly. "The 1971/72 season was one of the most exciting I can remember. We had a goal hungry striker called Wilson, Kenny Wilson. Boy could he score goals. There was nobody to touch him in the Scottish Second Division at the time. He was the reason we won the championship. He never failed to put the ball in the back of the net. The other teams just couldn't cope with him. He should have remained with the club for one more season, that way he could have proved he could do it in the First Division and live among the likes of Kenny Dalglish as goalscoring legends. I am sure he could have gone on to play for Scotland."

The 1972/73 season was always going to be difficult for Dumbarton. The better standard of footballer in the upper Scottish league meant that some of their players would be struggling to stamp their authority on the game. Pre-season friendlies had been arranged against some good quality opposition. Carlisle United were the visitors to Boghead Park late that summer. Kenny Wilson played his usual game, running at the defence and making life awkward for the Carlisle back four. He scored one himself and made the other two as the home side ran out 3-2 winners. Watching from the touchline was United boss Allan Ashman and scout, Hugh Neil. It was Hughie who first saw the potential of Wilson and made mention of it to the Carlisle boss. Ashman, though, wasn't interested at that time. Sure, he had been impressed by Wilson's presence and striker's guile, but he had other targets in mind. Players with proven ability, like Gil Reece of Sheffield United and Frank Carrodus of Manchester City. Both targets visited Brunton Park for contract talks after fees for their transfers had been agreed with their respective clubs. In the end, terms could be agreed with neither, leaving Ashman with the prospect of being without a proven goal scorer for the 1972/73 season. After the opening few fixtures, it was clear that Carlisle were short of firepower, so Ashman told Hugh Neil to go and take another look at the boy Wilson, who was now playing his football along with Scottish football's elite, and whilst he didn't score in the club's opening fixtures, he put in some extremly impressive performances. The goals would surely continue to flow.

Neil told Ashman that Wilson could, in his opinion, make it in English league football. It would be a massive gamble for the club and a huge step for the player himself, since he was part-time at Dumbarton. He had taken the opportunity to have a chat with a couple of the Dumbarton folk and confirmed that they would be open to discussion for a suitable transfer fee if Carlisle were interested. The surprising thing was that they were prepared to cash in on their largest asset. Ashman, after losing out on his first two targets, was desperate for a competent and consistent striker and told Neil to go back and find out how much it would cost to prise him away.

NEWS OF THE CARLISLE transfer record being smashed was first revealed by the *Evening News and Star* on 25 September 1972. The nightly paper anounced in bold back page head-lines: 'Ashman will tell Wilson to keep scoring'. It revealed how United had been watching the 26 year-old Wilson after being impressed by his performance in the pre-season friendly. A fee of £40,000 was at first anounced as the cost of Wilson's signature. Ashman seemed quietly pleased with his new capture. "We won't try to change the way Kenny plays. He can't play in midfield or anything like that – he is a goalscoring forward, plain and simple."

Ashman, it was revealed, believed that Wilson was the man to put away the chances which the strikers had been missing that season. A Scottish newspaper correspondent described Wilson as 'an outstanding capture'. It was further revealed that Wilson was still in employment in Scotland as a joiner, but one of his first tasks would be to tie up the loose ends of his job. Ashman went on to explain his hopes for the new man at Brunton Park. "I am hoping that Kenny will settle down quickly and if he can get off the mark soon it will be a decided advantage to him."

There was much speculation as to whether Wilson would start the following evening's league game at Brunton Park, an important clash with rivals Blackpool, then managed by Bob Stokoe. The questions were answered the following day when Allan Ashman announced: "The first appearance of Wilson should ensure a bumper attendance for tonight's game."

With the club also playing under the four brand new floodlight pylons for the first time there was much anticipation in the city. The scene was perfectly set for new Cult Hero-in-the-making Kenny Wilson to embark upon his English football career and get the local and very vocal and partisan home crowd for this derby fixture well and truly behind him. There was no doubting that the greater majority of those inside Brunton Park that evening were Carlisle United supporters, all desperately keen for their new signing to do well and to get one over their old manager at the same time. In that sense there was a massive responsibility placed upon the player's shoulders before he had kicked a ball in earnest.

Prior to the game, Bob Stokoe, never one to miss the opportunity to do psychological battle with the opposition, was to pour scorn on the signing when he said: "I can't say I've heard of this Kenny Wilson, but speaking to Hughie he seems to have a decent goalscoring record. I wouldn't have signed him had I got that money behind me. £36,000 seems a lot for what amounts to an untested part time footballer."

So the game kicked off and it has to be said that as far as Kenny Wilson was concerned it wasn't the best debut any Carlisle United footballer has ever had; indeed, that any footballer has ever had. Many of the players in this book and in the historical records of Carlisle United and other clubs have the enviable record of scoring on their debuts, not so Kenny Wilson. It was apparent from his first touch of the ball, as Stokoe suspected, that he was lost in the full-time professional game. He didn't understand the pace and certainly didn't know all of his colleagues' names come kick-off. Added to which it was an emotive local derby, the pace of which was fast and furious. One reporter recalled Wilson looking fraught and at times manic as he chased everything that moved on the pitch, but never actually got close to it.

Carlisle had desperately needed a win. Blackpool, meanwhile were fired up by Stokoe, a man desperate to get one over his old employers, who he had left in, let's just say, acrimonious circumstances. United had endured a woeful start to the campaign, worsened that night as they lost the encounter 2-3 before almost 11,000 fans.

This author was among the fans at Brunton Park that evening, my ultimate recollection being that everyone was moaning about Kenny Wilson being a waste of money and an awful signing. Personally, I felt sorry for him. It was, after all, his first game for the club. As a 13 year-old I hardly had the experience or the knowledge of the game to contradict my elders. Yet deep down I was certain that Kenny was better than everyone thought and could and would prove his doubters wrong. He was after all, our record signing. He had to be brilliant, hadn't he?

The press weren't very kind either. In a rather dismissive way the *News and Star* reported on United's horrendous start to the new campaign and within an entire page coverage simply stated that Kenny Wilson had a 'modest debut'. Worse still, letters from the public asked why the club had dismissed a perfectly good and successful manager in the form of Ian MacFarlane to bring back Allan Ashman. Kenny had found himself in the middle of public furore from the outset. Trainer Dick Young was anxious because the club's record signing was well below his accepted fitness level and advised Ashman to get the player to resign from his work as a joiner immediately. The Carlisle trainer said: "Wilson would need to go through a strict fitness regime to bring him to the standard of the other professionals at the club. He has the skill, it's the pace and stamina he lacks." Dick Young's pressure forced the issue and a couple of days after his United debut, it was revealed that Wilson had resolved difficulties with his work and was now able to train full-time. Now there was no room for excuses.

Everyone, it seemed, questioned why Ashman had turned to Wilson as a solution to the goalscoring problems. Some even believed that he had signed the wrong Kenny Wilson! So devoid of football talent was the player who they had seen in that brief 90 minutes at Brunton Park.

Ashman, though, would continue to support his record signing and publicly said of his new star: "We saw a side of Kenny's game we were unaware of tonight." That was a reference to him being forced out of the game by the professional skill of the Blackpool defence, therefore Kenny had been forced to track back into midfield to chase the ball. Ashman, the great manager that he was, turned a decided negative into a real positive.

Thankfully, elsewhere in the Carlisle squad, over the next few games ex-Manchester City striker Bobby Owen and ex-Middlesbrough forward Joe Laidlaw held the scoring fort, firing in decisive goals to enable victories, thus keeping United hovering just above the relegation zone. Both worked hard with their fellow attacker and couldn't help but be impressed by his finishing during training matches. Despite this, as soon as he appeared for Carlisle in a competitive fixture Wilson struggled to make any inroads towards his first goal in English football. Readers may remember that a certain Peter Crouch suffered a similar problem when he first signed for Liverpool. Kenny Wilson, though, was no Peter Crouch; a man who went on to score more international goals in a calendar year than any other Englishman.

RESEARCHING HIS CAREER, a common thread throughout the match reports covering United was the obvious omission of Kenny's name within the said articles. Sadly, when his name does crop up it is generally part of a sentence which goes along the lines: 'Wilson shot but it was wide of the mark' or 'Wilson's shot was weak' or more frequently 'Wilson was caught offside.' Kenny was, though, a willing workhorse and never gave up chasing and running. He was a good provider and foil to the likes of Laidlaw and Owen and created space for his fellows, but when it came to him being given the perfect opportunity, such as being through on goal one-on-one with the advancing keeper, he just fluffed it every time.

Strikers tend to suffer robust and thoughtless tackles more than most players, and Kenny was no different. He had the will and desire to succeed and wholeheartedly threw himself into every tackle and challenge in an attempt to win. In one such incident in the 22nd minute of an away league game at Blackpool on 4 November 1972, chasing after a 50/50 ball, he was kicked into the air by a Blackpool defender. The end result was devastating damage to his knee, which exacerbated a previous minor injury sustained in October. Unable to move, his face distraught with pain, he was stretchered from the pitch and at once seen to by the club's physiotherapist, Herbert Nicholson. The injury was a bad one, serious ligament damage.

On Monday 6 November it was revealed that his knee had been put in plaster and that Carlisle's record signing would now be sidelined for several weeks. The prolonged period of rest was soon over and three weeks after the plastercast had secured the knee, it was removed. Kenny was back in light training, working harder and pushing himself more than he had ever done before. He was desperate to get back into first team action and get among the goals. On Wednesday 13 December he resumed full training with the first team squad. Those who saw him train said he looked meaner, leaner and fitter. His manager felt he would be ready to return to first team action after Christmas.

Tuesday 26 December 1972 was a day of great rejoicing in the Wilson household. Kenny had proved himself fit and returned to first team action at home to Preston North End at Brunton Park. It was a miserable dank sort of day, the floodlights had been on since the kick-off, and United expected a tough battle against their Lancashire opponents. In what was an incredible game played out before 9,939 spectators, United romped into a 5-1 lead. With 15 minutes remaining, United winger Dennis Martin broke free down the right, attacking the Warwick Road End. Looking up he saw the Preston defence were square and moving out away from goal, with a jink of his hips and nod of the head he was past one man, before slipping an exquisite pass through to the middle of the pitch which effectively sliced open the North End defence like a knife through butter. Racing onto the ball was Kenny Wilson. The Warwick Road End roared the United striker on. Alan Kelly, the Republic of Ireland international goalkeeper, in the Preston goal moved out to narrow the angle and spread himself out, making himself big, very big. Kenny had no sight of goal now. Over nine thousand people muttered the same thing in unison: "For fuck's sake, Kenny. Hit the fucking ball!" And he did, with some venom too. Time stood still as the ball hit the goalkeeper, looped into the air over him and towards the Preston goal. Wilson followed it through, but it needed no further encouragement as it landed in the net; the Warwick Road End doing their bit by trying to suck the ball in.

At last, Kenny Wilson had scored. He'd made hard work of it, but he had finally done it. On his comeback too; very similar to a debut, but not quite. Brunton Park erupted, Kenny Wilson erupted, the Carlisle players went wild in celebration. In fact there wasn't one person who wasn't pleased for the club's record purchase. For the remaining 14 minutes the Brunton Park faithful sang his name and danced in jubilation. Kenny's goal was much more than just the sixth for United in that game, it was a moment of fulfilment, a bonding. Kenny was now one of us.

In the bigger scheme of things, it mattered little. As a forward in the English game he was plain awful. Dick Young had never been too sure about him. "Kenny was as nice a foot-baller as you would ever meet," he told me. "But he simply wasn't up to the type of game we played. Allan regretted signing him. I advised him against it, but he felt that the player was more than able to do it for us. The game is littered with Scottish footballers who couldn't make it in the English game and vice versa. He never settled in Carlisle and was really out of his depth."

Two games on and Kenny was on the substitute's bench. Despite the goal his perform-ances hadn't improved. In fact if anything they had deteriorated. A regular and somewhat infamous shout from the paddock area of the ground could be heard when Kenny was warming up pre-match was: "Get in here, Wilson. You are bloody rubbish." Hardly conducive to building his self esteem.

As the season progressed and the fans warmed to the club's record purchase, he became anonymous. The country had 'Where's Wally?', we at Carlisle had 'Where's Kenny?' One look to the United substitute's bench would reveal all. When he did appear for the team he failed to impress and his body language clearly showed him to be very unhappy. There were also times when he was simply dropped as apathy set in and he languished in the stands, an onlooker to a team who worked hard for each other.

He never formally asked for a transfer from Carlisle United, but made mention of the fact that he would like to play first team football and gain experience away from the club, perhaps on loan somewhere. Unbeknownst to the player, Allan Ashman had finally listened to Dick Young and now appreciated that his star striker couldn't cope with the rigours of Division Two football. By the start of the 1973/74 season his Carlisle career was over. He was loaned out to York City in September 1973, joining the Bootham Crescent club at the same time as experienced Nottingham Forest striker Barry Lyons. He made his debut for City on 1 October at Bootham Crescent against Chesterfield in a tame 0-0 draw. Five days later he appeared at Cambridge United in another goalless game.

It didn't work out for Wilson at all in Yorkshire. He didn't like the travelling and to be honest, hadn't set the place alight with his flair. Soon he was on his way back to Brunton Park, but not for long.

In October 1973, along with Bob Delgado, he was loaned to Workington Reds, then struggling at the foot of Division Four. His Workington debut was somewhat ignominious. It came at Layer Road, Colchester in a 3-0 defeat. As at Carlisle, the Workington boss George Aitken believed the striker would hit form sooner rather than later and persevered with him in the starting line up. There followed starts at home to Brentford (lost 2-0), away at Gillingham, (lost 4-0) and finally a victory with a 1-0 home win over Bradford City. His final game came as a substitute in a 1-1 draw with Rotherham United at Millmoor. The burden of weight was lifted from his shoulders on 20 November when he was recalled from his fortnightly reviewable loan spell at Borough Park.

It came about as a result of a telephone call from an official at Hamilton Academical who were sounding United out about a possible transfer. Eric Smith, the Accies boss, was keen on the record-breaking goal machine, initially he was put off by Carlisle's asking price of around £20,000. There followed much to-ing and fro-ing before finally Kenny ended his English nightmare and signed for Academical for a fee believed to be around £8,000. Wilson made his return debut in the Scottish game on 16 February 1974 at Montrose in a 1-0 defeat. A week later he was substituted after a poor performance away at Brechin City, and another 1-0 defeat. Finally, on 16 March 1974, almost a year and three months since his last competitive goal, Kenny managed to get on the scoresheet for Hamilton in a 4-1 victory over Cowdenbeath at Douglas Park. One can only surmise what celebrations followed for the poor lad as the sense of release must have been incredible as that ball hit the net.

A rich vein of form, for Wilson at least, was to follow as, on 6 April, he banged in another goal in a 4-1 away victory at Airdrie. It was brief respite as soon he was fluffing chances once again and couldn't find the back of the net at all. The Accies had seen enough to know that he wasn't the player they thought he was. In a sad end to his professional playing career Kenny Wilson played his last game at Hamilton on 13 April 1974 against Queen's Park. He was second substitute.

OSTRACISED FROM THE game he loved so much and still plagued by injury, Wilson ended up at Brora Rangers, playing his football at Dudgeon Park in the Highland League. Brora had an unenviable record during his time there; in both 1973/74 and 1974/75 the club finished bottom of the Highland League. In the first season they won just five of their 30 league games and lost 19. Whereas during his second campaign they won just three of their 30 games, drawing four and losing 23. For Kenny it was the end of his career.

It's hard to rationalise just what went wrong with a footballer who was scoring goals at a terrific rate in the Scottish league only to lose the knack in such spectacular fashion. Certainly it seems that his brief spell at Carlisle signalled the end of him as a rated star. He was injury prone and perhaps it was that he never really recovered from the serious knock sustained at Blackpool. One thing that is for certain, he was a costly commodity to Carlisle United and sadly he will always be remembered for being so crap! The fans, though, those who remember him, do so with great affection. The terrace chant of 'Oh Kenny Wilson, Kenny Kenny Kenny Kenny Wilson' echoed round Brunton Park for just a few months of the 1972/73 season. He was a player who endeared himself to the support not by his skill or goalscoring, but his sheer determination to give it a go. Kenny, wherever you are, good luck to you mate. Your place in this tome is a worthy one for you were a Cult Hero, albeit one of a different kind. Had fate been kinder, it could all have been oh so different. Couldn't it?

STAN BOWLES

'THE MAN'

1971-1972

UNITED CAREER

Games 33
Goals 12
Caps 5

MAGIC MOMENT

Stanley stood head and shoulders above everyone else at White Hart Lane as his shrewd and intelligent, and sometimes magical play earned United a draw in the FA Cup

YOU know the sort of player Stan Bowles was. You can liken his kind to Tony Currie, George Best, Rodney Marsh, Paul Gascoigne et al; footballers who, although a little troublesome to their managers, possessed bags of skill and were geniuses with a ball at their feet. At times they were known to burn the candle at both ends, enjoying long days and even longer nights – mostly partying. They are the sort of players that delight and frustrate in equal measure. And they often divide fans as to their worth and contribution to their side. Without doubt they are born entertainers.

Football fans of all ages know the name Stanley Bowles. Widely regarded by many true Blues as the most skilful footballer ever to play for Carlisle United, he was also known by a broader football audience as a player who couldn't quite match for any sustained period the dazzling potential he at times displayed. But when he was at his best, so good was he that many believe that he could have progressed to become one of Britain's if not the world's most devastating players. Instead, his name conjures up countless stories of a somewhat reckless and anti-authoritarian prima donna, of an impudent, carefree young man with a cheeky smile, rather than a man blessed with immense talent and footballing skill.

MY FIRST RECOLLECTION of the player who United fans often affectionately refer to as 'Our Stan' came in the car park behind the main stands of Brunton Park. It was to be his debut performance for United. Surrounded by a posse of press and photographers Bowles had difficulty moving through the assembled crowd. Step by step he gradually made his way towards the tiny blue door which marked the players' entrance. My first youthful impression of the player was that he didn't seem to fit into the surroundings. For a start he was wearing a long cream trench coat more commonly known as a 'flasher's mac'. His long fair hair was matched by a pair of unkempt sideburns and he looked painfully thin. My mate (we were just 12 years old) somehow got to within touching distance of him as Bowles was about to disappear through the door and for some inane reason shouted: "Stan, you're a poof". At which point Stan reappeared, looked at the slip of a kid standing before him, laughed and offered to sign the kid's programme (which he did). Like a true professional he ignored what was a pathetic comment. As he turned to return inside the ground, he suddenly stopped in his tracks, turned back round to face the gathered few souls. He looked down at my mate, laughed and jokingly raised two fingers at him before disappearing inside Brunton Park. Everyone, even my mate, saw the funny side of it. That's what sort of bloke Stan Bowles was – in fact still is – easy going, relaxed and not one to get all wound up about nonsense.

He made a lot of friends on his arrival at the ground that night, but on the pitch he didn't have the greatest of debuts and really failed to have any impact on the game whatsoever. He seemed short of fitness and was so slight that he was knocked off the ball too easily. At times he looked uninterested, meandering around the Brunton Park pitch aimlessly arousing great damnation from the ever-so-critical paddock area of the ground. One man who stood close to where I stood seemed hell bent on rejecting Stan from the outset. "Fuck off back to Crewe, Bowles. You are crap!" he cried. When Stan was substituted the man seemed to believe it was his doing and applauded enthusiastically. He wasn't alone in voicing his criticism of the new-comer. I felt saddened by the vocal attacks on a player who, after all, hadn't had time to get to know his playing colleagues' names, let alone been given a fair chance to settle in. United's opponents that day were Oxford United and it was another ex-Manchester City and Bury player who made the Carlisle headlines. Bobby Owen scored both goals in a 2-1 victory.

I resolved to get to meet Stan afterwards and capture his autograph on my programme that evening. In that way I might make him feel a bit better about things and that would provide me with the opportunity to tell him not to listen to the blinkered vision of many of the paddock critics. Sure enough, I waited around and got to meet Stan after game. I told him not to worry and to stick it out at Carlisle, telling him we had some very good players like Chris Balderstone, Alan Ross, Stan Ternent, Tot Winstanley, and John Gorman. He was very nice about it and told me that he agreed, we did have some very good players, he said he had heard the man in the paddock but was used to dealing with people like him. He signed my programme, told me not to worry and to go home before it got too dark. Stan Bowles had arrived at Carlisle United.

THE STORY OF STAN BOWLES is filled with drama and incredible off-the-pitch incidents, matched, of course, by some equally bizarre on-pitch antics, but always eclipsed by some wonderful exhibitions of the art of professional football.

Raised in Manchester, he first began working in a raincoat factory (which might explain the dodgy macintosh he wore when he arrived at Carlisle). He claims that he was just 15 when he made his first bet and was a well-established gambler before he became established in football. It was while he worked in the factory that the gambling habit was formed. Like so many, he had heard of a red hot horse racing tip, walked into a local bookmakers and backed the horse. It won, bringing him about £40 in winnings. "It was a lot of money to win for a boy of 15," Stan said. "I reckoned it was an easy way to earn money. I was right, but what I didn't realise at the time was that it was also an easy way to lose all your money. The losing bit gets lost in the euphoria of a good win, a bit like football really, but, as it takes hold of you, the money becomes almost valueless if you like. It's more about the winning and how good it makes you feel."

On the football front, Bowles was playing locally and had been watched by the likes of Manchester City for some time. He eventually signed as an apprentice for the Maine Road outfit where he earned about £7 a week. City at the time were managed by Joe Mercer and his assistant Malcolm Allison. Mercer was the gentleman of the two, whereas Allison was known to take no nonsense from his players and could be both volatile and ignorant, not only to his charges but to anyone at all. It was Allison who was Stan's greatest critic, not of his football, but of his attitude. Gambling had become second nature to the player and soon he was mixing and running with some less desirable elements of Manchester society. Late nights and long days soon took their toll on the young star. He began to lose focus on the game which offered him so much as the gambling habit took hold. Despite these frustrations for all concerned, Bowles was still a player with extreme potential and was once described by the late Joe Mercer as the 'greatest football enigma' he experienced during his long career in the game.

Gradually Bowles made sure he was targeted for attention by Malcolm Allison, time and again he would arrive late for training, a fact which infuriated the assistant manager. Warned as to his attitude and conduct, matters came to a head one day on the training ground when Allison openly told the player what he thought of him. Stan, never one to take the statesman's position, yelled back at Allison and threw a punch at him which connected with Allison's head. The incensed Allison flew at Bowles. The outcome was never going to be in any doubt. Allison was a valued member of the managerial staff. Player and assistant manager were quickly separated, but the assistant manager, claims Bowles, was never the same with him again.

Not satisfied that he had yet made a complete mess of things at City, Stan continued to flaunt rules and disobeyed just about every club regulation. On one occasion he failed to catch a plane to a European destination with the rest of the playing staff and management. Incredibly no disciplinary action was taken against him for that breach. So Stan continued to be late for training. One can only suspect how such lack of respect riled Malcolm Allison. Eventually, the pair came to physical blows again, this time in a nightclub in full view of the Manchester public. This was to be Stan's final act of rebellion at City, and shortly afterwards he was effectively sacked from the club.

Only 'effectively' because, although he would never play for the club again, City refused to release Bowles from his contract, taking the view that he was still worth something to them financially at least. No-one made an offer for him, so Stan, early in his career, found himself on the soccer scrap heap.

LOWLY BURY OFFERED salvation with an offer of a three month trial. Bowles seized the opportunity. From day one he made his presence known. A fall out with new manager Colin McDonald over his pay demands quickly followed and then there was the predictable lack of punctuality for training and other club events. McDonald was never really in control of Bowles and it seems that the player knew it. For his part the manager persisted in playing Stan out of position, a matter that was discussed within the dressing room but never resolved. The player never had a positive word to say about the manager, a fact which soon found its way back to McDonald. The local media, keen to sensationalise Stan's off-the-field exploits, dug about for any garbage news story linked to the player they could find. It was a tough world, but Stan had already laid the foundation to his own football downfall.

Five games and seven weeks later, his three month trial at Gigg Lane was terminated, Bury had won just one the five games Stan had appeared in, and he failed to score for the Shakers.

Ernie Tagg, manager of Crewe Alexandra, had seen the potential in Stan and brought him to Gresty Road. "It was the best thing that happened to me," Stan recalled. "Ernie was a genuine bloke. He ran a pub as well being manager at Crewe. I learnt a lot from him. He was a good manager, who knew how to get the best out of his players. He did me alright anyway."

Whilst at Crewe, Stan reinvented himself, his desire and belief in the game returned. Surrounded by many other promising professionals he worked hard to repay Ernie Tagg and Crewe. Tagg himself said Stan was a model professional during his spell at Gresty Road, a solid statement in support of the player's new-found hard work and dedication. Having made

51 league appearances and netted 18 goals, Stan was suddenly being linked with clubs higher up the league ladder. Media speculation grew linking him with Fulham, Newcastle United, Sheffield Wednesday and Northampton Town to name but a few.

Eventually, a call was received at Gresty Road. It was from Ian MacFarlane, manager of Carlisle United, a man who had once acted as coach to a youthful Stan at Manchester City. MacFarlane received the go ahead to make an offer for the player and consulted with his board. The maximum they could raise was £10,000, Crewe had asked for £25,000 but MacFarlane pleaded poverty. A few days passed and the transfer looked like it was dead in the water when MacFarlane once again rang his Crewe counterpart and offered to meet them about half way, this time offering £12,000. The fee was accepted and so Stan Bowles became a Carlisle United player.

It has been claimed by Stan himself that Carlisle actually deceived Crewe by pretending to be hard up and thus unable to meet Crewe's financial demands. The evidence supporting this being that United striker Bob Hatton signed for Birmingham City later the same day for £80,000. So upset were Crewe officials by this that allegedly they said they would never do business with Carlisle again! Even before he had kicked a ball for United, Stan Bowles was involved in controversy.

The late Dick Young was first team trainer at Carlisle during the Bowles era; he spoke fondly of the player who arrived with a dubious reputation and big gambling habit. "Ian MacFarlane knew Stan from his youth days and was keen to get him signed up for us. I had been down to Crewe a few times to watch him with Hugh Neil. It was clear that he was a class act, some of his trickery with the ball left us breathless. Hugh was as keen as Ian to sign him, but I wanted to make sure he was performing consistently. To me, when he was at Crewe he lacked a bit of confidence. He wasn't keen on putting his foot on the ball and stopping the game dead. Good midfielders need to be able to do that from time to time.

When we signed him, he was a bit nervous. Big Ian didn't mess around and told Stan that he expected him to perform and be loyal to Carlisle. He told him he knew every journalist in the area and if anything untoward got back to him, then he would tear his balls off one at a time. Stan was like a naughty schoolboy and said his wayward days were behind him. He wanted to knuckle down to make a name for himself in the game and to prove to him that he was able to do it on the pitch. Ian told him that Malcolm Allison was the one who made the final recommendation for Carlisle to take a gamble on Stan. He was a bit surprised by that I think.

I've got to say that when he was with us he could be an absolute pain in training, messing about with his ball tricks. He liked to wind the other players up with his back chat and skill. At times you felt you would have loved to kick him black and blue, but he was well liked and just about made it for training on time. He hated the medicine ball and did his best to avoid working with it, which made me all the keener to work him harder with it.

As a player, though, he was something else. Even Chris Balderstone was amazed by his talent with a ball at his feet. The one player Stan didn't get much from was Alan Ross. Somehow Rossy was his match during training session games and he couldn't get the ball past him no matter how hard he tried. Albeit, I think he did manage it when he returned to face us in a competitive league game. I have to say, Stan Bowles was as talented a footballer as I have ever worked with, but you just never really knew what was going through his head at any time, particularly when he was on the pitch."

The late Alan Ross, the Bowles nemesis in so many training sessions, had nothing but fond memories from Stan's time at Carlisle.

"He was a bloody pain, talk about vain!" Ross told me. "He believed he was the new George Best and acted like a multi-millionaire, throwing his money around like it was loose change. We all really liked him. He brought something really special to the club, and he was an inspiration in the dressing room and suffered a lot of friendly abuse from the rest of the players. He took it all in his stride and always had a smile on his face. It always seemed that he got more fan mail than most of us, he liked that a lot I think. After a win he would ask us all if we fancied a pint with him. He wasn't slow on the social interaction bit, but it seemed that when you did have a pint with him he never ever paid, so we would avoid it if we could, making up excuses not to go out for a drink with him. I remember on one occasion the boss telling him that he knew every move he made in Carlisle when away from the game. Fact was Ian had contacted all the bookies in the city and asked them to let him know if Stan had been in. A few would let him know, but the majority it seemed were happy to take Stan's money. I think when he went, we were all a bit saddened. He was class and could turn on a sixpence."

AFTER A STEADY, IF unspectacular, start and integration into his new surroundings, Our Stan began to flourish on the field, creating a strong understanding with Chris Balderstone in particular in a midfield which was as good as any in Division Two at that time.

The understanding the entire team developed of Bowles' style of play engendered a new optimism at Brunton Park as suddenly United had not only dogged determination, but equal amounts of flair too. And, while it may not have been entirely due to Stan, no matter what he may tell you, he was undoubtedly the catalyst. Bowles came of age in the 4-1 drubbing of Bristol City at Ashton Gate. It was a quite outstanding performance from United with Bowles creative and innovative with his vision and superb dribbling skills. Bobby Owen grabbed a brace, both of which came courtesy of Bowles' artistry. Stan found the net himself after some amazing dribbling had freed some space, allowing him to almost casually stroke the ball home. Elsewhere in the team, Frank Barton seemed to have found a new lease of life following the arrival of Bowles, making the kind of darting runs through defences that Dick Young had so enthused over a few seasons earlier.

With the likes of Balderstone and Martin alongside him, and with some strong and reliable defenders allowing him freedom to take risks, Stan seemed happier in his game. "It was great to see him develop so quickly," Young told me. "He really listened to Chris Balderstone during a game, and Stan Ternent was constantly at him to play the ball forward. I had been at him to take control of games, to put his foot on the ball, stop play and look for the player making a run and find the space with the ball. At Bristol he showed he could do it, from there he played the game with a smile on his face."

Suddenly, Stan was part of a team, a team he enjoyed playing in. The manager had the skills to control him, and on the odd occasion when he did go off the rails, MacFarlane was quick to remedy the situation with a few words of wisdom. Witness the occasion when Stan apparently hadn't shown up for a night game. It was getting close to handing the team sheet in and still no Stan. MacFarlane got on the phone and telephoned each and every bookmakers in Carlisle. The search paid off as MacFarlane finally tracked Stan down and the gruff manager told the bookmaker to get him to Brunton Park now, advising him to tell the player that if he didn't show, then he would come out to get him and drag him by the balls to the ground. Stan showed up!

MacFarlane didn't mix his words where he felt discipline was necessary, unlike Malcolm Allison who had lost control. He was able to take a step back and make assessed decisions, which worked. Having spent some time with MacFarlane at his home in Market Harborough discussing United, I know he had a real desire to do well at Carlisle and felt he was building a team more than capable of challenging for a place in the top flight. Stan Bowles was an integral part of that jigsaw.

Twelve goals from 29 appearances in his first season, including a brilliantly contrived effort against Tottenham Hotspur in the FA Cup, saw Bowles become a firm favourite with the fans. A quite amazing hat-trick against Norwich City before Christmas was the performance which really catapulted Bowles from being a player of supreme quality to a Cult Hero. Norwich had been challenging for top spot in the league and ultimately went on to be Champions, but at Carlisle that day, Stan ripped them apart with such insouciant nonchalance that he actually had the audacity to talk to the crowd during the Canaries' annihilation. Bowles' goals were well executed and one in particular was spectacular in as much as he weaved through a cluster of defenders before firing high into the net from a difficult angle.

Leading 2-0 at half-time, United continued to push forward with exhilarating style. Everything Stan did turned to gold. On one occasion, in front of the Scratching Pen, he took the ball off a defender's toe, flicked it up into the air, controlled it on his knee, before lobbing it towards the Warwick Road End goal, with a scrambling keeper striding back and somehow tipping it over the crossbar. Stan meanwhile turned to the fans in the Scratching Pen, bowed and winked.

On another occasion, when taking a throw in, he asked the fans behind him if they thought the right-back was as crap as he thought he was. The supporters loved it and lapped as much of Bowles up as he could offer. By the time the third goal had flown in, he was jubilantly kissing his fingers before thrusting them in the air as a salute to the United faithful. Those are, without any question, the deeds of a Cult Hero.

BY THE SUMMER OF 1972 many First Division sides were rumoured to be watching Bowles' progress at the club. There was little time for distraction as soon the pre-season friendlies and tournaments began.

United took part in the Anglo Italian Trophy that year and were drawn against Stoke City, AS Roma (then one of Europe's top sides) and Catanzaro. On Saturday 1 June 1972, United ran out as clear underdogs against the mighty AS Roma at the Olympic Stadium. The Roma coach, Helenio Herrera, said scornfully of United: "We have similar sides in the lower levels of our leagues." In an incredible game United ran out 3-2 winners, with Bowles and Balderstone, in particular, running the show.

The rest of the tournament saw United remain unbeaten, but fail to reach the final on goal difference. One match stands out in the memory from that tournament, versus Catanzaro at home. United needed to win comfortably to stand any chance of going through to the final. Bowles was at his brilliant best in this encounter, tearing at the Italian defence from the kick-off. Back flicks, body swerves and nutmegs followed each time he received the ball. On one occasion he dribbled past five defenders before curling a beautiful shot towards the goal from the edge of the area, the ball striking the joint of crossbar and post and bouncing to safety. His performance was simply awesome as United went on to win the game 4-1. Afterwards, he was deflated with United's failure to qualify for the final on goal difference. He told a local reporter: "We are unbeaten and have been the best English team in the tournament. It's not right that we don't qualify for the final. We have come through a very strong group. This club deserves to be there, not Blackpool, who beat an unheard-of village team."

Bowles was now displaying real passion for his game and in particular the club. His stock was as high as any player's in United history. Then, suddenly, it was all over. His mentor and advisor Ian MacFarlane was dismissed as manager in extremely curious circumstances. There was a real belief that the directors couldn't deal with his straight and direct manner, added to which Allan Ashman had revealed he wanted to return to the English game and returned to Carlisle as manager. Bowles was immediately given the cold shoulder by the new manager, who knew of his reputation, but clearly didn't want to chance any confrontation.

After just six games under Ashman's management Stan was gone, sold to Queen's Park Rangers for £110,000, an excellent profit for the club, but leaving behind a huge void in terms entertainment and creativity. Ashman had little to say to the outgoing Bowles, simply saying good luck to him as he left the club for the last time. He was to later admit: "I never really liked footballers like Stan Bowles. He was a maverick and didn't conform well to discipline. They are fantastic entertainers, but lack consistency and aren't really the team players we need."

STAN SPENT ALMOST EIGHT seasons with QPR, including a superb campaign in which Rangers finished as runners-up in the First Division in 1976, when the championship was lost narrowly to Liverpool. At Loftus Road the gambling worsened, as Bowles could regularly be seen putting bets on in a local William Hill bookies just before kick-off. Legend has it that he wore his long 'flasher mac' over his playing kit, complete with football boots as he dashed out to place his bet.

I was fortunate enough to meet with and interview George Best before his untimely death. During our chat the subject of Stan Bowles came up.

"Stan was an absolute legend wherever he played," Best told me. "I knew about him when he was at Man City. They said he was my opposite number at Maine Road. We both loved a drink and a bit of fun. We often met up with Rodney (Marsh) too and would go out to entertain! Stan was a great player, but he had the gambling thing quite bad and that spoilt his game. He would bet on two flies walking up a wall. I loved him, though; quite a personality and a person who loves and lives life to the full. I saw him play for Carlisle a couple of times. When he was running at players you could see he was just like me. It gave him a real buzz. At QPR he got the recognition he couldn't get at Carlisle and from there he became well-known for his football talent."

From fashionable west London, Stan moved to the more countrified surroundings of Nottingham, when he signed for Brian Clough's Nottingham Forest. Clough knew Bowles was at best temperamental, but believed he could manage him and squeeze a couple of further seasons of quality play out of him. Stan, though, had other ideas. For a start, he received a £15,000 golden handshake from QPR, followed by a £15,000 signing on fee from Forest; two deals which he believes were among his best in football. Clough had a reputation of bringing players who he believed were too big for their boots down to earth. Stan, meanwhile, had a reputation for irritating managers and not conforming as they wished, effectively winding them up at every opportunity. With two opposite personalities working together in such close proximity there was only going to be one end result, confrontation. So it went, as row after row followed, with Cloughie looked to press buttons to find how his players would react.

The gruff north-easterner was not one to suffer fools gladly, but at the same time he didn't like smart arses either and he thought Bowles fell into both categories and made it his business to provoke the player. The partnership never worked and conflict simmered close to the surface all the time. Others at the club seemed to humour Clough's whims, but not Stanley Bowles. No, he was his own man and would always do what he felt was right, not what others told him was right.

EVENTUALLY IT ALL FELL apart in 1980 when Stan walked out of the Forest camp before their European Cup final against Hamburg. It was because of a set of differences, which effectively meant that Clough had won and maintained control, telling the player that he wouldn't be playing in his big pal John Robertson's testimonial game which was coming up shortly. Bowles reacted badly and told him that he didn't want to play for him or Forest any more. Clough appeared to enjoy the confrontation and allegedly responded to the angry player: "You are turning down the chance of a European Cup medal because of that?" To which the player is said to have replied: "Yeah, fucking poke it." Understandably, Clough shut him out, denied his existence and wouldn't speak of the player again. Indeed, a few years before his death when I spoke to the ex-Nottingham Forest manager and mentioned Stan to him, Clough made no comment. It was as though I was speaking of a player he had never heard of. Neither of the men ever spoke to the other again.

So, after just one season at the City Ground Stan was moved on, spending the last few seasons of his career at such places as Leyton Orient and then Brentford before he retired from the game in 1984. He can still be found in the Brentford area of west London, regaling anyone who will listen – and there are plenty – with tale after tale of his footballing days.

At Carlisle Bowles still holds the respect of the people and the fans. Supporters of Carlisle United still recall almost 40 years later, their own personal moments of brilliance which came from his dancing football feet. Stan often refers to Carlisle as a remote place snowbound in the winter and wonderful and picturesque in the summer. One thing that is for certain, for 11 months in the early 1970s he lit up the football skies of Cumbria and created marvellous memories for a devoutly loyal band of supporters. No doubt he made a few book-makers and publicans happy too.

To this day, Stan Bowles remains one of Carlisle United's favourite sons. Who knows how his career would have unfolded had it not been for Ian MacFarlane believing his instincts and bringing him to Brunton Park? Thank God he did.

PETER BEARDSLEY

1979-1982

UNITED CAREER

Games	121
Goals	21
Caps	59

MAGIC MOMENT

Workington simply had no answer to the consummate skill and finishing of the young Beardo in the 1980 FA Cup tie. He scored two and dominated the game

'OUR FAVOURITE ADOPTED SON'

'He was down to earth and would help anyone, even the tea lady, if he felt she needed some assistance. It was a pleasure to work with him'

Alan Ross

TO say that Peter Beardsley needed Carlisle United as much as Carlisle United needed Peter Beardsley would be an understatement. United were still smarting and hadn't recovered from the hurt of relegation from the First Division at the end of the 1974/75 season. Three managers later (Ashman, Young and Moncur), a further relegation had seen the club settling into life in the old Third Division, aspiring to mediocrity in the top half of the table. Apart from a truly memorable FA Cup battle with Manchester United – during the game a blatantly poor refereeing decision, dismissing a clear penalty appeal when George McVitie was hacked to the ground when charging into the Red Devils' penalty area, robbed Blues of a much-deserved victory at Brunton Park – there was little else offered in the way of long term aspirations for the future of the team.

The arrival of Bobby Moncur as player/manager in November 1976 was viewed as a positive step. In an early fans forum he exclaimed: "This is a huge job, but we are all big enough to take it on. I expect your support. I have a lot of contacts in the game and I will be calling in a few favours to get this club back on its feet and challenging again for a place in the First Division. As long as I can remember, everyone in football has been impressed by the stylish football Carlisle United play. This in no small way was down to Dick Young. He had an eye for bringing in quality players and making them even better before selling them on. I want to replicate and continue what Dick has achieved at this club. I will be looking at local talent at all levels. My network is vast. I will leave no stone unturned in my quest to bring the very best to Brunton Park."

At the end of his first season in charge, 1976/77, Moncur's side were relegated, agonisingly on goal difference, with Leyton Orient and Cardiff just keeping their heads above water. However, true to his word, within 12 months he had introduced into the first team three local players in the form of Andy Collins, Geoff Fell and Keith Sawyers, none of who seemed distinctly out of place in the Third Division, albeit most played bit part roles, covering for injuries or acting as substitutes. Collins fared better than the others and managed 47 starts. With no disrespect to these players, they were hardly what United fans had hoped for. What the side needed was players with flair and imagination; confident footballers to supplement the goalscoring skill of experienced players such as David Kemp, who sadly left the club for Plymouth Argyle after just one full season as the main striker. It was rumoured that he was hugely disappointed that insufficient quality was being added to the squad.

Back in Moncur's native north east there was much in the way of new talent being discovered, though it has to be said that the likes of Newcastle United and Sunderland were creaming off the best of these players. So in 1979, when Moncur recruited the much-respected scout, Brian Watson to the Carlisle ranks, it was in the hope that he could persuade some of the youngsters to move to Brunton Park. Watson was very much involved at the famous Wallsend Boys club, along with his friend Peter Kirkley. One good example of how good these two men were in spotting and nurturing talent is that in recent years they produced the likes of Alan Shearer and Steve Bruce.

It didn't take long before Watson was in contact with the Carlisle boss advising him of a raw young talent playing at the Boys Club, who had been attracting the attention of other clubs, such as Burnley and Plymouth Argyle. Watson also explained that Newcastle were aware of the youngster's potential and were sniffing about, monitoring the situation. Moncur said he was interested and wanted to look at the lad, offering him a full game in a trial match against Blue Star the following Thursday. It looked as though the offer was too late, as the player at the same time received and accepted an offer from Geoff Allen, the youth coach at St James' Park, to work out with the youth team at the club's Benwell training ground. Brian Watson informed Moncur of the situation with the youngster and Newcastle, but the Carlisle boss wasn't about to be put off. He insisted that a place in the Carlisle team in the Blue Star game would be held open for the young lad should he change his mind.

On the Thursday morning (for the record, 8 August 1979), Watson received the call notifying him that the player was interested in turning out for Carlisle in the Blue Star friendly fixture which took place close to Newcastle airport. Introduced to his peers in the dressing room, the youngster looked every bit a confident footballer. Moncur himself elected to play in the game, which United won 3-2. But the result mattered little. Moncur and Watson knew they had unearthed a real gem. The youngster scored one of the United goals in the game, but it was his overall contribution and skill that caused Moncur to make an instant decision. As the Carlisle players and trialist relaxed in the privacy of an upstairs room at the Diamond pub in Ponteland, downstairs Moncur and Watson discussed offering the young lad a contract. Finally, the pair removed themselves to the upstairs room and it was a content Bobby Moncur who asked the youngster, Peter Beardsley, if he fancied signing for Carlisle United. The answer was instantaneous and positive. The following day, in the sanctuary of the Darlington manager's office (United were playing a friendly fixture there), Peter Beardsley signed a two year contract with Carlisle United, worth £60 a week.

Initially, reaction to the signing was muted, since nobody in Carlisle outside those who had seen him play at Blue Star and Darlington were aware of the youngster's pedigree and potential. Beardsley joined the club at the same time as Stan Gate, a young lad who never quite possessed the same ability as Peter. Curiously enough, Gate ended up leaving the playing side of the game, instead entering a career as a Football League official. As an assistant referee he has officiated at Brunton Park several times and covered Blues games frequently.

THE 1979/80 SEASON kicked off with an away game at Southend United, but things didn't go at all to plan for United. The game was lost 1-0, a Micky Tuohy strike sufficient to snuff out the Carlisle threat. Behind the scenes, main striker David Kemp was clearly rattled by rumours of other clubs' interest in his services. He had made it clear to the United management that he wanted away if the right club should come along. Speculation has it that Plymouth had in fact made an approach immediately prior to the season's start. Whatever, Kemp's performance that day gave the impression that he wasn't interested in playing for Blues. One can only feel for a manager with such a player in his ranks. Does he ignore the petulance and simply persevere or does he punish it? Moncur was his own man and wouldn't stand for childishness. Kemp was suitably omitted from the first team for two successive games, while the intricacies of a permanent transfer were discussed with Plymouth. Kemp was clearly on his way out and few supporters really cared about the loss of his services. He had a arrogant temperament and wasn't a fans sort of player or favourite. Despite this, he was an intelligent footballer and undoubtedly a first rate finisher in front of goal.

Elsewhere, while the first team were putting in a dismal performance at Southend, the reserves, under the guidance of ex-United keeper, Alan Ross, included in their line-up one Peter Beardsley. The fixture was a Lancashire League game against Wrexham at Brunton Park. Ross told me of his first insight and opinion of a raw Peter Beardsley. "I was told to look after him by Bob, nurture him and bring him on and through the ranks slowly. In the kickabout before the game he was quiet but full of confidence. I asked him if he was alright. He said he was a bit nervous and just wanted the game to start. I told him to do the easy things and not to try to be too flashy, always look for the easy option.

He was just a boy. I couldn't help but think about protecting him. I didn't want him kicked up in the air or anything like that – it could damage his confidence and future. When I got the team together in the dressing room before the kick-off I told him to go out and score goals. I told him that to score goals is the greatest thing you can do to build your reputation and confidence. I said to him that the boss would want to know how he got on, so if he could score a hat-trick that would be a good thing for me to be able to tell him. I also told him I would get him one of the new club jumpers as a reward if he did score three goals for us in the game.

When the game started he looked every bit the best player out there. His control of a football was something I hadn't seen the likes of for many years at Carlisle or anywhere else for that matter. The last player who could kill a speeding ball dead, control it and distribute it was Chris Balderstone. What I saw in Peter Beardsley was equally as exciting. He dominated the game, put everything into it. I had to remind him about stamina as he was chasing every ball, even back in defence!

Anyway, that night I made contact with Bobby Moncur and told him that the young Peter Beardsley had done alright. So much so that he had, indeed, scored a hat-trick! For a few seconds Bobby was speechless. He asked me if I thought he was good enough for the first team. I had no qualms in acknowledging that he was. Two days later Peter was in the starting XI for the home game against Blackburn Rovers. There was never any doubt in my mind that he was going to make it big in the game. He was so committed, so full of bounce, so full of enthusiasm. More importantly, he was down to earth and would help anyone, even the tea lady, if he felt she needed some assistance. It was a pleasure to work with him."

THE BRUNTON PARK FAITHFUL, this author amongst them, caught their first glimpse of a fresh-faced kid called Peter Beardsley on the evening of 21 August 1979, when he ran out against a physically tough Blackburn Rovers team. First impressions were that he didn't look like the world-class footballer that he was to become. He looked like a young boy playing a man's game. Within minutes he ended such thoughts, collecting a waist-high ball on the inside of his right thigh, dropped it to his feet, shimmied one way then the other, before rounding two players and delivering a perfect through ball to Hugh McAuley on the left wing. Everything seemed to come through him that evening. He was an instant success and the fans took to him immediately. More exciting was the prospect of him partnering and running off Paul Bannon. That evening, there was hardly anyone inside Brunton Park who missed the presence of David Kemp. Carlisle United fans had a new hero to worship, Peter Beardsley had arrived.

I didn't manage to get my first interview with the player for several weeks. Carlisle had Beardsley wrapped in cotton wool, treatment, I would suggest, which served him well in his future career. By the time I met with him he had continued to flourish and had even scored his first professional goal, against Chester. I wasn't expecting nor prepared for our meeting. I hadn't really too many questions to ask him. He had been consistent in his performances and was proving himself on the pitch in each game. As I sat in the Brunton Park reception area Beardsley suddenly arrived and I was introduced to the shy and very youthful player. I resolved to be informal and to chat about his life in football to that point.

"I really love football, playing is what it's all about," he told me. "I like it here. The manager has been great to me and so has everyone at the club. The other players tend to look out for me, look after me on the pitch, but I know it's a tough game and I am capable of looking after myself too. I think this is a good club and a nice city, I am looking forward to a long and happy future here.

I still have to pinch myself to make sure all this is happening. I am so lucky to be playing football for a living. It's a great feeling to run out in front of the fans each week. I remember the feeling I had when I scored my first goal against Chester a couple of weeks back. I wanted to shout and scream. It was like nothing I have felt before; pity we didn't win, mind. The one thing I have learned since signing for Carlisle is that in football you can't take anything for granted, which is why I appreciate being given the chance to play."

Unknown to anyone outside the club at that time was the fact that Moncur had taught the young player some tough football lessons. Having brought Beardsley into the first team, he dropped him for a fixture at Millwall, just when his confidence must have been growing. Thereafter the youngster made himself a virtual ever present in the United line-up through his tenacity and never-say-die spirit. Beardsley became a beacon of hope to the Brunton Park faithful, a role he fully embraced. Soon, before even the end of his first season, he was no longer the cheeky and impudent young footballer he'd initially been regarded as, but a mature and talented player.

Lifelong supporter of the Cumbrians, John Harrison, recalled his Peter Beardsley memories for me: "I remember all the disappointment of when we were relegated from the First Division, and the period after just seemed so glib. We had players like Billy Rafferty and Phil Bonnyman who provided some hope and good memories, but it was Peter Beardsley who I think really provided us with the stepping stone to launch ourselves back into a decent standard of football. Division Three football wasn't the best in the late seventies. Some big clubs were in there, but it was pretty much kick it and run football. We seemed to sign so many inept players who clearly weren't up to it, it came as a real shock to us all I think. Then, when Peter arrived, it [Brunton Park] just seemed a brighter place to go.

He had a certain style and way about him on the pitch, arrogant almost. He could change a game single-handedly, it was a real pity that he didn't have a couple of other players of such quality around him or we could have progressed through the league.

A couple of performances stick in my memory, one when we destroyed Workington in the FA Cup in 1980. In the first half we really weren't at the races and Workington looked like they were going to win it. The supporters were getting on the players' backs a bit and our nervousness was showing. Then Peter weaved, in that characteristic way of his, past three Reds defenders and fired home. It was the predecessor of all those cheeky dribbles we would grow to love during his time at the top of the game over the next 15 years of his career. He completely took control of the game from then on, chasing lost causes and making opportunities for himself and others. We finished up winning 4-1, Peter scoring twice, but it was very much his grafting which won us the contest.

The other game when I think he was at his brilliant best was against Plymouth Argyle in 1981. Little Gordon Staniforth actually scored a hat-trick in this game, but it was Peter Beardsley who was the outstanding player of the match. He made all Stan's goals and must have fired in 20 shots himself. He performed some on-the-ball tricks, nutmegs and even put a Plymouth defender on his arse by weaving round him three times and twisting him all over the place until he finally lost his balance. I don't think many Peter Beardsleys come round in one lifetime. He was an exceptional talent, but what made it even better was that he was OUR exceptional talent."

BY THE 1980/81 SEASON the newspapers were full of speculation as to who the player was going to leave Carlisle for. Manchester United were apparently keeping an eye on him, as were Liverpool, Everton and Tottenham Hotspur and just about every other major club in the land! With such an abundance of rumours in circulation, the end result is very often negative for the club who hold the player's contract. Week after week the Brunton Park main stand area was filled with high profile ex-players now acting as scouts for bigger clubs. It was clear who they were coming to watch. Beardsley. Offers were made, but drastically under market value for a footballer whose ability and class stood out among the majority of his peers.

When Vancouver Whitecaps scout, Peter Lorimer, was seen in the main stand one evening there was little in the way of interest. Why would a player of Peter Beardsley's ability leave the English game to play overseas? Yet it came true. Within weeks a deal had been struck with Vancouver, £275,000 plus a loan back deal during the close season. It was great business for Carlisle United AFC Ltd, but on the terraces the deal was met with much disappointment.

Beardsley was very much more than just another footballer who made the grade at Carlisle. He wasn't a journeyman looking to extend his career, nor a wannabe one game wonder desperate to make his mark and prove himself. Peter Beardsley was adopted by every Blues supporter. He was Brunton Park's favourite son. Someone we nurtured, cared for, winced for every time a clumsy opposition defender clattered into his tiny frame, someone we celebrated with at each point of his wonderful career, both at Brunton Park and after.

I don't know one supporter of Carlisle United who didn't feel a sense of pride when the player went onto bigger and better things, be it winning trophies at Liverpool or collecting international honours for his country. As the compliments on his ability expanded to worldwide circulation, we all recalled that it was at Brunton Park where that boy first learned his trade. I can still see him at Carlisle in my mind today, racing round in United blue, dictating the pace and style of a game, or finishing a move he started with a goal. No Carlisle player since has been afforded such heartfelt acclaim.

There has been speculation linking him with a return to the club, this time in a managerial role. Perhaps it is best that it remains idle speculation, as, for the Carlisle faithful, Peter Beardsley remains a paragon of virtue, a footballer who can do no wrong. Few players maintain such integrity and adulation having moved on from a club, thus Peter Beardsley holds a thoroughly unique honour.

Also unique about him is that Beardsley holds Cult Hero status at Carlisle, Newcastle, Liverpool, Everton, Bolton, Fulham, Hartlepool and very likely in Vancouver. I am sure that, unanimously, his name would be the first one every Blues supporter expected to see in this work. After all he merits it. My closing words on this absolute legend are a pertinent reminder to those who almost dismiss our club as being unimportant. Despite the likes of Sir Bobby Robson, Arthur Cox and co. staking their own claims as to finding and producing this pure diamond, it was actually Carlisle United and Bobby Moncur (not forgetting Brian Watson) who first provided Peter Beardsley with his professional opportunity in the game. So when the ex-England supremo Sir Bobby Robson refers to Beardsley as "my" little gem, sorry Sir Bobby, he is OUR little gem. Arthur Cox is, quite inappropriately in my opinion, often accredited to being first in identifying Beardsley's talents and trying to sign him from Blues for Newcastle, but claimed financial restrictions prevented him from doing so. The cheek of it. It's almost as though the role of Carlisle United in the progression of the player's career can be dismissed. The first time Cox knew of Beardsley was when he [Cox] was manager of Chesterfield. Surely, if he had his finger on the pulse, Cox would have snapped the young player up for the Spireites before Carlisle did? Reality being that Cox signed him from Vancouver AFTER his Carlisle career, so he played no part in unearthing the legend that is Peter Beardsley.

It cannot be denied that the player did learn a great deal after his time at Brunton Park, particularly at Liverpool, but it should never be forgotten that it was Carlisle United who took a chance on the young player. It was at Carlisle United where he first learned his trade and blossomed and not Newcastle or anywhere else.

One final point of note: during Peter's time at Carlisle, he met his wife, a Carlisle girl [then Sandra Devlin] who was also a member of the club's staff, evidence indeed (if there is any need to provide such) of Peter's links with the city and our wonderful football club.

JOHN HALPIN

'HALPS'

1984-1991

UNITED CAREER

Games	148+5
Goals	17

MAGIC MOMENT

Halps ran with the ball fully fifty yards, weaving in and out of the Blackburn defence before rolling it into the net in front of the Warwick Road end. The best goal ever seen at Brunton Park

AS a football club we have been blessed with more than our fair share of creative and intuitive dribblers, players who somehow seem to have the ball permanently fixed to their boot and whom no amount of kicking and harassing from defenders can dispossess. The one thing these players love is to run at defenders, turning them inside out, often gliding past them with ball at feet as though performing some surreal form of dance. Players who are a catalyst to an end product. Players who, on receiving the ball, create an air of positive anticipation and expectancy amongst the watching crowd.

Today, many managers and coaches still profess that the most difficult ball for defenders to deal with is the one cut back from the byline. At one time the players who practised this art were known as out-and-out wingers. They possessed pace and ball control and, more importantly, a direct mindedness to get behind their opponent and deliver the ball across the goal. Many fans claim that Billy Hogan or George McVitie are the finest wingers the club has had. Others claim that accolade should go to Frank Barton or Tommy Murray, both of whom could be equally as merciless and incisive with ball at feet. As good as those fabulous players were, one player, one winger seems to stand out above all others as an all-time great. A player whose maverick individuality could turn a game with a display of exquisite skill; a swerve of his hips, a drop of the head and he was off towards the opposition goal. John Halpin is the player who above so many others could raise the temperature inside the ground when he set off on one of his runs.

During my time researching and writing about the club I have heard no-one say a bad thing about John Halpin, either as a player or a person and, certainly, he has more than proven his loyalty to Carlisle in recent times with his football work in the community.

John was born in November 1961 in Armadale, a town situated about 20 miles west of Glasgow, which had expanded significantly in the middle of the nineteenth century, mainly due to the extra demand for coal and ironstone. There was a recorded population in 1841 of 121, but by 1861 this had grown to 2,500. As was the case in so many rural areas of Scotland, football was an extremely popular pastime and sport. This was reflected in Armadale itself by the existence of a number of junior teams. Armadale Star had for many years been the primary club in the town. It was they who first played their games at a ground known as Volunteer Field. This later became Volunteer Park, home to Armadale Thistle, and the ground where a young John Halpin first displayed his undoubted football talent.

As a young player he shone in schoolboy football and, like most of the other top talent in the area, was quickly snapped up by Celtic Boys club. He then moved to Armadale Thistle, who, it should be said, are a well respected junior side who are renowned for producing some quite prodigious talent over the years, including players who went on to become full internationals such as John Walker 1895-1904 (5 caps Scotland), Willie Robb 1926-1928 (2 caps Scotland), George Farm (at Blackpool) 1953-1959 (10 caps Scotland), Jackie Plenderleith (Manchester City) 1961 (1 cap Scotland), Colin Stein (Rangers) 1969-1973 (21 caps Scotland)

and Joe Baker (Nottingham Forest & Sunderland) 1960-1967 (8 caps for England). Whilst working as an apprentice joiner and playing football part-time, John found himself in some demand. In 1978 Hibernian offered him a trial. Shortly after he returned from this, on 5 September 1978, Celtic signed him on professional terms. Soon he was playing for Celtic reserves, alongside players such as Pat Bonner, Paul McStay and Charlie Nicholas. On 8 May 1979 he made an appearance in Celtic's 3-2 Glasgow Cup defeat of Clyde. In July 1980 he was drafted into the Celtic first team pre-season tour of Holland and Germany and produced some tantalising performances which saw him ensconce himself as an integral part of the first team options. Despite this, he had to wait until January 1982 before making his full debut for the Celts at Parkhead in a Scottish cup tie against Queen of the South which was comfortably won 4-0. Also tasting first-team action for the first time that day was Paul McStay. A certain John Halpin tapping home Celtic's fourth goal of the game and later recalled: "I remember all the noise as I walked down the tunnel... for Paul McStay and myself it was the biggest day of our lives. When I scored, yes it was a tap in, but I didn't care whether it was from one yard or thirty, it was still a fantastic feeling to score."

Despite this, competition for places at Celtic was vast and John couldn't manage to claim a regular first team berth. A loan spell to South China in May 1983 saw him try to gain more experience for himself and appeared to have given him some confidence in the goal scoring department. During the following 1983/84 season, he scored 18 goals in 27 games for Celtic reserves. At the beginning of the following season there was a brief loan spell at Sunderland, before he moved to Brunton Park, actually signing for the club on 24 October 1984. He told the author in a 1984 interview the reason why he opted to come to Carlisle: "I had worked hard at Celtic, but for one reason or another I just wasn't able to do myself justice and make the first team regularly. It was then that I was told that Carlisle manager Bob Stokoe had made enquiries about taking me there. In September his assistant, Bryan 'Pop' Robson came up to watch me in a reserve game. He must have been impressed because he recommended me to Bob. To be honest I wanted to play regular first team football. I had been given a taste at Celtic and I was hooked and wanted more. I came down to chat with him and he assured me it was the right move for me so here I am. This is a decent-sized club and I believe I have made a great career move coming here."

John made his first team debut at Brunton Park in a forgettable 0-1 league defeat to Huddersfield Town. There followed another appearance, this time in a disappointing 1-1 draw with Leeds United at Elland Road. It was during this fixture that he showed why Bob Stokoe had signed him. Out wide he consistently gave Leeds defenders Denis Irwin and Gary Hamson a torrid time, taking them on and often leaving them kicking at thin air as he whipped the ball past them in pursuit of a goal or a cross. It wasn't long before he had big centre-back Andy Linighan trying to kick him up in the air too, but the skilful new signing out-manoeuvred all such attempts and was already being noted by the gentlemen of the English media. Jim Nicholson, a Leeds-based freelance journalist, told me after that game: "Halpin looks a good prospect. He's quick and agile and clever, reminds me a bit of Eddie Gray in his heyday."

Rich praise indeed and there were countless others too who admired Stokoe's skill in identifying exceptional talent and bringing it to Brunton Park. As a supporter at the game I remember feeling disappointed that we hadn't won, but excited by the prospect of what we had found in John Halpin. I hadn't seen anyone in a Carlisle shirt look so comfortable with a ball at his feet since Peter Beardsley had left. And in fact to me, Halpin was a far more exciting proposition.

Sadly, in just his third appearance for the club, at Cardiff City, he received an elbow to the face. The blow was so ferocious that it broke his cheekbone and effectively ruled him out for almost a two month period. Returning to action on Boxing Day and a 0-3 home defeat to Middlesbrough, Halpin struggled to hit form and, despite scoring his debut goal for the club a few weeks later at Fulham, it was a season of trials and tribulations for the player. "My wife and family were still up in Scotland when I signed for Carlisle," he told me. "The injury didn't help with me settling in the city, but Bob Stokoe was great. He really helped me and my family settle down and assured me he would keep me in line for first team football as long as I showed a desire for it. Bob was an old school-type of manager. He had a great knowledge of football and knew his staff inside out. I learned a lot from him. He realised that the English game was a lot different to the Scottish game I had been used to. That awareness helped me a lot too."

The following 1985/86 season was, by his own opinion, his best ever in football. The supporters had taken to a player who had provided them with glimpses of real skill, a talent which excited them and got them talking about how good he could become. If the previous season had only provided the odd snap of his potential, then this season was to provide concrete evidence that the player was outstanding in all areas. Yet he was omitted from the first game of the season, with an arrogant young winger called Mark Gavin taking the outside-left slot in the United line-up. Stokoe told me that he regretted bringing Gavin, who he had signed from Leeds, to Brunton Park. "Mark Gavin was a footballer who had ability and pace, but he wasn't the right player to bring to Carlisle. Some players just can't perform at some clubs, Mark was a mistake. I didn't make many in my career, but he was one of them. I grew to dislike his attitude. He wasn't a patch on Johnny Halpin either as a player or a person."

Stokoe, by his own admission, had made a mistake in dropping Halpin. He soon reinstated him, for the next game in fact, a 3-3 draw at Crewe Alexandria. It was soon after this game that Stokoe announced his retirement from the game and told his players that Bryan 'Pop' Robson was to be his replacement. The new manager told Halpin to go out and express himself, and to enjoy the game whenever he played. It wasn't to last long for, within a few weeks, Pop, unable to take the pressure, resigned.

Brimming with confidence and now with an ability to score goals too, Halpin prospered. Stokoe returned to manage the team and dispensed with a lot of the dead wood which had been brought to the club; players like portly goalkeeper Kevin Carr. Out went Mark Gavin and Wayne Entwistle too. Stokoe replaced them with younger, more astute talent such as striker Rob Wakenshaw, who came in on loan from Everton and goalkeeper Scott Endersby from Swindon Town. More pertinent for Halpin was the permanent acquisition of a talented midfielder from Sheffield Wednesday in the form of John Cooke. Cooke was a gifted player who complemented Halpin's style. With as creative a midfield as any United side has ever fielded, John Halpin began to enjoy the freedom his play so richly deserved.

Without doubt, Halpin played his best football during this period and was time and again voted Man of the Match. From the terraces, supporters chanted his name and in the media there was speculation; desperately woeful speculation so far as fans of Carlisle United were concerned. He was soon being singled out as one of the most exciting players in the then

Second Division and clubs were monitoring him game by game. Every day there seemed to be another team interested in signing Halpin. Middlesbrough and Sunderland were but two clubs apparently 'closely monitoring' the situation.

THEN IT HAPPENED – Saturday 18 January 1986 – the day John Halpin transformed from plain hero to one of the great Cult Heroes. Blackburn Rovers were the visitors to Brunton Park that day. The Lancashire side weren't the greatest of footballing clubs, regarded by many as kickers and spoilers. Some may say that things haven't changed. Anyway, both clubs that day were fighting for points to pull them away from the relegation zone. It was United who won the contest, 2-1, a fair result on the day. It wasn't the result that had everyone at the game talking, even the Blackburn fans were provoked into after match discussions. The focus of all this chatter was the scoring of what is perhaps the greatest goal in Carlisle United's history.

The myth that has subsequently been created about this one strike is of urban legend proportions. I can only retell it as I remember seeing it as a supporter stood in the Scratching Shed side of the ground. With United attacking the Warwick Road End, John Halpin collected the ball in his own half. He was but a few feet from where I stood adjacent with the half-way line. The Blackburn defender that day had been run ragged. He was visibly wilting each time John ran at him. In an attempt to compensate for this, Rovers had dropped a couple of players into the right side of midfield to protect the defence from his divisive runs into their territory.

Pushing the ball forward, Halpin rounded one defender, then a second before cutting inside another. His way towards the Blackburn goal was blocked by a wall of Blackburn players keen to knock him off the ball. Weaving his way back outside onto the left wing, he calmly cut back inside the defence. I swear Brunton Park stood silent, in awe of what it was witnessing. With the ball still at his feet, almost rhythmically he moved from side to side, leaving Blackburn players in his wake. Then suddenly he was confronted by the giant of a goalkeeper. Now at this point, most players would slam the ball as hard as they could towards goal, not John Halpin. No, he had the coolness and confidence to stop, throw experienced keeper Tony Gennoe a dummy, before calmly rolling the ball beneath him and into the net.

Brunton Park erupted. If a player had ever received a standing ovation from all sides of the ground then it happened that day. Blackburn were single-handedly destroyed by Halpin. Although Andy Hill was also on the score sheet it is destined to be regarded as Halpin's game. Each time he got the ball thereafter he ran at Blackburn, with the fans screaming out: "Skin him, John!" and the player smiling and thoroughly enjoying the freedom he created for himself. I think it worth mentioning for the record books the identity of the Blackburn defenders who were torn apart by John that day; Derek Fazackerley was the centre-back who couldn't get near him. Then there was the vastly experienced defender Jim Branagan, who just happened to be the poor soul tormented relentlessly by the taunting feet of the United winger, along with Mike Rathbone, who was his young counterpart in defence. Interestingly, up front for Blackburn that day was one Simon Garner, father of recent United favourite, Joe Garner, who himself scored a spectacular goal for United at Port Vale during the 2006/07 season.

IT WAS AFTER THIS game that rumours abounded about a possible transfer of the United star. Liverpool, it was said, would be making a bid for him before the end of the season. Everton and Newcastle were said to be interested too. The fans were resigned to the fact that a player of his ability could not dwell in the lower reaches of the Second Division. Here was a superstar in the making, a footballer who would without doubt, prove himself far superior in all round skill and ability to Peter Beardsley.

Tragedy then struck. During a 3-1 away victory at Middlesbrough in April 1986, Boro full-back Brian Laws clattered into Halpin in a challenge for the ball. Always a fair player, Laws had not meant to cause any injury to the United star, but like so many other defenders who'd faced Halpin that season, he was frustrated at being given a real roasting. Halpin did not realise at first that his leg had, in fact, been broken. "I knew it was badly injured because it hurt when I tried to stand up. I came back to Carlisle with the team that evening and went straight up to the hospital for an x-ray. They told me immediately that it was broken." The injury was to keep him out of action for six months.

It was midway through the following season before he returned to action. United had been relegated with many attributing this to the loss of Halpin for key games. Now in the Third Division, Carlisle were struggling both on and off the field. Bob Stokoe had again retired and been replaced by the well-respected Harry Gregg. With United desperate to succeed, John was drafted back into first team action too early. Ten games later in January 1987, his leg was again broken, this time in a Freight Rover Trophy tie with Preston North End.

It was a devastating blow for the player. The fans and the club, including yet another new manager, Clive Middlemass, stood by him throughout his awful spell of injuries and, almost a year later, he returned to first team action in an away fixture with Swansea. Over the next 12 months Halpin's form returned, although he was never the sparkling performer he had been. Yet despite this, clubs at a higher level continued to monitor his performances.

At an away league fixture at Rochdale on 25 November 1989 he suffered yet another blow to his career. "I somehow managed to dislocate my ankle and break the leg again," Halpin said. "I was in awful pain. The specialist told me after that third break that at best it was 50-50 whether I would be able to play again. I was upset and ready to call it a day, I have never been as low as I was then."

As incredible as it seems, John Halpin returned from this third leg break to play professional football again, this time though, not with Carlisle United. He was released by the club in July 1991 and moved to Rochdale to play out the last throws of his career. Maintaining his roots in Carlisle, he opted to travel up and down the motorway to the Spotland club. The journey isn't an easy one and eventually took its tiring toll and caused him to announce his retirement as a professional player. After a brief stint at Gretna, the highlight of which was an FA Cup encounter with Bolton Wanderers, John finally packed up playing the game he loved so much.

IT WASN'T, HOWEVER, too long before he was back at Brunton Park, this time working as Football in the Community Officer for the club. Completing his full coaching badge in 1998, he has been an asset to the club ever since. Indeed, during a time of crisis he shone like a beacon, his honesty and integrity being an example that helped keep the playing side of things firmly focused.

John Halpin remains part of Carlisle United to this day, genuine and bona fide evidence that loyalty still exists in a modern game which at certain levels is said to be filled with greed and avarice. A true ambassador for the club he continues to extol the virtues of Carlisle United to youngsters and schools throughout the county. He takes time to talk to fans and is forever a true blue. If there is a modern day 'Mr Carlisle United' then John Halpin is that man, a god, a legend, a hero, a cult hero. More than anything else, John Halpin is the man that scored THAT GOAL!

MALCOLM POSKETT

'SUPER MALLY'

1982-1985
1986-1988

UNITED CAREER

Games	175+11
Goals	60

MAGIC MOMENT

Mally destroyed Crystal Palace single-handedly. He was better than any Brazilian that day, scoring four goals

WHAT links Elton John, Watford and Carlisle United? No, I'm not thinking of the recent concert that was held at Brunton Park. No, it isn't feisty little striker Rod Thomas who was a big hit at Carlisle in the 1990s. My answer to this question pre-dates both these connections. My answer is Malcolm Poskett.

Malcolm or Mally, as he became more affectionately known by the Brunton Park faithful, will never know the adulation this author and many others once held him in. Sure, we had heard of him before he joined Carlisle, after all he had played in a decent Watford side alongside the likes of Ross Jenkins and emerging Nigel Callaghan and the infamous Steve Harrison of sitting on a wardrobe fame. Before that he had played for Brighton and Hove Albion, which was where I first heard of him, playing alongside footballers like Mark Lawrenson. Mally, you see, was known as an adept scorer of goals. Not simple taps in the Gary Lineker mould, but goals from all over the park, coming from both feet and very often from his head too, but more of that later.

There are those who claim that Mally in his heyday was a dead ringer for the spaghetti western actor Lee Van Cleef. Poskett too was tall, lean, brave, very brave in fact, especially when there was a goal to be scored. It was then that he possessed nerves of steel. Yet, more interestingly, just like Van Cleef, he wore a suave and distinctive, and dare I say, distinguished-looking drooping moustache. That moustache was to become synonymous with Poskett almost as much as the wonderful goals he scored. It somehow gave him the edge over his competitors. Hell, that tash was special, so special that I grew one myself. I still have it in fact. In honour of Mal!

To be less light-hearted about matters, Poskett was undoubtedly a goalscorer supreme, not only at Carlisle but wherever he played. At United he joined a side which was going through a period of transformation, yet, in what must have been difficult circumstances, Mally proved himself to be a gifted and talented footballer; from a Cult Heroes perspective, a true crowd pleaser. His finishing was at times instinctive and sublime. He can be best described as a warrior who led the front line by example, never saying never and giving everything for the team.

THE FOOTBALL STORY OF Mally Poskett begins in Middlesbrough on 19 July 1953, his birth date. Growing up in the Teesside region as a young footballer Poskett made his mark first with North Riding Schools, then in the Teesside Leagues with Acklam Steel Works where his consistency in front of goal saw him move to Northern League outfit, South Bank FC in the 1972/73 season. A plater by trade, he was a prolific goalscorer at local non-league level. In one appearance for South Bank he fired five goals against Stanley United, scoring all five with his head!

It was a display in a 3-2 defeat in the Northern League by Middlesbrough reserves, during which the striker scored twice, that caused Boro to sign him. The transfer cost? A donation of just £100 made to South Bank. It wasn't a great time for the player as the club's management was in fiasco mode, Stan Anderson departing in December 1972 and no permanent replacement seemingly forthcoming. Left to languish in the reserves, and having made just one first team appearance as substitute at Ayresome Park, it became clear that his future lay away from Middlesbrough. It wasn't long before he was released and accepted a move to Hartlepool United, where again he wasn't given an opportunity to prove himself by manager Len Ashurst and he found himself playing much of his football in the reserve side which, to be fair, were of lesser quality than South Bank FC.

The situation wasn't good, though his self belief remained intact. Poskett took the brave decision to turn his back on the professional game and left the Victoria Ground to sign for non-league Whitby Town in April 1973. Whilst concurrently working in the oil industry, at Whitby he made a real name for himself, scoring 90 goals in two seasons, form which soon attracted Football League clubs, including, you guessed it, Hartlepool United. So, Malcolm returned to the Victoria Ground for the cost of a set of new first team strips, going straight into the first team where he scored 20 goals in 51 games in the Fourth Division. After two outstanding seasons at Hartlepool, finishing as top scorer in the 1976/77 season and also being voted as supporters' Player of the Year, Poskett had clearly turned himself into an asset United could make money from.

Alan Mullery, then manager of Brighton and Hove Albion, moved to bring Poskett south in a £60,000 transfer in February 1978. It was to be the highest fee Hartlepool would receive for a player for over a decade. On his Brighton debut Poskett scored at Hull City, but Seagulls fans recall most fondly the day he destroyed Charlton Athletic at The Valley, scoring a hat-trick. The Brighton fans were in good voice around that day and chanted "P-O-S-K-E-T-T, Poskett, Poskett" for most of the game! As is the case wherever he has played, Mally provided satchels full of good memories for the Brighton supporters, who might have hoped he'd spend a little longer on the south coast. After two good seasons at the Goldstone Ground during which he helped them to promotion to the First Division in 1979, however he fell out of favour with boss Alan Mullery, who had, it was claimed, simply brought him in as a stopgap for the injured Teddy Maybank. Whatever it was that caused the disruption, the writing was clearly on the wall. Matters came to a head when the manager made it perfectly clear that he no longer saw Poskett as a first team option and duly signed Ray Clarke from Bruges for a reported £200,000. Money not well spent one has to say! Clarke managed just eight goals in 30 games for Brighton. Mally's continued work rate mattered little to his manager. He was now a fringe player.

Two months later Poskett moved on, this time to Watford for a fee of around £110,000. Graham Taylor, their manager, said of the signing: "Malcolm Poskett is a proven goal scorer, the type of player I like. He will do a great job for us." He did too, for a while at least. Sadly, due to illness and injury he was unable to fulfil his full potential at Vicarage Road. Yet, despite his setbacks, he did continue to score goals; 17 from 63 league outings isn't a bad return by any standards.

His striking partner at Watford, Ross Jenkins was a solid and experienced professional. Playing alongside him allowed Poskett the freedom to develop his game and to become an all-round better player. Soon, dribbling and calculated running became a natural part of his game. Those attributes made him all the more effective. It is often said that when fans sing derogatory chants about an opposition player, it is because they see him as a threat. Mally became an object of Chelsea fans' displeasure after he humiliated their goalkeeper Petar Borota in a February 1981 league encounter. Borota, as might be recalled, was something of an eccentric, confident and at times plain foolish keeper. On this day Borota had dribbled the ball fully 30 yards from his goal and was teasing the Watford forwards. Poskett could see that Borota was in fact beginning to panic, the Chelsea players and management were screaming for him to clear the ball and he wasn't aware of the impending danger that loomed. Poskett, quick as a flash, moved forward and tackled the unsuspecting goalkeeper, dispossessing him. He ran forward, leaving the Yugoslavian in his wake and calmly stroked home the only goal of the game. The Chelsea fans booed, hissed and called him all the names they could muster; and that was just Borota. Imagine, then, what they called Poskett!

DESPITE THE FACT THAT Watford fans held him in some reverence, Poskett left the club shortly after they had won promotion to the First Division; the second such achievement of Poskett's career. This coincided with a time when one Elton John was ploughing wheelbarrow loads of cash into Watford in an attempt to invigorate the club's fortunes. Mally was expendable and was now on the open market. It was 1982 and Graham Taylor who, two seasons earlier, had hailed the arrival of Poskett now opted to cash him in.

It wasn't a high profile transfer, but Carlisle boss Bob Stokoe somehow managed to jump ahead of a few other clubs, such as Hull City, Grimsby Town and Darlington all of whom wanted the services of the lean striker. It was Stokoe who struck the deal with his Watford counterpart, and snapped him up for a bargain £20,000 in August 1982. The player joined around the same time as another striker who was to make a huge impact at the club, Alan Shoulder. Both hailed from the north east and both were very keen to carve a good name for themselves in the annals of Brunton Park history.

Now 29, Poskett took over the No. 9 shirt from Bryan 'Pop' Robson. He quickly settled into the side and scored on his debut, a 3-0 away win at Derby County. The Shoulder/Poskett partnership had looked good in the season's opening fixture. Mally Poskett was now a name on every Carlisle supporter's lips.

The transition from player to cult hero status wasn't long in coming and Poskett, no doubt, took double satisfaction from a result whereby he rubbed one of his previous managers' noses in it. On 18 September 1982 Malcolm Poskett single-handedly demolished Alan Mullery's Crystal Palace side at Brunton Park, scoring all four Carlisle goals in the 4-1 rout. Bob Stokoe said of the performance: "I've never had any affection for a big name manager who has no right to be in such a position. Alan Mullery to my mind was a lucky man to manage a club as big as Crystal Palace. He was a top footballer, but as a manager he still had a lot to learn. Malcolm really taught him a football lesson that day. It was as brilliant an individual performance from a footballer that I can recall. The goal where he managed to backheel the ball over his head and into the net was fantastic, all but Brazilian in its execution. He had the Midas touch that day, but then that's what I knew he was capable of when I signed him. He was a clever footballer."

United fans still talk about those goals to this day, but more was to come from the player. The start of the 1983/84 season was hardly inspiring, no goals had been scored in the opening four league fixtures, then in a crazy three day spell in October 1983 it all happened. Malcolm Poskett became the first ever Carlisle player to score four goals away from home in a Football League fixture, as Derby County were thrashed 4-1 at the Baseball Ground. After the game, Poskett was almost apologetic about his performance. "Today was one of those days when it all goes right," he said. "I am a bit disappointed to be honest because I missed easier chances than I scored. As a striker you want to put away every chance. Derby were shambolic. I was expecting a real battle today, instead they went down without a fight. You just don't expect to see a club as big as Derby County capitulate like that. I really enjoyed it out there."

It goes without saying that Derby's defence was awful on the day, but that's not to take anything away from United and Poskett. This was a Rams team full of internationals, Archie Gemmill, John Robertson and Dave Watson to name three. Then there were up and coming stars like Bobby Davison, Bobby Campbell and goalkeeper Steve Cherry. Further, they were managed by none other than Brian Clough's ex-right hand man, Peter Taylor. Essentially Derby had ploughed lots of money into trying to buy success for the Baseball Ground, yet the two things they had not accounted for were poor management decisions and ineffective transfer activity. This meant that they were a team without leadership, a club spiralling out of control. Worse still, they were fast becoming the whipping boys of the league.

It was Derby's first home League defeat of 1983, albeit the week earlier, Simon Garner had scored five against them for Blackburn at Ewood Park. This time the defeat was not accepted as easily and local newspaper the *Argus* rather disparagingly claimed: 'It could hardly have been a more shattering defeat because Carlisle are an ordinary side.'

Matters were made worse by the fact that Carlisle fielded three former Derby players in their line-up, goalkeeper Dave McKellar, defender Don O'Riordan, who came to Carlisle by way of Tulsa Roughnecks and Preston North End, and finally Andy Hill, who had signed for Blues for £15,000 less than a fortnight earlier.

So, unbeknown to anyone at the time, the scene was set for a real upset. Pre-match media comments centred on Derby making amends for the woeful defeat the previous week. It took just 11 minutes for Poskett to silence the home fans when a through ball from Tommy Craig caught Cherry and Watson in limbo. Watson stuck out a toe and knocked the ball past his stranded keeper leaving Mally with the simple task of running the ball into an empty net. The second, after 26 minutes, came about as a result of good work by Alan Shoulder, who dispossessed Futcher and centred to give Poskett a free header.

After 72 minutes, with Poskett wreaking havoc, he poked in a rebound for his hat-trick. Incredibly United had scored only twice in their previous seven games. Rampant, every United player galloped forward and tried their hand at scoring as Moore then hit the bar. In the closing stages, with Derby piling forward and even missing a penalty, Poskett received a ball on the half-way line and ran at the Derby defence, twisting one way then another before shooting home his fourth goal.

Derby boss Peter Taylor, interviewed after the game, was clearly a man lost at sea: "Any team managed by Bob Stokoe is going to be resilient. They were very lucky today to beat us. Had we taken our chances we could have scored a couple more goals. Our players need time to settle in. It's our first home defeat and it hurts. Time will tell and we will be pushing for a top six place by the end of the season, Carlisle will be struggling to avoid relegation. I thought Poskett was lucky to score at all today and Andy Hill was hardly in it at all."

The fact that Andy Hill went close several times, including hitting a post, and was provider of one of Mally's goals seemed to have bypassed Peter Taylor's match summary. Poskett himself had missed a couple of other chances to enhance the Carlisle lead. Further, even if Derby had scored a couple more goals they would have still lost. Taylor seems to have missed the fact that Poskett and Carlisle had scored four! Bob Stokoe, meanwhile, was rather more gracious, saying: "Bloody fantastic. I thought each and every one of my players was outstanding. Young Andy Hill gave them a torrid time and Malcolm Poskett was at his usual lethal best. Derby don't look like a good side to me. It says it all that their manager has completely ignored me today. I'm satisfied with the win."

Three days later, Football League leaders, Southampton, who had so far been unbeaten and hadn't conceded a goal, arrived at Brunton Park for a second round League Cup tie. Managed by Lawrie McMenemy, the Saints were flying high. In goal for them, Peter Shilton was enjoying some of the best form of his career. This truly was a test of Carlisle's character. Once again it was Mally Poskett who stole the headlines, grabbing a brace as United cruised to a comfortable 2-0 victory. McMenemy, one of the game's gentlemen, raved about the Carlisle performance. "I knew Malcolm Poskett would be a threat," he said. "I told my players before they left the dressing room not to give him any space on the pitch or in the area. He was the difference between the two teams tonight. That's six goals in two games he's scored for Carlisle now. That tells you how good a player he is. I haven't seen my defence look as worried about a player so far this season. He's a typical north-eastern striker, devastating in front of goal."

POSKETT TOPPED THE Carlisle scoring chart for that season once again before things took a decided turn for the worse during the following campaign. There was a lack of quality arriving at Brunton Park as part of Bob Stokoe's summer squad building. Less than average players such as Garry MacDonald, Dave McAughtrie and Steve Tupling were hardly likely to set the division on fire and were less than inspiring to the club's support. Despite this somewhat turbulent spell in his Brunton Park career, Poskett still led the front line and scored plenty of goals. However, no-one can blame him for being disappointed with the overall calibre of player coming into the club, although the arrival of three decent players in the form of Ian Bishop, John Cooke and John Halpin did steady the ship for the remainder of the season.

By now it seemed clear that Poskett was not part of the club's future plans and much to the shock of the supporters, he was allowed to leave, moving to Stockport County. It was clear Poskett hadn't wanted to move on, but he accepted the transfer with some dignity. His stay at Edgeley Park was short-lived and a loan spell at previous stomping ground, Hartlepool United, quickly followed. But then, joyous news, Malcolm Poskett returned to Brunton Park in the 1987/88 season, brought back by new boss Clive Middlemass. Awarded a hero's welcome on his return, Poskett rewarded the manager's faith by becoming the season's top scorer with 12 goals.

It was to be Poskett's last season with the club as he retired from playing aged just 34. During this time there was also a brief spell as caretaker-manager, after the departure of Middlemass, before he finished with the professional game. He then played for spells at Morecambe, Workington and Cleator Moor Celtic before, at the age of 36, hanging up his boots for good and leaving the game behind to earn a living selling cars in Carlisle.

There are supporters at Morecambe who believe Poskett could have played on for a couple more seasons. Such was his level of fitness and commitment to the game they grasped an immediate affinity for him. Before he passed away, Bob Stokoe described Poskett as: "a modern-day Derek Dougan, a unique brand of footballer with drive and determination, strong and with an appetite to score as many goals as he could."

Mally was someone who could communicate with supporters not only by speaking but by the international language of football, where scoring goals is a form of art. What Bob didn't say was, that just like Derek Dougan, Mally also sported a smashing tash!

STEPHANE POUNEWATCHY

1996-1998

UNITED CAREER

Games 103
Goals 5

MAGIC MOMENT

Strutting around the Wembley pitch as though it was his own. Colchester could do nothing to get past him. He was magnificent as United lifted silverware under the Twin Towers

'THE GALLIC GIANT'

BOTH on and off the pitch, football clubs need leaders. Individuals who possess that special something, the instinct and awareness to make them that bit different, to cause them stand out above their contemporaries. After a woeful season in Division Two (now renamed League One) in 1995/96, which had ended so cruelly with Carlisle occupying the final relegation spot, United were back trading their wares amongst the basement clubs. Coach Mick Wadsworth had left to pursue a career elsewhere in the game, which would take him via Newcastle to Congo and finally to Gretna. The Wadsworth departure allowed United to promote from within and appoint Mervyn Day as first team manager. It was his first managerial appointment and Day was to prove without doubt a coach/manager with great foresight and tactical ability. He quickly built an excellent reputation for himself, sufficient to be regarded as one of the top young managerial talents in the English game.

Disillusioned by some of the abject performances from the United team of that relegation season, Day resolved to rebuild Wadsworth's team. During the summer transfer scramble leading up to the 1996/97 season he was keen to bring in the right calibre of player to enhance the side. His main priority was to shore up the defence and to transform it into a formidable and resilient rearguard. He had seen one of his previous managers, Howard Wilkinson, then at Leeds United, build a team capable of becoming Football League champions by building a defence fit for purpose. Day had played in a Leeds side that had some of the toughest and hardest defenders in the game within its ranks. Defenders who when mentioned would cause the hardest of strikers to wince at the thought of doing battle against them. Players such as Vinnie Jones, Chris Fairclough and Noel Blake were not blessed with bagfuls of skill, they weren't there to play pretty football or to spray the ball all over the pitch. No, they were there with one aim in mind, to stop opposing players playing and scoring against them. These were footballers who, if we're being honest, lacked many qualities, but what they all did have in abundance was passion and a desire to win at all costs. These were players who wouldn't always go the for the ball. No, if they couldn't get that then it was their purpose to stop the opposition dead in their tracks and if that meant kicking a player into the stands then so be it.

So it was in August 1996 that Day proudly announced the capture of an unheard of French defender called Stephane Pounewatchy. Outside of France the player had not created an international stir. In fact most people who heard about the signing dismissed it as another average foreign import trying to break into the English game. United fan Dave Brown recalls: "As a supporter of Carlisle United, it was a really depressing time. Mick [Wadsworth] had left us in the lurch the previous season by clearing off to Norwich, where he was a miserable flop. Mervyn Day had been moved up from within the club to replace him. Sad thing was, Mervyn had to take the blame for us being relegated, but it wasn't actually his fault. It was down to the fact that the club didn't invest in the team and we were fielding, at times, second rate players who weren't up to it. There were some concerns that we would flounder in Division Three and that, again, no money would be invested in the team. When it was announced that we had signed Stephane Pounewatchy it never really had any impact on the supporters. Most of us honestly thought: 'who the hell is that we've signed now?'"

STEPHANE POUNEWATCHY WAS born in Paris on 10 February 1962. He was the youngest of three brothers and two sisters and excelled in what he loved best, school sports. Like so many youngsters he enjoyed nothing more than playing football with his older brothers and by the age of six he was competing as a midfielder in the junior leagues of the French capital. A strong and athletically built youngster, he was good in the air and quick on the ground. Further, he could shrug off the challenge of most strikers which made a role in central defence seem an obvious conclusion for his natural talent. Yet somehow he found himself consistently assigned to midfield roles.

At the age of just 15, he signed schoolboy forms with a Paris-based league side and a professional career in the game became a reality. Just over 12 months later young Stephane found himself being invited to sign for the then French First Division club side Sedan, a club based in northern France. Discussions were held with his family and the move was agreed, and so at the age of 16, Stephane Pounewatchy made his bow in the French league.

Two years later he hadn't really progressed as he would have liked at Sedan. His father, keen that Stephane should have as many options in life open to him as possible, guided his son towards academic qualifications. Football was and remains a tough career. Despite the riches on offer to those who do make it, only the very best earn sufficient to retire in comfort in their mid-thirties.

Respecting his father's judgement, Stephane left the professional game and Sedan, returning to college to complete his schooling. He still found time to play part-time football as and when he could in and around Lyon. With academic qualifications achieved, Stephane sought a career as a professional footballer as the break from the game had not doused his flame. He sat down with his parents to consider his options and was thrilled to learn that his father would now support whatever decision he made in his professional life. So came about his love affair with Football Club de Martigues.

THE FRANCIS TURCAN STADIUM, home ground of FC Martigues, has a capacity of just 15,000. Although it was rarely filled during the early years of Stephane's career there, the club played some good football and were generally competing for promotion to the French Premier League. He soon found himself offered an extension to the three year contract he had originally signed. Few footballers at any level find themselves on six year contracts, but such was the esteem that FC Martigues held for the strong central defender, who was adored by fans of the club, that he was offered such a stay. By 1994, he was captain of the team and it was no coincidence that Martigues won promotion to the Premier league.

The inaugural season in the Premier league was not the greatest for Stephane. He managed just 12 appearances and a further three as substitute. Injuries and competition for first team places meant that every player had to be consistently at the top of their game. That aside, the personal high point for him as a player that season was scoring the winning goal in a 1-0 home victory against Girondins de Bordeaux, regular competitors in the Champions League. FC

Martigues, meanwhile, finished the season in a very respectable 11th position. The step up to Premier league football where he was playing against the likes of Youri Djorkaeff, Lilian Thuram, Bixente Lizarazu, George Weah and Christophe Dugarry was tough, but Stephane and his colleagues were up to the challenge and fared well against such exalted company.

FC Martigues coach, Rene Exbrayat, was slow in offering his captain a new contract. Realising that his time at the club looked over, Stephane considered his options. He didn't have too long to ponder his future as newly promoted Premier league side FC Gueugnon offered him a one year contract. FC Gueugon had won promotion by virtue of finishing in third place the previous season behind Olympique Marseille and Guingamp, but many regarded them as the best side in the Second Division that season. Hence the acquisition of Pounewatchy in central defence would further help their progress and desire to remain alongside the French footballing elite. Unfortunately, the club couldn't sustain its success in the top flight. Injuries ravaged the team and there were insufficient funds being ploughed back into the team to allow cover. The end result, despite some encouraging late season form, was relegation, by just one point.

That brought about a rethink of the club's strategy and so, after one season, Stephane Pounewatchy was released. FC Bastia showed some interest in acquiring his signature, but by now, the player had his mind set on higher aspirations. He wanted to move out of the French game altogether and try his luck in Britain, with the challenge of a new culture and environmental changes. Southend United were one of the first clubs to offer him a contract. However, discussions between the player's agent and manager, Ronnie Whelan, broke down. It was then that his agent, through contacts, learned of Carlisle's interest. Whilst Stephane was ideally looking to play in the English Premiership or First Division, the opportunity to join such a club didn't exist. Pounewatchy was told that his best bet of breaking into the English game and being noticed by the top clubs was to join an ambitious lower league club. Carlisle United matched that profile exactly. Mervyn Day sold the positive attributes of the club to the player and in August 1996 Stephane Pounewatchy made club history by becoming the first official overseas signing. Some 103 appearances and five goals later, he had become an absolute Cult Hero to the Brunton Park faithful.

To say that the supporters of Carlisle United needed Stephane Pounewatchy as much as he needed them would be an understatement. It was a perfect marriage from the moment this Gallic giant of a player first met with the fans in the player car park of the Brunton Park stadium. Karl Armstrong remembers meeting Pounewatchy prior to a game. "A whole load of us had gathered outside the players entrance behind the main stand," he told me. "We didn't recognise some of the players coming into the ground and I certainly didn't recognise Stephane Pounewatchy. While we there, this strong and casual-looking bloke walks up to us and smiles, holds out his hand to shake and introduces himself to us. It was Stephane Pounewatchy. It was surreal. He smiled and spoke to us. It was in broken English, but he had manners and a certain way about him that grabbed your attention. He shook many hands that day and took the time to speak to the fans. It was something he always did when he was with us. Brilliant bloke, he really was."

Carlisle romped away at the top of the Third Division table as they started the season superbly. After ten games they led the table by two points from Fulham as United sought to right the wrong of relegation the previous season. Four clean sheets from the start of the season showed where the side's strength lay as Day built a team that excited the natives of Cumbria once again. At its heart was a giant, black French defender. We literally had not seen his like before! And how we loved him.

In November 1996 Pounewatchy scored his first league goal for the club at Brighton and Hove Albion; the 27th minute strike being the first of United's three goals in a comfortable 3-1 victory on the south coast. The goal was greeted with great excitement by the travelling Carlisle army of supporters. It was seen as some small reward for the great work he had put in since joining the club. Defensively, playing alongside Dean Walling, Pounewatchy ensured that United were a far tougher proposition. What is more, both were good players and could outplay most forwards who they came up against.

That victory was the third in a run of 12 games that brought 11 wins and a draw, including three FA Cup wins which brought about a meeting with Sheffield Wednesday in the fourth round. United went down 2-0 in front of a huge Brunton Park crowd of 16,104, but showed that they could compete with a Premiership side.

The season rolled on with Wigan and Fulham, both on a long term collision course with the Premiership, challenging for the divisional title alongside Carlisle. A solid series of results, with Pounewatchy resplendent in a defence that was conceding fewer than one goal per game – the best in the division – saw United top the division in late March, with just eight games remaining. By this stage only six points were needed to guarantee promotion, but Carlisle took their foot off the gas, failing to win any of their next eight matches in all competitions, allowing Wigan and Fulham back into a three-way tussle for the title. Eventually the trio finished comfortably clear of the chasing pack, although Carlisle ended up in third position, 12 points ahead of Northampton, in fourth.

Promotion was secured by a goalless draw away to Mansfield on a Friday night, not the most glamorous way to do it, and in truth the most important result that April evening was Swansea's 3-1 defeat at Colchester, which confirmed that United were back in the third tier of English football at the first time of asking.

THERE WAS TO BE further glory when, after some weak performances in the early stages of the Auto Windscreens Shield competition, United reached Wembley Stadium on Sunday 20 April 1997, to face Colchester United. A crowd of 45,077, mainly supporting Carlisle, watched a tense and nervous battle between the two CUFCs. It was never going to be one of Wembley's more classic finals, but at least Carlisle did try to play the more attractive football.

Blues, well versed in the pressure of a Wembley final after their previous appearance in the Auto Windscreens final defeat by Birmingham City in 1995, settled from the outset. As early as the second minute Dean Walling went close, then Allan Smart just missed connecting with a dangerous cross from Owen Archdeacon. United fans leapt for joy when they thought Dean Walling's flick from Rory Delap's long throw-in had gone in, but it went into the side netting instead. Colchester, by now growing in confidence, began to push forward and looked like they had scored when Abrahams flicked a loose ball over the advancing Caig in the United goal only for the ball to drop onto the roof of the net.

The second half was notable for its lack of goalmouth action. One incident was rather curious as Rory Delap chased after a loose ball and seemed unaware of a corner flag until he collided with it. It took a full six minutes before a suitable replacement flag was found. A member of the Wembley Stadium groundstaff received one of the loudest cheers of the day as as he charged around the perimeter of the playing area carrying a stick/broom handle! But that was a mere sideshow to the commanding performance of Stephane Pounewatchy, who was a giant in everything he did that day. He intercepted crucial passes and made decisive tackles on the Colchester strikers, preventing them from breaching the Carlisle defence. Despite having the majority of possession, Carlisle couldn't break down a similarly resolute Colchester defence. To be fair, such was the strength of both back fours neither side looked likely to score throughout the 90 minutes of normal time, nor, to be fair, the further 30 minutes of golden-goal extra-time. United had an early chance to score, when Aspinall and Hayward made some neat inter-passing movements on the edge of the box. A split second of hesitation and the chance had gone. Hayward went close minutes later but his effort was well turned away for a corner. After two hours of intense tactical battling it was down to penalties.

This was the first time that United had ever had to endure the ordeal of a penalty shoot out. Colchester buried their first three penalties successfully. United, meanwhile, were struggling; Paul Conway had put away the first, Owen Archdeacon, who had been United's regular spot-kick expert, saw a rather insipid shot saved by Carl Emberson. Dean Walling restored hope when he shot home a third kick, now the pressure was on.

It was Tony Caig's turn to act the super hero. First he pushed Karl Duguid's kick onto a post. At 3-2 to Colchester it was Warren Aspinall who calmly despatched United's fourth penalty to level the score at 3-3. Peter Cawley stepped forward for Colchester, it was their final kick of the initial allocation of five, so effectively sudden death. Caig psychologically unnerved the player and managed to turn the ball away. United now had the upper hand as just one penalty remained. Steve Hayward fired his shot wide of Emberson's despairing dive and into the net. The Deckchair Army behind the goal were ecstatic. Quite incredibly, Carlisle United had won at Wembley! Stephane Pounewatchy in his first season in the English game had won a trophy at Wembley Stadium. Furthermore, he was voted clear Man of the Match for what can only be described as a classy performance. The player himself was reduced to tears of joy and could only speak of his love for the club and how fortunate he felt he was to be part of Carlisle United. His commitment to the cause cannot be denied, as he purchased and moved into a house in Wiggonby, near Wigton. It seemed that he was laying down roots and expected to be part of the club for a considerable time to come.

THE FOOTBALL FAIRYTALE continued as the player performed with consistent quality at the heart of the United defence. With the club again selling players, notably Dean Walling and later Matt Jansen, and replacing them with inferior quality signings, things on the pitch took a turn for the worse. For some inexplicable and never quite understood reason, Mervyn Day was sacked after six games of the new 1997/98 season, to be replaced as team manager by club owner Michael Knighton. Turmoil reigned at Brunton Park as the club became the laughing stock of football in an extremely embarrassing episode.

Despite the chaos taking place around him, Pounewatchy maintained a dignity that was sadly missing throughout the entire club. He became a constant to the supporters who desperately needed someone to stand up and be counted. The player revelled in the relationship he built between himself and the fans, for at least 90 minutes each week he gave all he could for them. Whilst most supporters despised what was going behind the scenes at Brunton Park, almost all rejoiced in the fact that Stephane Pounewatchy displayed devout loyalty and remained at the club.

The Auto Windscreens Shield, once again, offered respite from the calamity occuring at Brunton Park. In the early rounds, Oldham were beaten 1-0, followed by a 6-1 demolition of Rochdale. Spectacularly, a Pounewatchy hat-trick was the most memorable event of that evening. Other goals came via a brace from Nicky Wright and a solitary strike from Graham Anthony. But it was Pounewatchy who grabbed all the headlines. He told the author. "I don't score many goals, so to get three in one game was very different for me. It was one of those games. Every player in our team did everything right; passing, movement and finishing, it all happened for us in that one game. I felt bad for Rochdale. They were not a poor side, they just couldn't control us on the day. My goals were all fine goals, I was very proud to be playing for Carlisle United and serving them well."

With the fans singing his name from the terraces, elevating him to cult hero status, Stephane became a positive focal point at the club. But certain people behind the scenes didn't like the attention being drawn away from them. Perhaps it made them feel even more insecure than they were, who knows, but at the end of that 1997/98 season, with United, under the management of Michael Knighton, relegated back to the Third Division, Stephane Pounewatchy was released by Carlisle United.

The bulk of the United support turned against the club owner claiming that he allowed Stephane to leave in order to hurt them more. A general belief existed that Knighton could no longer subsidise nor had the desire for success at the club, but was keen to cash in and sell it off at a huge profit. Certainly, he did himself no favours in allowing the Gallic giant to leave the club, for Pounewatchy held a mystical sort of spell over the club's support, much in the way one of his countrymen, Eric Cantona, had done at both Leeds and Manchester United. At Leeds, the sale of Cantona caused questions to be asked about Howard Wilkinson's judgement. At Carlisle, releasing Pounewatchy ended any relationship the owner aspired to with the club's support.

Despite all this, rumours persisted that Pounewatchy had been allowed to leave after making wage and contract demands over and above what Carlisle could afford, thus leaving the owner with no alternative option but to allow him to leave. We shall probably now never know the truth as to why Stephane left, but for sure, the reverberations of the decision were to be felt around Brunton Park for many seasons after the player had departed.

AFTER A BRIEF SPELL IN the Scottish league at Dundee United, during August 1998 Pounewatchy returned to the English game with Port Vale, but he never truly settled into his game at either club. Most felt his heart still lay at Brunton Park. After a miserable time at Vale Park, in February 1999, at the age of 31, he joined Colchester United, a team who had three weeks earlier revealed Mick Wadsworth as their new manager. Joining his Layer Road team-mates for training for the first time Pounewatchy said: "I am very happy to be in the shop window again and relishing the challenge of helping Colchester United stay in Division Two. I am signing until the end of the season and it is good that I will be finishing the season here. I am very happy to be in the Second Division because when you are a professional footballer you want to play at the highest level you can."

Wadsworth, meanwhile, claimed the signing of Pounewatchy would be great for the club. "Stephane is a class player. We worked out the deal with him yesterday and I am very happy that he has come to us. But now he is here he is going to have to fight for his place in the side. The lads already in the team have done exceptionally well since I arrived and there is no way I am going to rock the boat."

Back up in Carlisle there was much in the way of discontent among the club's supporters. The signing by ex-boss Wadsworth of ex-United favourites, Pounewatchy and Warren Aspinall signalled a revolt. Supporters began to vote with their feet. Attendances dropped and United sat either bottom or uncomfortably close to the bottom of the Football League for long periods. In Essex Aspinall and Pounewatchy led by example, steering Colchester away from the Division Two relegation zone. In the 15 games in which he featured for Colchester, Stephane inspired the team around him and endeared himself to supporters by his desire and ability to win every challenge he made.

At Brunton Park the infamous Jimmy Glass moment, which saw Carlisle escape relegation to the abyss that is the world of non-league football at the last possible moment of the Football League season in dramatic fashion, epitomised how tenuous United's link to the professional game actually was. There was a desire that the club should never find itself in the same position again. To drop out of the Football League would have been unthinkable during that era. So to this backdrop, rumours began to circulate. In Essex, there was talk that Stephane longed to return to Carlisle and couldn't settle in the south east, even though it was closer to his French roots. In Carlisle just about everyone expected him to return. Rumour built, but the longed-for move never happened. The rumours were just that; pie in the sky assumptions. With heavy hearts Carlisle fans had to live with the fact that their Cult Hero was not going to return.

In June 1999, it was revealed that he had been released by Wadsworth. One Essex local newspaper surmised that the central defender could be heading back to Carlisle. The *Colchester Recorder* claimed: 'Out of contract Pounewatchy has been linked with his former club Carlisle, who only salvaged their Football League status at the end of last season with an injury-time goal by loan goalkeeper Jimmy Glass.'

Wadsworth revealed that he had personally told the giant defender his services would not be required by the Us next season after the Frenchman rejected a new contract. "We made Stephane an offer which was not acceptable to him," said Wadsworth. "I'm sorry to see him go because he did a marvellous job for us. But he has a record of pricing himself out of the market. That's why he has floated around the professional circuit in recent years. At 31 Stephane is not going to get any better; that is why I signed Sagi Burton from Crystal Palace."

Once again the rumours of high wage demands appear to have been used as a reason to move the player on. This time it had an air of finality about it.

AFTER THE COLCHESTER United experience, it seems that Stephane was wounded enough to leave behind the British game. He returned to his roots in France and moved into the world of players' agents where he has proved equally as successful. There can be no doubting that Carlisle United played a major role in this footballer's career. Regarded highly wherever he played, Stephane had a very special place in his heart for United.

Many years ago during his time at the club I was fortunate enough to meet with him to discuss his thoughts on Carlisle as both a city and the football club and its supporters. The following is an extract from that encounter.

"I had not heard of Carlisle when I played football in France, but when I heard they were interested in signing me I soon learned about the city and the football team. Carlisle is a very noble city. I enjoy its history very much. The castle and the cathedral have a royal feel about them. I see the castle and am in awe of what it stands for. The cathedral is very beautiful, like French cathedrals, holy but gothic. It captures me in a spell.

The people here are very welcoming and friendly, I like being part of this, I enjoy the area very much, so much scenery and so close to the city too. It is rural when compared to Paris and other cities in France. I want to stay here as long as I can. This is how I wanted England to be and I am very happy.

Carlisle United are a good club, a big club with wonderful fans who follow the team with passion. As a player you need passion to be able to compete, you must have desire to play for your team, at Carlisle it makes me want to play for the fans also. I am surprised at how many fans come to away games to watch us. No other team I have seen here in this league bring so many to us. The fans are the best I have known. They deserve a big club. They deserve success. I want to be part of that success with them.

I like Mervyn Day very much, he is a good coach and a manager also. He is well known in France as an excellent goalkeeper. I was very proud to sign for Carlisle with him as the coach and manager. I think I will be very happy if Carlisle can go to the Premier League. That is where I want to play. I want to play there with Carlisle United. They have been in the top league before. I see no reason why we cannot do it again. There are some good players here. Dean Walling is strong like me. He has passion and desire. We read each other well and he can play football also. It is curious how the fans like him too. Dean and I are on very good terms with the fans. That's important, to have an understanding of what they expect and what we can deliver. My family all watch for Carlisle's results now. They want us to win, to know I am doing well.

I cannot see myself wanting to leave Carlisle United for a long time, I enjoy my football here, I am settled, relaxed, I have found my inner self and am confident I can do well for the future of the team, the area, the city the team, its fans are all an important part of my life now."

Hardly the words of a demanding footballer; more like those of an ambitious player who desperately wanted to succeed alongside the club he played for.

Sadly, Carlisle United couldn't match his ambition. He became a mere pawn in the often political world of football management, ruthlessly cast aside at the apparent whim of club hierarchy. No matter how hard the club tried, Stephane Pounewatchy was never adequately replaced, Kevin Gray perhaps coming closest to enjoying the adulation and terrace worship which was bestowed upon Pounewatchy.

He may only have been at Brunton Park for two seasons, but the Gallic giant's legacy of being honest, dedicated, loyal and passionate about a football club he had never heard of before coming to England will forever remain part of Carlisle United's history.

JIMMY GLASS

'SIR JIMMY'

1999

UNITED CAREER

Games	3
Clean Sheets	1
Goals	1

MAGIC MOMENT

As the ball fell inside the box, Jimmy, fully 100 yards from his own goal, rifled the ball into the Plymouth net to send Brunton Park into ecstasy and create one of football's greatest moments

SOMEBODY, generally believed to be ex-player and television pundit Jimmy Greaves, once coined the phrase: "It's a funny old game." I can think of no other statement which truly sums up the tale of Jimmy Glass, or Sir Jimmy Glass as he is so often referred to by United fans. You don't have to be a football geek or a statistician to know who Jimmy Glass is or what he did for Carlisle United. His name and antics are permanently etched into the history and folklore of the game. So high profile was the incident that it has been said that the coverage provided by the world's media ensured that it was and remains to this day, the most featured and watched goal of all time, yes up there with Maradona's pair against England in 1986, the fourth Brazilian goal in the 1970 World Cup final scored by Carlos Alberto and Gazza's impudent strike for England against Scotland at Euro 96. So it was, that one day in May 1999, in the Cumbrian city of Carlisle, that Jimmy Glass, a workmanlike journeyman goalkeeper found himself catapulted from being just another loan player to absolute Cult Hero status, not only in Cumbria, but around the world (except Scarborough, of course).

THE LEAD UP TO WHAT actually happened on 8 May 1999 can be easily traced to times long before Jimmy actually arrived at Brunton Park. The off-field proceedings had been (during this turbulent period in the club's history), to say the least, farcical. Instability reigned as one of the brightest and best managers the club had seen was sacked. Fans' favourite Mervyn Day had gone, replaced by the club owner who installed himself as Director of Coaching in July 1998. With his tales of UFOs and Aliens, the football media clamoured for as much of Michael Knighton as they could get. Whatever any Carlisle supporter may feel about him, Knighton did get the name Carlisle United into the newspapers!

During the pre-season build up and presumably to help motivate supporters, the Director of Coaching duly announced to the press: "This is the best squad I've assembled in six years". The quote failed to convince anyone. However, no-one can condemn the man for the immense self belief he had in his own ability. Unfortunately for him it was less than inspiring to others, especially those who knew and loved Carlisle United. Incredibly, Knighton somehow assembled virtually a new squad for the 1998/99 season including many of the trainees who had graduated through the excellent system set up by Mervyn Day and others before him. Wheeling and dealing in the transfer market was what Knighton excelled at, many deals being without any real financial outlay. Damon Searle arrived from Stockport County, followed by David Brightwell from Northampton Town and Stuart Whitehead from Bolton Wanderers.

The season started brightly with a 1-0 home victory against Brighton and Hove Albion, but there followed, consistent with the rest of the campaign, three straight league defeats and an exit from the Worthington Cup (over two legs) to Tranmere Rovers. It was clear that this was to be a season blighted by inconsistent, and to be perfectly honest, poor performances. The fans voted with their feet as attendances at Brunton Park dropped to new depths and tended to hover around the 3,000 mark. Just 2,106 turned out for the return leg of the Worthington Cup fixture with Tranmere Rovers.

The turmoil continued as United floundered at the foot of the table, courting relegation and what would undoubtedly be oblivion and the end of the football club as it was then known. By December, there was some welcome news from Brunton Park, as Michael Knighton elected to stand down as Director of Coaching. The club had, in fact, been in the bottom three of Division Three for some time and it was obvious to all that they would be unable to claw their way out. Rumours abounded that Peter Beardsley was interested in returning to the club as player/manager. It was typical press speculation, fuelled by a desire to portray all things being good inside the club. The reality was that a well paid manager was never in the equation. Talk of the Beardsley move finally ended on transfer deadline day when mysteriously it was revealed from an unknown source within the club that the deal was now dead.

With such high profile names being banded about, it was with great anticipation that in December 1998 the media gathered for a press conference to reveal the club's new Director of Football. It turned out to be the ex-Middlesbrough and Sheffield Wednesday defender Nigel Pearson. Without being disrespectful to Pearson he was hardly the revelation anyone expected or wanted. To his professional credit, Pearson was a respected footballer and he wanted to make a name for himself as a manager. He immediately set about changing the playing side of the club. New, more intense training methods were introduced to help sharpen fitness and maintain focus. He talked to players and told them what he expected from them and told them what an honour it was to play for Carlisle United. Despite all this, few outside Brunton Park gave him any chance of steering the club away from relegation. The simple fact is that Pearson took over a losing team, a club in freefall.

As the season drew to a close, the team were deeply entrenched in the relegation mire. Pearson had managed to instil some self belief in his players and there had been an improvement in results. However, as others before him had found, just when you think things can't get any worse, someone pulls the rug out from under your feet. This time it was a bombshell of phenomenal proportions.

Reliable first team goalkeeper Tony Caig, who had been one of the few players who displayed consistently solid performances on the pitch, was sold on 25 March to Blackpool for a ridiculously small fee of £5,000. The whole affair deteriorated when it was revealed that the club had no suitable reserve keeper available in the squad. Pearson had to act quickly to replace him for the final few games of the season, bringing in Richard Knight, a rookie keeper without any league experience on loan from Derby County.

You simply couldn't script this farce as, in an incredible twist of fate, with just three games of the season remaining, Knight was recalled to the Baseball Ground by Derby after the Rams' regular first choice keeper, Russell Hoult had been sent off and suspended. Derby urgently required cover for reserve keeper Mart Poom. This entire scenario now left Carlisle without any kind of goalkeeper! After some despairing communications with the Football League, special dispensation was granted allowing United to sign a replacement goalkeeper on loan. It was down to Pearson to find someone, anyone who could fill the gap between the posts. One can only feel sorry for him as a manager. Few find themselves managing teams in such a precarious position. Now to exacerbate matters he found himself without a goalkeeper. Desperately, he rang round other clubs. At this late stage of the season no-one with any lengthy first team experience was available. Eventually it was suggested that Jimmy Quinn, manager at Swindon Town, may have a keeper on his books who was virtually redundant. So the phone call was made and it was announced that Jimmy Glass was to fill the goalkeeping void at Carlisle United for the remaining three fixtures of the season.

ON HIS UNITED DEBUT, Glass conceded three times in what was a 3-3 draw with Darlington. The team now sat second from bottom of the Football League with just two games remaining, two points ahead of bottom club Scarborough. Relegation to the Conference had become by simple mathematics, a two horse race between Carlisle United and Scarborough. Jimmy played a major role in United gaining a vital point in a 0-0 draw at Hartlepool in the penultimate game of the season, though it was, it seemed, too little too late. Scarborough had managed to beat Plymouth Argyle, the three points saw them leapfrog over Carlisle to go second bottom, dumping United to the bottom of the league and owning the sole relegation position going into the final game of the season.

Ominously, Saturday 8 May 1999 threatened to be the darkest day in the club's history. Plymouth Argyle came to Brunton Park with nothing to play for but pride. It would be to their benefit to see Carlisle relegated, after all it was the longest journey they and their fans had to endure in the season. Blues needed to win the encounter, and even then they could only hope that Scarborough, who entertained Peterborough United, would draw or lose. A sizeable crowd of 7,599 turned out to witness what everyone expected to be the club's final game in the Football League.

I cannot recall a more emotional day in my entire life. I swear, from the moment every United fan awoke, there, swinging above Brunton Park, hung the sword of Damocles. Few wanted the kick-off time to come round. Inside the ground the tension was more real. There were no smiling faces anticipating success or victory. This was the real hardcore of the club's support. Sure, everyone believed the team could raise its game and win, but thereafter, it was still down to what happened at Scarborough. Much of the clearly visible angst on the terraces was directed towards the club owner, who found himself taking the brunt of the blame for the predicament the club currently found itself in.

The Brunton Park Tannoy announcer made every effort to get the fans emotionally and positively aligned and behind the team prior to the kick-off. The game started, Plymouth wearing their usual and no longer unique green playing strip given Eddie Stobart's recent sponsorship of Carlisle, United wearing the blue and white colours, which representatives of the team had so proudly worn for around a hundred years. The obvious tension on the terraces transmitted itself onto the pitch with neither side attempting or being confident enough to take a chance. It was pretty dire stuff. Then, at seven minutes past three, a sudden change swept through the terraces of Brunton Park. It started with a buzz which quickly turned into a cheer, then a roar. Those with radios pinned to their ears (there were about 3,000 folk with those, I reckon) announced that Peterborough had scored at Scarborough and were leading 1-0. On the field things improved too, the whole place went wild when a Scott Dobie header flashed into the back of the Plymouth net, only for it to be ruled out by the referee who had blown for an earlier infringement in play. The passion from the terraces was clear, as everyone screamed for the players to attack the Plymouth defence at every opportunity. Yet still the game had not ignited into the thunderous affair which United fans had every right to expect. It seemed as though both sides were playing out a draw, then disaster! Right on the stroke of half-time the storm clouds gathered over the stadium and gloom and despair descended upon the terraces. The worst possible news emerged from East Yorkshire, a goal flash revealing that Scarborough had equalised, making it 1-1 at the McCain Stadium. Should scores remain the same Carlisle would be relegated at full time.

With Plymouth attacking the Warwick Road end in the second half, United, it seemed, had played a psychological stroke, realising that the United fans in that area would do their utmost to intimidate the Argyle forwards. The game desperately needed a goal. The reality was that Carlisle desperately needed a goal, a goal which never looked like coming. Suddenly, Plymouth began to press forward and the United defence were on the back foot. Jimmy Glass pulled off a couple of decent stops to prevent what would be a devastating blow, conceding a goal. It always strikes me as being played out in slow motion, but when Phillips of Plymouth received the ball on the left and ran through the United defence, everything seemed surreal. Surely nothing so bizarre as Plymouth scoring could happen. But it did. The Blues' defence opened up wide, very wide allowing the player to fire easily past the despairing dive and outstretched arm of Jimmy Glass. The ball flew into the Carlisle net to give the visitors the lead. All around me Carlisle fans were in tears. This was bleak and things looked bad, very bad.

Despite the setback most of the crowd responded positively, but the majority of the shouting was supporters voicing their feelings against the club owner. 'Knighton out' echoed around Brunton Park and could, I am told, be heard as far afield as Botchergate and Rickerby Park. On the pitch United never looked like equalising, Jimmy Glass made a couple more saves and was at every opportunity launching the ball up field in the hope of mounting a United attack. One such clearance found the influential Graham Anthony, who controlled the ball and played it forward past a Plymouth defender and hared after it. He eventually crossed and the ball was cleared, dropping into the path of team captain David Brightwell. Twenty five yards from goal, he lashed it back towards the Plymouth goal and into the net. At last, Brunton Park went wild. Suddenly out of nowhere the team had given themselves a fighting chance of survival, the scoreline now read 1-1.

On the touchline Nigel Pearson was clearly ecstatic. He jumped and punched the air, celebrating as though this game meant everything to him. Pearson was in my opinion a devoutly loyal and honest manager. He showed a real passion for the club which the fans recognised and respected enormously. As he stood on the touchline that afternoon, every other second he glanced down at his watch, desperate for time to stand still, anything to give his side a longer period of time to score another goal. As the clock ticked away, the emotion on the terraces worsened. United fans young and old could be seen crying tears of despair. Between sobs they still managed to scream their support to their heroes in blue.

From my position in the stand I focused on the referee. The 90-minute mark approached and he started his countdown, glancing at both linesmen and like every Carlisle supporter in the ground, constantly looking at his watch, though for him it was for evidence that injury time approached. Plymouth, it seemed, had given up the fight and began to aimlessly hoof the ball up field to waste time. They simply wanted to get the season over and go home. Once again, the crowd began to act in an agitated manner. This time, though, it was with excitement. News filtered through that Scarborough's game with Peterborough was over. It had ended in a 1-1 draw. That in itself simplified matters. Nothing short of a win was the result required by the Blues. The 90 minutes were up and the fourth official revealed four minutes of injury time. Just where that had come from I didn't know. However I was more than pleased to accept it. Plymouth, though, were out to spoil the remaining minutes and continued with their time-wasting tactics and Carlisle, it seemed, could do nothing to prevent it.

By now, every Blues fan in the ground had eyes welling full. Like everyone else they knew that with things as they stood this would be the end of Carlisle United. Tears began to run down my face and I could hardly see what was happening on the pitch through my now flooded eyes. I looked down at my wrist watch. We were in the absolutely final minute of injury time. This was it, last chance saloon. I had to interview players after the game and knew that this would be an impossible task in my present state. I was an emotional wreck, and I was not alone either.

When Scott Dobie won a corner for Carlisle, I saw the referee look over at his linesman. No words or signals were given, but I just knew that he was saying: 'as soon as the momentum of this attack is over I am blowing the final whistle.' I hadn't noticed that Jimmy Glass had sprinted upfield into the Plymouth penalty area for the corner. I glanced round at the fans, some were leaving the ground, no doubt muttering disparaging remarks and blaming the whole world for the fate that they felt was to befall their club. I am not a religious person by any standards, but I silently prayed for a miracle, some act of divine intervention which never happens. I didn't care what it was as long as Carlisle scored.

Supporter Geoff Strong recalls some of the tension he witnessed during the last few minutes of the game: "With about five minutes to go I was shouting for Carlisle to attack Plymouth with more conviction. It wasn't going to happen and my frustration turned to anguish. The bloke in front of me was actually physically sick. He wasn't a youngster either, but a supporter in his forties I would reckon. Everywhere I looked, women, children and grown men were in tears. People hugged as though consoling one another as the inevitable approached. It was like a scene from a film showing people waiting for the end of the world."

Meanwhile at Scarborough, the home support was celebrating on the pitch with their players as erroneously, a Tannoy announcer had revealed that the Carlisle game was finished. They believed that relegation had been avoided. Back at Brunton Park, the seconds ticked by as Graham Anthony confidently strode up and swung in the corner. Perhaps, he thought it was to be United's last ever as a professional club. It had to be good one. It was, the ball was whipped in and quick as a flash Scott Dobie reacted, powering a header towards the Plymouth goal. I jumped to my feet believing it was in, only to see the strong upright frame of the Argyle keeper reacting quickly and parrying the ball out with both hands. In despair I shouted: "FUCKING WANKER!"

I stood there opened mouthed, my mouth forming the last syllable of my previous description of the Plymouth custodian. Brunton Park momentarily fell into complete silence as the ball fell to the feet of United goalkeeper Jimmy Glass, who had managed to get into the Plymouth penalty area virtually unnoticed. Time stood still. I looked over at the referee to the left of the goal. I'm certain he glanced towards his watch. I flicked my eyes back towards Jimmy Glass as, with his right foot, he lashed out at the ball, firing it into the back of the Plymouth net.

Time and life actually stopped for about three seconds. There was a moment of eerie silence, even the Plymouth players stood seemingly paralysed. Then there was pandemonium. The joyous shout of 'GOAL' roared from the lips of every Blues supporter in the ground and I would imagine from those who had been listening on the radio. Even the Plymouth fans celebrated their part in football history. Within seconds, Jimmy Glass had disappeared beneath a mass of blue bodies. Fans of all ages rushed onto the pitch as everyone clambered to congratulate the scorer. The pitch invasion was a good humoured affair and the Plymouth fans joined in the celebrations having witnessed a remarkable piece of football history. Even the referee was knocked off his feet, hugged, kissed and hugged again. It truly was a football miracle and Brunton Park celebrated it to the hilt.

The referee, keen to play out the final moments, somehow cleared the playing area of supporters and made Plymouth restart. One touch then two, then the shrill whine of the final whistle signalled the end of the game. United had won 2-1, Scarborough were relegated. At the McCain Stadium, the mass hysteria which had followed their 1-1 draw with Peterborough and the belief that they had avoided relegation saw players, fans and officials on the pitch jumping as one and celebrating with champagne. Suddenly it all turned sour as news of the Jimmy Glass goal was revealed. In the days that followed it was reported that Scarborough were set to appeal against the loan signing of Jimmy Glass. However, such intent was clearly nonsensical and nothing materialised.

At Carlisle, the joyful celebrations saw fans fill the playing area to form a sea of blue and white. Attention was focused towards the directors' box located centrally in the main stand. The players emerged to rapturous applause, the greatest of all being saved for the saviour Jimmy Glass, the hero of the day and sporting a bloodied nose suffered during the mass goal celebration. He was clearly delighted and elated and could hardly contain his emotion. Manager Nigel Pearson also took centre stage and somehow, over the singing and chanting, managed to thank the club's supporters and directors for their support and efforts since Christmas. The speech will be remembered for two reasons; firstly it was clear from its content that he was leaving the club and secondly, he failed to acknowledge the support or efforts of the club owner in any manner shape or form, a notion which most United fans supported.

Nine days later it emerged that club had actually sacked Pearson a few days after the miracle; a typically tragic end, to what had been a bizarrely surreal event. There was the usual speculation that Sir Jimmy would be signed by the club on permanent deal as soon as possible. For whatever reason, it never happened.

AND THAT WAS IT. Those three games, and that one special, vital, emotional goal were Jimmy Glass's sole contribution in his Carlisle career, and yet his name will be writ as large across the club's history as any long-serving hero such as McConnell, Broadis, Stokoe, Ross or Balderstone. The incredible circumstances and nature of his goal will always mean that Jimmy will be held in whispered reverence by all supporters of Carlisle United. He said in his own autobiography *One Hit Wonder* that he would never return while the then owner was in place. For that reason alone, it was, in fact, the one club he would never sign for. Amazingly, United tried to sign him on loan the following season. Understandably, Jimmy refused point blank. Who could blame him?

I got to interview Jimmy right after the game. It was brief, it was direct and it was emotional. "It's fantastic, I never knew what was happening at Scarborough, I was too busy concentrating on getting the ball forward as often as I could. The dressing room was tense before the game but the boss was brilliant. He kept us all together and held our nerve. He believed we would do it and now we have I can't believe it. When David Brightwell hit the equaliser, I believed we could win the game. I didn't know how long was left, but thought: 'These people don't deserve to see their team lose league status.' So I signalled to the boss to tell him I was going up for the corner. Next thing I know I am hitting the ball into the net. It was a fantastic feeling, the best ever. I love it here, I would love to stay. I am the happiest person in the world at this moment. Where did all those people come from, I can't believe I got out of that unhurt."

Jimmy moved around to other clubs after his miracle at Brunton Park, eventually drifting out of the professional game and moving into the world of information technology. But due to this one defining moment of his career, 8 May will always be celebrated by Blues supporters as Sir Jimmy's Day; a day when you can just take a moment to pause and feel the lump in the throat, the incredible rush and the elation of seeing Jimmy's right boot swing and the ball hit the back of the Plymouth net.

Perhaps he wasn't the greatest goalkeeper to have graced Brunton Park, perhaps not the most agile and certainly not the most talented. But without question, if you are looking for a Cult Hero that made that vital difference in a special moment of the club's history, then look no further than Jimmy Glass.

KEVIN GRAY

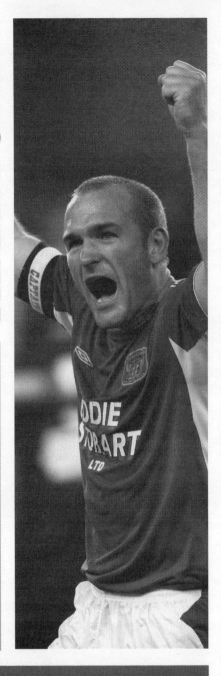

2002-2007

UNITED CAREER

Games	134+4
Goals	13

MAGIC MOMENT

A colossus during our entire campaign in the non-League and a leader on the pitch. Kev dragged us back into the Football League thanks to that wonderful victory over Stevenage

'A COLOSSUS'

> '**We were knocking on the Stevenage dressing room door and singing: 'We are going up, say we are going up'. It was an excellent time. I think we partied for about three weeks.**'
>
> **Kevin Gray**

LET'S not beat about the bush here. This is the player who joined us when the odds were heavily stacked against us, when others had turned their back on us as a club and either moved on or, worse still, denied our existence. United were a club in freefall following relegation to the Conference and were a club with a terrible reputation, thanks in the main to a certain eccentric egotist who dreamed of butterfly farms, moving pitches and somehow managed to find subsidies to fund irregular-looking stands; oh, and who also had a friendly chat with some aliens on the M62. This was a man who claimed to know football inside out, as a player, a coach and a manager; a man who claimed to be an astute businessman yet was so easily fooled by a tin pot curry house waiter into believing he could sell Carlisle United for a song.

If truth be known, United had been in freefall for longer than any of us care to admit. The Jimmy Glass moment was all but a distant memory as we sat, countless points adrift, rock bottom of the Football League in 2004. It felt like it would take many years before we could recover from the legacy of Michael Knighton's tenure. Having witnessed way too many Houdini escapes, this time we all realised there was no escape.

Paul Simpson, our latest manager, had joined the club after a miserable spell at Rochdale where his managerial training had come to an abrupt end with the sack. I think it fair to say that most supporters at the time felt he had been a decent enough player, but as manager, well, let's just say that at Rochdale he did little to inspire anyone.

Simmo had initially joined us as a player. But now he was not so much gradually immersed into the cosy managerial surroundings of Brunton Park as absolutely chain-ganged into a managerial position which to all intents and purposes had disaster stamped all over the rest of the season. Despite this Simmo was a winner. He demanded nothing less than being winners from his players and soon he set about transforming the ailing football ways of the club. First he acquired the services of the multi-talented Dennis Booth as his assistant, and pretty soon the managerial pair began to wheel and deal. Boothy, as Dennis was already affec-tionately known, had a vast knowledge of the game at most levels, while, in the background, we as supporters wondered, and wondered more. Firstly, had Simpson and Booth got what it takes to lead us from the depths of football hell? And secondly, did they have the contacts to bring in the leaders and characters we so desperately needed on the pitch? It was an obvious question to ask... who in the playing world would seriously be daft enough to join Carlisle United? The answer proved quite simple. It wasn't someone who was daft or desperate, it was a true leader and inspiration, the absolute legend and Cult Hero that is Kevin Gray.

FAST FORWARD TO WHAT can only be described as a beautifully sunny Cumbrian day in late May 2007. I am gradually weaving my roadster through some of the most picturesque and beautiful country lanes of Cumbria. I am tense. My wife, Mandy, who accompanies me, notices my anxious state and tells me to slow down. The reason I am anxious is because we are on our way to a rendezvous with Kevin Gray, honoured to be invited to his home. I am concerned about how our meeting will go, this after all is a player revered by the loyal support of Carlisle United. For me, though, the problem is that he has recently, just a few days earlier in fact, been released by the club. Surplus to requirements? I ponder how could this happen to someone who has been an inspiration to so many both on and off the pitch during his spell at the club.

I am filled by mixed emotions. Some feel he has been exploited, that the club used him, drained him of all his drive, determination and motivation which led us onward and upward, only to discard him when he had given us his all. The guy is in his mid-thirties. Mandy asks me what I think he is going to do now he has been released? Whereas I am more concerned about how he will react to my telling him that, despite everything that has happened recently, he is a Carlisle Cult Hero through and through, regarded by many to be thoroughly deserving of such a title, as much as anyone else contained within this book.

All these thoughts are flooding through my mind when suddenly my mobile phone rings. I pull off the country lane, well, theoretically anyway, and answer the call. Before I can muster a greeting, I hear a deep and honest voice. It's Kevin Gray. "Paul, you daft bugger. You have just gone past me house, turn round and come back." I look round and see his house set in what I would call idyllic surroundings. Turning round and pulling up beside his house I think to myself: 'for god's sake, this is Kevin Gray I am going to interview, the same Kevin Gray who was a leader on the pitch and a player with a heart as big as Brunton Park.' Putting it bluntly, as I got out my car, I was crapping myself.

I need not have worried as a voice boomed out: "Alright mate?". I looked up to see there, sitting basking in the midday sun, genuine Carlisle United football idol, Kevin Gray. Strangely this wasn't the person who the fans associated with, the solid rock at the centre of the United defence, the captain who marshalled his ranks with almost military precision, the leader who drove his men forward squeezing every last ounce of passion, determination and energy from them. No, here before me was a very proud dad and husband, rocking a pram which contained his beautiful five day-old baby daughter, Elise. No words or descriptive passage could ever describe the bond that clearly exists between Kevin Gray and his family, I quickly note, and admire that he is their rock as much as he was ours.

The chances are that he is minding his new-born daughter after spending a few hours tinkering under the sizeable bonnet of the other obsession in his life – a 10-ton Robey compound cylinder traction engine, built in 1916 and handed down to Kevin by his grandfather, who inspired Gray's own interest in this mechanical leviathan. It does seem a more suitable scenario for Super Kev than cradle-rocking. After all he was the man who was the solid engine, the heart and soul of United's rise back up through the divisions to the brink of the play-offs into the second flight of English football for the first time in 20 years.

Some supporters may recall Kev turning up with his engine to the 2005 United open day, a sight which left many mouths agape. But that's one of the wonderful things about a succession of Carlisle's Cult Heroes, that ability to do something just that little bit different, on and off the pitch. Relaxing by stripping down a grimy century-old engine wouldn't be top of my list of ways to prepare for a new season, but then I'm not a total football legend.

My first question to Kevin is: "Have you sorted yourself out with another club yet?" He tells me it's still confidential, but Chesterfield had offered him something and he intended to accept. Inside, I groan, I had hoped that he would tell me that Carlisle had offered him another contract. As with all things in life, things move on, and so here we were, discussing history. Having interviewed footballers of all types over many years, I have to say that my meeting with Kevin was as good as it gets. We connected straight away. Few footballers are able to carry the respect they hold on the field away from it. Kevin did so with consummate ease. And so, in the midday sun we sat down with coffee, family, which included a cat called Socks, and the spirit of Carlisle United.

THIS COLOSSUS FIRST learned his trade at Dunham-on-Trent primary school in Retford, Nottinghamshire. His first position in the school team was as a left winger. His headmaster, who had noted his athleticism and skill with a ball at his feet, was desperate to get young Kevin Gray into the school team and as soon as he was old enough and strong enough to compete, his playing days began.

A change of schools naturally followed as Kevin moved up to Tuxford Comprehensive, again in Retford. It was here that his strength as a defender and leader was first noticed, as first he was tried out at left-back, before swapping roles to centre-half, a position he was to excel in for the rest of is playing career. "I just sort of settled into the role in centre-half and found it natural to tell other players around me what to do. I don't think its something you think about at that age, being a captain or a leader, you just want to play football and do well. That something that has never changed with me. I just get on and do the job on the field. If I have to I will push other players to give more or tell them if they aren't giving enough. It's all about heart and commitment to the team."

It wasn't too long before young Kevin Gray was being noticed by club scouts, not least those who had contact within the Nottinghamshire Football Association. Kevin was representing the county at football at all levels. His consistent performances at the heart of defence supplemented by some motivated leadership set him above many of his peers. Bob Shaw, chief scout at Mansfield Town was as well respected as anyone in the local game. A shrewd and talented scout he had unearthed many a gem for Midlands club sides and others. Bob made contact with Kevin's family and offered him terms at the Field Mill club. "I was really excited to be joining Mansfield. They were a decent enough side and had some quality players, like Trevor Christie, playing for them. Trevor was merciless in front of goal, a real goalscorer."

Manager of the Stags at the time was George Foster, himself a no-nonsense defender. He very quickly warmed to the young Kevin Gray and moved him into the first team, his debut being in a home game against local rivals, Chesterfield, which the Stags won 3-1. "To be honest, everything happened very quickly when I joined Mansfield. I just seemed to progress very quickly. I was nervous when I realised I was making my debut against Chesterfield. I was only 16, who wouldn't be nervous at that age? It was great being part of the first team, and I really knew from that day on that I didn't want to play anywhere else but in the first team. I learned an awful lot from George Foster. He was probably one of the best managers I have had. He was a real motivator. You didn't dare upset him or else. Bill Dearden was his assistant at the time and he was sound, a tough man who knew the game and how to play it. He used to play for Sheffield United. In fact, he's back at Mansfield now as manager."

Some 155 games (plus 15 substitute appearances) and six goals later, Kevin Gray said his farewell to Field Mill and took the step up to Huddersfield Town, then managed by the warhorse that is Neil Warnock. "It was typical of football at the time. It was July 1994. I had just bought a house in the Mansfield area," Gray told me. "I had only been in it a couple of weeks when the boss rang me to say that Huddersfield Town had offered £20,000 for me. There was a bit of silence. I knew that £20,000 was a lot to Mansfield and could help them rebuild. For me, though, the chance to play at a higher level was too good an opportunity to turn down. Neil Warnock had a bit of a reputation of sorting players out and making them better, so I thought it would be a good move."

As was the case at the time, football, and in this particular instance, Huddersfield Town, was going through a period of change and transformation. It wasn't long before Kevin Gray was playing under different managers. "There were a few at Huddersfield; Brian Horton, Peter Jackson, and Steve Bruce. In their own way they were all good. Huddersfield was a nice place to play football, what with the stadium and the passionate fans. I settled in well and I like to think all the managers I played under felt I was professional and gave 100 per cent in all I did for the club. There was, as is the case with all professionals, though, a low point in my career at Town."

That low point came when Gray was involved in a tackle which broke the leg of Bradford City striker Gordon Watson on 1 February 1997 at Valley Parade. The match was only Watson's third game for the Bantams after he had become the club's record signing in a £550,000 transfer from Southampton. Watson suffered a double fracture of his right leg and Gray's challenge was condemned in the media. Watson underwent surgery in which he required a six inch plate and seven screws inserted into his leg, an operation, it turned out, which sadly effectively ended his career. Worse still for Gray, in a landmark case in the High Court in October 1998, Watson successfully sued Kevin for negligence and was awarded £50,000 in interim damages as well as a later £900,000, the bulk of which was to compensate for the loss of anticipated earnings.

Coping with being the perceived deliberate wrongdoer in these circumstances must have been difficult. "I felt I needed to move on to help my career," says Gray. "I tried a change of scenery at Stockport County, on loan, another nice club, but it didn't happen there for me."

Eight years after he joined Huddersfield, Gray moved on, a press statement released by Huddersfield at the time told how Gray's stay at the McAlpine stadium had come to an end. 'Kevin rejected our offer five weeks ago and we genuinely tried to negotiate a deal and did offer him an improved deal.' He told me: "There were a lot of changes going on behind the scenes at Huddersfield at the time. Effectively the improved deal offered was half my previous salary. As a player, you have two options, take what's offered or try to better yourself and seek an offer elsewhere. So I moved on. It was at this point that I reasoned that footballers are a commodity. They have relatively short professional careers as players and have to make the most of what's on offer while they can. A free transfer to Tranmere Rovers soon followed.

The manager of Tranmere at the time was Dave Watson, the ex-Everton defender. He had a massive reputation as a player and seemed to being doing okay as a manager, I thought so anyway. He asked me to join Rovers and I thought at the time it was going to be a positive move for me career-wise. Tranmere have always been regarded as a good footballing side, so I was moving upwards, I felt. The Huddersfield supporters were great during my time there, really supportive and got behind the team. I was a bit sad to leave them, but I had decisions to make and I had to do what was right for me."

Whilst no-one could disagree that the move appeared to be a progressive one for Kevin, it proved to be anything but an inspirational one. "Injuries just seemed to happen. I wasn't known as being injury prone. I always kept myself a hundred per cent fit, but I think it just happens to every player. One injury turns into two, then it's long term and you can't seem to get yourself back to peak fitness. It didn't help me that Dave Watson, the manager who signed me at Tranmere, was moved on fairly sharpish before I had chance to settle in. It was a bit unnerving for me as well as everyone else. New managers bring with them changes to style of play, as they want to stamp their authority on the team or club.

At Tranmere it was Ray Mathias who replaced Dave Watson. We never seemed to hit it off and I don't think he liked or rated me as a player. I was unsettled because of this, despite the fact that I was team captain and the fans seemed to appreciate me. I only managed 15 games in total for Tranmere, and I wanted away, but I wasn't going to rush off at the first chance this time. I wanted to select a club that was right for me, a club where I could add value and enjoy my game."

SO IT WAS THAT AFTER three years at Prenton Park, Kevin Gray received a somewhat curious, but much welcomed telephone call. "At Huddersfield we had a playing kit that had what I can only describe as having snug-fitting shorts. They didn't leave a lot to the imagination if you know what I mean! Anyway, this one day, my mobile phone goes off, I answer it and this voice says to me: "How you doing tight pants? Do you fancy coming to play for Carlisle United?" It was Dennis Booth. I knew a lot about Paul Simpson and Dennis Booth and, after Boothy had discussed the club's position to me, I said 'yes' without any hesitation at all. It was the best move of my professional career. The club signed Tom Cowan around the same time and I knew I was joining something very special. They needed experienced players and I honestly warmed to the challenge."

The signing of Gray made an immediate impact on a very leaky United defence. Suddenly, gaping holes were plugged and players were finding an extra yard in their pace. Slowly but surely, with United being cast adrift at the Football League for so long, there was hope. A run of wins closed the gap as United moved off the bottom and, incredibly, escape from relegation looked a real possibility. Sadly, it wasn't to be, injuries and suspensions cost points as the team were soon back in the relegation pack. It all hinged on a home game with Cheltenham Town. Kevin Gray was suspended and missed the game. "I got sent off at Orient which I still think was unjust. We appealed, but I received a punishment of a two games on the sidelines as a result meaning I missed the last two games of the season. It was a bad deicision really. The boy had clattered into one of our players, a real nasty foul, so I ran up to him and told him there was no need for it and he collapsed on the floor, I never touched him."

Kevin had the full support of boss Paul Simpson, who looked at the incident on video, evidence enough that he didn't touch the player. But no, the Football Association still went ahead and backed the referee. Simpson was incensed at the thought of losing such an influential player during a crunch period of the season. "It was a scrappy, aggressive game. I thought it was a disgraceful challenge by an Orient player that led to Kevin Gray's sending-off. Kevin ran 15 to 20 yards and put his hands on his chest. The player went down. The referee's assistant on the far side claimed Kevin struck the player, but Kevin swears blind he didn't. He's an honest sort of fellow. He's an aggressive player, but by no means a dirty one and I'd be very surprised if he'd hit him."

Kevin continued: "It was terrible. We all really thought we could get out of it [relegation] Simmo was a top boss and motivated us. There was a real belief that we were part of something special. Fred Story then came in as owner and he too was a leader. He inspired us all and there was a real spirit which I hadn't had before in my career. The Cheltenham game was terrible, we needed to win, but we didn't. I was suspended and couldn't play, but still wanted to back the lads in the dressing room. After the game, the dressing room was like a morgue, players cried, everyone was depressed and down.

Despite this, we knew that the team was a good one, a team which could win things. We didn't ever believe we were losers. The fans, well, they were just brilliant. We all felt we had let them down. Dennis Booth chased everyone round and told them that we might be relegated this time, but next year we would be back, bigger and better. Fred Story and the directors were gutted by it all. We as players owed them something. We were ready to come back to the league within a year and committed ourselves to that cause."

TO SAY THAT THE Football Conference was an eye opener would be an understatement. Brunton Park was and is a relative football palace compared to some of the venues in the non-league game. It was said at the time that Carlisle United were the biggest club to ever drop into the non-league arena. Certainly some of the clubs rubbed their hands together at the potential of Carlisle United bringing 800-1,000 away fans to their ground. Most upped the admission fee for away fans, with clubs like Gravesend and Canvey Island disbelieving at such an away following. In some towns beer prices were raised in club hostelries, especially for away fans. The Conference cashed in on Carlisle United. One club even referred to Blues as the Manchester United of non-league football…what an insult!

"Oh Paul, let me tell you, it was drastic, worse," Kev continued. "I had never heard of a football team called Canvey Island. They were one of the better teams we played, but rough, crikey, they knew how to mix it with us. Danny (Livesey) and me really cruised through that game. I think they had two players sent off, strikers, so we hardly had anything to do. We won thankfully, but was I glad to get out of that place. Great experience though.

Then there was Gravesend. I think most of us thought Gravesend was a place in a horror film, if it wasn't it should have been! Bad isn't it, especially when that was one of the better places we visited! We stuffed a few teams during our time in that league, then it all went a bit pear shaped both on and off the field."

After a defeat at Crawley in January 2005, the players returned to a scene of complete devastation at Brunton Park and throughout the city of Carlisle. A torrent of water had swept through the city, causing damage beyond belief, also costing lives. Football in Carlisle during this period was not a priority as everyone mustered to the call to support families and victims of the flood damage.

"It was terrible," recalls Kev. "We were all in a state of shock at the club. We all wanted to do anything we could to help the community. Fred Story was brilliant. He helped everyone he could and was a real ambassador during that time, something I still hold him in great regard for."

DESPITE ALL THE problems in the city, football had to continue. Carlisle organised to play home games at Morecambe and Gretna whilst Brunton Park was relieved of the water which had rendered much of the stadium destroyed.

"Getting to play our games back at Brunton Park was a relief," Gray told me. "It was the turning point for the whole city. Our form had dropped off and we were no longer top of the table or in the promotion places. But we dug in as players and kept believing. Eventually we got to the play off final at Stoke City's ground, the Britannia Stadium. It was half full, most fans were from Carlisle, what a brilliant atmosphere. I remember the manager of Stevenage, our opponents, Graham Westley, he was full of himself and there was player called Dino Maamria. In all my time I have never played against such a player who thought he was better than he was. Danny Livesey and me played our usual game, keeping it tight at the back. He was all over the place, hardly getting a touch, but giving it large. "Do you pair not know who I am?" He kept reminding us. Best of it was, neither of us knew who he was.

Anyway, Westley, their manager, was giving it all to us, saying we were crap and didn't deserve to be in the play-offs. Then Murph got the goal and we won. As we went to collect our medals, me and Danny walked past Maamria, and Danny turns and says to me: 'Do you know who this man is?' I replied: 'Yeah, some Conference player I have never heard of.' I then burst into song: 'We are going up, say we are going up!' While Danny said: 'Yeah and he is a loser.'

I won't repeat what Maamria said.

It got better too. As we walked past Westley I told him he was still some unheard-of bloke managing a Conference team. Danny thought I went a bit overboard, but Carlisle was my team. I was proud. I wouldn't let anyone, especially someone else's manager, say anything bad about us.

Afterwards, just about every player in the team went wild in celebration. We were knocking on the Stevenage dressing room door and singing: 'We are going up, say we are going up'. It was an excellent time. I think we partied for about three weeks."

THE FOLLOWING SEASON back in the Football League saw United storm through the table to clinch the Championship in some style. Football pundits nationally raved about the team's style of play and, in particular, the goals from Karl Hawley and Michael Bridges. Kevin Gray coordinated and marshalled his team as well as any captain. Time and again he produced intervening tackles which prevented goalscoring opportunities against United. He even weighed in with a few goals himself. "I think the League Two Championship-winning season was the best I have had in football." Kev told me. "There was a real belief about the club that we were on the up. I managed to get on the scoresheet a few times too which was nice; mainly headed goals like virtually all my goals really.

There just seemed to be so many highlights. One of my favourite moments was at Darlington. Their boss, David Hodgson, had gone public in his condemnation of us, saying Darlington would beat us. He was really winding us up, which did us no harm at all really. We absolutely stuffed them at their place 5-0. It ended up with Lummy [Chris Lumsden] and me banging on their dressing room door after the game, singing: 'We are going up, say we are going up' and reminding them inside that dressing room what the score was. Great stuff!"

On the claims in some areas that promotion was down to Michael Bridges and Karl Hawley, Kevin has strong and persuasive argument. "It was a real team effort that season. We had a couple of players come in who did well for us, complemented our style of play, but there is no way that anyone can seriously say it was down to just Michael Bridges or Karl Hawley that we won the championship that season. There was and still is a real good morale in the dressing room. We didn't miss either player when they had gone or were out the team. Honestly, some of the stuff that happens is unbelievable, like the time Dolly (the trainer) brought in a mannequin to training. He dressed it in goalkeeper Tony Williams' clothes and brought it out to the side of the training pitch. We were always winding Tony up about his dress sense. I think we were all wondering what the hell Dolly was doing. Then suddenly he pours a bit of petrol or something over the dummy and Tony's clothes and sets fire to the lot. We were wetting ourselves as Tony looked on absolutely mortified. He took it all in good spirit though!

Then there was the time that Dolly set Tony up again, this time with some FA coaching coursework he [Tony] had been doing. Dolly swapped the contents of the folder with some bogus paperwork. Tony took his coursework really seriously and was always studying. Well Dolly only does it again, setting fire to it beside the training pitch. Tony went mad, but saw the funny side of it in the end, when he realised Dolly was winding him up. That's what I mean, it was team spirit and morale, as good as anywhere I have known it, if not better. We were all in it together like one big family. We took defeat badly and celebrated the victories, brilliant."

In the summer following the League Two championship season, Paul Simpson left the club and moved to Preston North End, taking with him assistant manager Dennis Booth. "I think we were all a bit surprised by Paul leaving, but I understand he was ambitious and wanted to progress himself. Good on him, no-one would deny him that opportunity," continued Kev. "When the new boss [Neil McDonald] came in, it was different. We were worried about how things would change and how it may affect us players, but he done a great job. Training and day to day stuff changed, but the morale remained high. He is a decent enough bloke who knows his stuff. At one point of the season, I really thought we were going to make promotion again, but key injuries meant the loss of form and momentum."

It was in January of 2007, during such a dip in form, that Kevin was dropped from the first team. Typically he took it like a true professional. "There's no point sitting crying into your hands about not being in the team. It's happened before and it will probably happen again. You've just got to get your head down and keep working hard, because you never know what's going to happen. Everyone in the team, not just the centre-halves, are fit and doing well and it's up to everyone else to train hard, keep them on their toes and make sure nobody becomes complacent."

Then came the devastating news both he and United fans had never wanted to hear. Kevin Gray had been released from the club at the season's end with no offer of a new or reviewed contract.

"Naturally I was really upset about being released by the club," he confided. "I love it here, love the fans, love the area. I am really settled. I don't really want to go anywhere else.

But, being realistic, these things happen in football. It doesn't do to rest on your laurels. You have to expect the unexpected. Carlisle United Football Club is such a great place to work, especially as a player. The support is incredible, fantastic. Words can't describe what they mean to the players. For the past few seasons it's been like playing every game at home, the amount of travelling fans we take to away games is unbelievable, Championship league quality."

Then there is Fred Story, he is an amazing bloke. He has turned the club around and set it on an even keel. He's a real character too. I had a little bet with him once about fitness and the club's rowing machine. He said he could beat my time, so I had a little wager with him. The chairman never loses. I lost and as part of the deal, had to sing an Elvis song in one of the club bars. I sang *In The Ghetto*. I thought I was excellent, but apparently it was dreadful, which is probably why I am a footballer and not a pop star!"

KEVIN GRAY, LEGEND and absolute Cult Hero signed a one year deal with Chesterfield (our loss, their gain) in the summer of 2007. He also achieved level one towards his FA coaching badge and currently awaits a final assessment on this work. Typical of the nature of a loyal and dependable father and husband, he opted to miss the assessment in order to be with his family for the birth of baby Elise.

As we sat in the garden of his home, his older daughter Grace, devotedly proud and loyal, tells me how good her dad is at football and brings out for me to see, his winners' medals from his days at Carlisle United. Kevin smiles in appreciation. When I tell him he is in this book on merit and that the majority of Carlisle fans rate him highly, he doesn't seem to believe that he deserves such accolades.

The Kevin Gray I met that sunny Cumbrian day was unassuming and an extremely nice man. I recall the late Bill Shankly telling me once: "It's nice to be important, but it's important to be nice." Kevin Gray achieves just that in impeccable style. I can only wish him good luck at Chesterfield and his further career and hope that, one day, he will return to his beloved Brunton Park as part of the coaching set up. Whatever, he will be welcomed with open arms by each and every supporter of the Blues, who will never forget the colossus who dragged our ailing team by the scruff of the neck and led us all back to days of glory graced by the likes of McConnell, Shankly, Hogan, Broadis, Ackerman, Ashman, Whitehouse, Young, Ross, Balderstone, Stokoe, McIlmoyle, Wilson, Bowles, Beardsley, Halpin, Poskett, Pounewatchy and Glass. We salute you, legends and heroes one and all.

Bibliography

The Lads In Blue
Paul Harrison
Yore, 1995

The Carlisle United Story
Ronald Cowling
Lakescene, 1974

Carlisle United – Fifty Seasons On
Keith Wild
1984

Rothmans Football Yearbooks
Jack & Glenda Rollin
1970 & 1990

Shanks
Dave Bowler
Orion, 1996

Football League Records
Barry Hugman
Queen Anne Press, 2005

Football League Player Records 1888-1939
Michael Joyce
Soccer Data, 2002 & 2004

McIlmoyle
Gordon Routledge
Arthuret, 2004

The Sporting Life
Titus Wilson & Sons, 2002

Additional Archive Sources:

Newspapers:
Carlisle Evening News & Star
Bethlehem Globe Times
Cumberland Evening News
Cumberland Times
Derby Evening Telegraph
The Journal

Online:
Carlisle United Online
Official Carlisle United website
Vital Carlisle United
Soccerbase.com
History of US Soccer

Other:
Transcripts of private interviews carried out by the author with Carlisle United players
between 1971 and 2007
Official Football League records

Subscribers

Derek Anderson
Steve Ashcroft
Alasdair Blain
Ian Bone
Carol Bracegirdle
Guy Brennan
Callum Brewell
Gary Broadbent
Barry Carr
Shane Cheetham
Ian Collins
Steven Coyles

Richard Dickson
John Ellwood
Tommy George
Stuart Gilbey
John Gray
Karl Gray
Samantha Gray
Sean Gray
Nick Hadkiss
Geoffrey M Hall
Kevin Humphries
Michael Lawton
Albert Mitchell
Tim Nabarro
James O'Toole
Dawn Peters
Alan Rankin
Richard Reardon
William Rice
William Stanley Rutherford
Adam Sheridan
Colin Smith
Tony Smith
Peter Smithson
Paul Tait
Peter Terry
Paul Thompson
Anthony Thorpe
Paul Tinning
Jon Veale
Bill Walshaw
Colin Warren
Andrew Watson
David Wood

John Gorman
Kevin Gray

Chris Balderstone
John Gorman
Peter Beardsley
Kevin Gray

Dean Walling
John Halpin
Hugh McIlmoyle
Chris Balderstone
Stan Bowles
Jimmy Glass
Dennis Martin
Stan Bowles
Dean Walling
Paul Simpson
Kevin Gray
Kevin Gray
Kevin Gray
Kevin Gray
Keith Walwyn

Keith Walwyn

Billy Hogan
Kevin Gray
Kevin Gray
Stephane Pounewatchy

Dennis Martin
Hugh McIlmoyle
Billy Hogan
Jimmy Glass
Kevin Gray
Stan Bowles
Kevin Gray
Dean Walling
Stan Bowles
Kevin Gray
Malcolm Poskett
Alan Ross
Kevin Gray
Dean Walling
Peter Beardsley

Stan Bowles

Top Ten Players Voted For

Player	Votes
Kevin Gray	12
Stan Bowles	5
Dean Walling	4
Chris Balderstone	2
Peter Beardsley	2
Jimmy Glass	2
John Gorman	2
Billy Hogan	2
Dennis Martin	2
Hugh McIlmoyle	2
Keith Walwyn	2